THE AUTHOR

FROM MONS TO YPRES
WITH FRENCH

A PERSONAL NARRATIVE

BY

FREDERIC COLEMAN

Attached to Sir John French's Headquarters during the Retreat
from Mons, and to the 2nd Cavalry Brigade Headquarters
during the advance across the Marne and Aisne, to
the 1st Cavalry Division Headquarters during
the fighting on the Lys, at Ploegsteert,
Messines, and Ypres, and at the
Front in France and Flanders
until June, 1915

OVER FIFTY ILLUSTRATIONS
WITH MAP

FIFTH IMPRESSION

The Naval & Military Press Ltd

in association with

The National Army Museum, London

Published jointly by

The Naval & Military Press Ltd

Unit 10 Ridgewood Industrial Park,
Uckfield, East Sussex,
TN22 5QE England

Tel: +44 (0) 1825 749494
Fax: +44 (0) 1825 765701

www.naval-military-press.com
www.military-genealogy.com
www.militarymaproom.com

and

The National Army Museum, London

www.national-army-museum.ac.uk

Printed and bound in Great Britain by
CPI Antony Rowe, Chippenham and Eastbourne

*In reprinting in facsimile from the original, any imperfections are inevitably reproduced
and the quality may fall short of modern type and cartographic standards.*

PREFACE.

THIS is a plain tale.

I am an American, and I have believed from the commencement of the war that the Allies' cause was just.

I am an admirer of brave soldiers, and willing to pay tribute to good work, from a military standpoint, by men on either side.

For ten months I was with the British Expeditionary Force in France and Flanders.

I am so greatly indebted to many units of the British Army for the opportunity afforded me to undergo experiences which form the subject matter of this somewhat rambling narrative, that I must make my acknowledgments, for the most part, collectively.

At the hands of Sir John French's Headquarters Staff I met unfailing kindness and courtesy throughout my sojourn in their midst.

Of General Smith-Dorrien I can sincerely speak as all speak who have met him, with profound recognition of his high attainments as a military leader, and of his great heart. Truly, a kinder man I have never met.

During the months I spent with the British Cavalry I felt an ever-increasing pride to have been attached to that branch of the Service. The officers and men

PREFACE.

of the 2nd Cavalry Brigade could not have been more friendly had I been of their own number.

My work with the 1st Cavalry Division brought me into somewhat less personal touch with the individual units, but I was most cordially treated on all sides.

To General Allenby and his Staff I have ever been grateful for the cheery welcome that made tired hours invariably brighten when I had the good fortune to come into touch with that efficient and energetic coterie.

The 2nd Cavalry Brigade Headquarters Mess, and later the 1st Cavalry Division Headquarters Mess, of which I was a member for so long a time, contained good fellows to a man. Among them I formed friendships which are the most cherished of all my priceless mementos of the most wonderful year of my life.

It is, however, to General de Lisle, personally, that I am under the deepest obligation. I have been brought, at one time or another, into close contact with the Field Forces in time of war of half a score of nations. Among them I have never met an army officer more keen upon his work than is General de Lisle. My personal affection for him, my admiration of him, and my sincere good wishes run hand in hand.

To Julian W. Orde and his efforts the Royal Automobile Club Corps owed its existence. To him I owe a great personal debt. No matter what the issue or how difficult of access that which was required, Julian Orde never failed a member of the R.A.C. Contingent —that hurriedly organized little band of whom Sydney

PREFACE.

Green (with General Hubert Gough from the beginning of the campaign) is the sole remaining active member.

Friends galore have given me those invaluable suggestions and opportunities whereby one gains a close insight into affairs, and oftentimes a pictorial record of them.

To none do I tender more sincere acknowledgment in that connection than to my old friend Percy Northey, a sometime member of the R.A.C. Corps.

Many gallant gentlemen mentioned in the following pages have gone on before, but, thank God! many have " come through."

Friends and readers, do not forget that most Americans feel much the same as I feel about the war.

An overwhelming majority of those of my countrymen who know the truth would do what lies in their power to further the success of the Allies and their righteous cause.

FREDERIC COLEMAN.

CONTENTS.

CHAPTER I.

CHAPTER II.

CHAPTER III.

CONTENTS.

CONTENTS.

CHAPTER IX.

CHAPTER X.

CHAPTER XI.

CHAPTER XII.

CONTENTS.

ILLUSTRATIONS.

ILLUSTRATIONS.

xiv

ILLUSTRATIONS.

1st Army H.Q'rs
Cambridge

27. Aug. 15.

Dear M' Coleman

You ask me to give you
a letter which will be certain evidence
that you were with the fighting troops
of the British army from the commencement of this great war —
I very gladly write such a letter for
throughout the time I was with the
army in France from the 19th Aug 14
to 7th May 15. I frequently came across
you — & always pretty close to where
the shot & shell were flying pretty
merrily — The first time we met
was in the Square at St Quentin during
the great retirement, the morn'g after
the battle of Le Cateau, the 27th Aug
(12 months ago to-day) when Lord Loch
introduced me to you & you kindly
gave me a lift in your car —

Y'rs si——
H Smith-Dorrien

29th Division
Dardanelles
31st August 1915

My dear Coleman:

I was so pleased to get your letter of August 6th containing the announcement and outline of your proposed lectures. The letter brings back vividly the interesting as well as dangerous journeys we spent together in your wonderful car. From August 31st, just a year ago today, until the end of May following, when I was transferred to this Division, my Cavalry were sent into action without your car moving backwards and forwards from the firing line to my Head Quarters, and I hope you will make it clear to your audiences that you did not view the fight from positions miles in rear, as is necessarily the case with Correspondents.

I see you have reproduced the photograph of the car after one H.Q. were blown up outside Messines but I wish I had a picture of your face when you missed your gears the morning that shell burst in our faces and smashed the radiator & windscreen.

Well, goodluck my dear Coleman. Whatever life may bring you; & I hope it will be all

xviii

prosperity and success, you will always admit that you never spent a more wonderful time, one that can never be forgotten, than the months you spent in the front line with my 1st Cavalry Division.

I need not say how much assistance you were to me during all this time; but you may not know that I reported more than once that without your car at my disposal I could never have kept in close touch with my Brigades round the Lisne, At Ypres and Messines

With all good wishes and kindest regards to Mrs Coleman & Ruth

Yours ever,

Beauvoir de Lisle

FROM MONS TO YPRES WITH FRENCH.

CHAPTER I.

On a pleasant August evening in 1914 I embarked on a troopship at Southampton. I was one of twenty-five members of the Royal Automobile Club who had each volunteered to take his motor-car and proceed at once to the General Headquarters of Sir John French's Army. That Army, the original British Expeditionary Force, was in France or Belgium, we knew not exactly where. It was generally anticipated by all and sundry that, if not actually fighting on that Friday evening, August 21st, it would soon be engaged with the Germans advancing towards France through poor Belgium.

The day before, Brussels had fallen. At the time I left Southampton the British 1st Corps and 2nd Corps, with a Cavalry Division, were in Belgium entrenching a position from Condé east to Mons and on to the eastward as far as Binche, on the road to Charleroi.

The twenty-five volunteer motorists who composed our party had been sent officially from London by the War Office to drive officers of the General Headquarters Staff at the Front. Our troopship arrived in Havre at an early hour on Saturday, the 22nd, but owing to lack of facilities for disembarkation of the cars night had closed in before the little band was ashore and ready to proceed across the North of France to the Belgian Line. Sunday morning the twenty-five cars were *en route* for

WITH FRENCH.

Amiens. Three of the party ran ahead with General T. D'O. Snow, commanding the 4th Division, and his staff, and the remainder lunched at Neufchatel, and reached Amiens at tea-time. Here the majority of the party remained, to be assigned on the morrow to various duties. Six of us pushed on that night to Le Cateau. Arriving after dark, we found that Sir John French's Headquarters were in a château near the town, and G.H.Q., as General Headquarters proper was termed, was located in a large school in the centre of the town. The drive had been long and dusty. After a late and meagre dinner at the Hotel du Nord, a hostel of modest pretensions, we spread our blankets underneath the trees of the schoolyard and were soon wrapped in sound slumber.

That Saturday and Sunday had seen part of the German invading army under Von Buelow take Charleroi from the French 5th Army and win the crossing of the Sambre. The Sunday had seen the first clash between the German and British armies. By the middle of the day the first great German attack against the British force had developed, and Von Kluck, with his German 1st Army, was outnumbering and, at one or two points, beating back the British troops before night had fallen. On Sunday night Sir John French had learned that the retirement of the French 5th Army on his right had rendered the Mons line untenable, and orders had already been given to fall back.

The great retreat had begun.

I awoke at daybreak on Monday, the 24th, to the sound of the guns. Drummond's 19th Infantry Brigade had disentrained at Valenciennes the night before. A new line from Jenlain, a few miles from Valenciennes, eastward through Bavai to Maubeuge was to be our new front, and we were retiring under cover of an attack by our 1st Corps.

I was asked to take two medical officers and two male nurses from Le Cateau to Landrecies. British wounded

MONS TO YPRES.

were being hourly brought into the town, where French wounded had arrived in some numbers already. At the door of one of the improvised hospitals, formerly a school, I had a chat with a wounded gunner. He was a corporal in one of the batteries attached to Haig's 1st Corps, and had a shell sliver through his right knee, another through his arm, and a flesh wound in his hand. He had little idea where he had been except that the fighting had been in Belgium. Four of our batteries of field-guns had been placed near each other on a hill, and the men told that the position was to be held at all costs. The German infantry and some of their cavalry had come within range and been badly cut up until the German guns got the range of our batteries. " Their shells burst well up in the air," he said, " throwing out dense clouds of smoke in three colours. The fumes of the shells were overpowering and bullets the size of marbles rained all about. Two of our lot were killed and thirty wounded while we were serving the guns. Finally, we had to leave the position, taking away our wounded. We had to abandon the guns, as the enemy's fire was too fierce to allow of our removing them."

High explosive shell made him and his fellows " go hot all over " when struck. These pieces of shell burnt him when they struck him, he said, a quick burning pain following the contact with the hot bits of projectile.

In the afternoon I ran from Le Cateau to Inchy, on the Cambrai road, to pick up General J. A. L. Haldane, who was in command of the 10th Brigade. While waiting in a lane by the road I spent an interesting hour watching a Battalion of Dublin Fusiliers, a part of the newly-arrived 4th Division, which had that day disentrained at Le Cateau, break camp in the adjacent field. Their eagerness to engage the enemy and their thirst for information were both great. The tension was high, for the significance of the French retirement on the right of the British Force was sinking in. I encountered a number of English officers from time to time

3

who openly reviled a retirement the strategical needs of which had not been explained to them, the plain necessity of it not as yet having become apparent.

I was back and forth between Inchy and Le Cateau several times during the afternoon. General Henry H. Wilson used my car to drive slowly and carefully over the road in order to reconnoitre the surrounding country. He explained to me his dislike of the best available ground in that vicinity as a defensive position.

During the afternoon stories of the day's fighting had begun to come into Headquarters. Le Cateau had seen but few wounded men until that Monday evening. In spite of the exaggeration which accompanied the tales of casualty from the Mons and Condé fighting, I gathered that Haig's Corps had effected a successful retirement and reached the protection of the guns of Maubeuge on the right, whilst Smith-Dorrien's 2nd Corps had retired cleverly during the afternoon and reached the vicinity of Jenlain. The retirement as a whole, therefore, difficult as it was, had been carried out admirably. A jumble of reports poured in regarding an action at Audregnies, where rumour persisted that the 2nd Cavalry Brigade under General de Lisle had been well-nigh wiped out. One dust-covered subaltern told me that the Brigade was going out of the village in column of sections when it was attacked by German infantry, with the result that but 240 men out of the original 1,500 remained. Ninety of the 9th Lancers, eighty of the 4th Dragoon Guards, and seventy of the 18th Hussars were, he said, all that was left of the command. Close on the heels of this first report was a more intelligible and infinitely more reliable one, brought in by Captain Francis Grenfell, of the 9th Lancers, who had been shot twice through the leg. He told me that the cavalry had charged a German infantry division well supplied with machine-guns, and never reached a point closer than 800 yards to them. Grenfell and some of his Lancers had that day saved the guns of the 119th Battery of R.F.A., for which he was subsequently awarded the V.C.

I spent several hours gathering a coherent story of that fight at Audregnies, which had covered the retirement of Sir Charles Fergusson's 5th Division as he was falling back not far south of the canal line between Condé and Mons. The Germans were working round the 5th Division left. Unless they were checked it appeared to Fergusson that his force would be cut off. General Allenby with his Cavalry Division was on the left rear of the 5th Division. When Allenby received word of Fergusson's danger the 2nd Cavalry Brigade was in and near the little village of Audregnies. The German infantry could be seen coming south in considerable numbers and heading straight for the town. A couple of squadrons of the 18th Hussars were a bit north of Audregnies and to the east of it under the shelter of a railway bank. The 9th Lancers and 4th Dragoon Guards were in and back of the village proper. Away on the left, to the west of Audregnies, was the 1st Cavalry Brigade, the 11th Hussars occupying a walled farm practically due west of the village, and the Queen's Bays in support a bit to the south. Still further west, in Baisieux and in front of it, was General Hubert Gough's 3rd Cavalry Brigade, which had to deal with another German infantry column coming down from the north.

Thus the 2nd, 1st, and 3rd Cavalry Brigades were facing the German advance, which was in two distinct sections. The Germans appeared to be in such numbers in front of Audregnies that de Lisle gave orders to Colonel David Campbell, commanding the 9th Lancers, to hold the Germans at all costs and to charge if necessary. One of our batteries was not far from the village, and the noise made by the German shells searching for it, and by our guns firing a reply, was incessant.

By some slight misunderstanding of the verbal order given by de Lisle, Colonel Campbell took it that he was to charge the enemy at once. The 9th Lancers pushed on through the village and galloped down a lane which converged into an open field in plain sight of the enemy. When the 9th Lancers had passed through the lane as fast as they could get through it, for it was narrow, tortuous, and thick with dust, they had not far to ride across the field when they were confronted with a stout wire fence. The 4th Dragoon Guards were coming on after them. The enemy's shell fire was at once directed at the approaching horsemen. The German infantry opened with machine gun and rifle fire at points variously estimated at from 500 to 800 yards distant. There was no getting across the wire. The only thing left to be done was to wheel to the right and gallop for safety to the eastward across the German infantry front, thus affording the enemy such a target as infantry rarely obtains. Swinging around to the right past a sugar mill, then out from the momentary protection of its adjacent piles of slack and cinders, they kept on to the eastward, then turned south, some seeking the cover of the railway embankment, others making for a cemetery which lay to the east of Audregnies, or scattering to the high ground to the south. Captain Francis Grenfell, who had been wounded, found himself under the railway bank with what he was convinced was the sole surviving remnant of the 9th Lancers. In fact, it was not until next morning that it was realised how many had escaped. The 9th Lancers lost in killed, wounded, and missing about seventy-five all told. The 4th Dragoon Guards' casualty list included two officers and fifty-four men.

The great value of the Audregnies charge was that it accomplished the object in view. It stopped the advance of the German infantry and allowed the 5th Division opportunity to retire southward. The German line did not make a further move forward from that position for at least four or five hours after the charge. The troopers themselves, as more than one of them told me,

" could not see what we were charging either going or coming." The field across which they had to gallop was so plastered by all sorts of fire that to do more than simply gallop and keep clear of fallen and falling comrades was all that the men could do. De Lisle issued a special Brigade Order at Le Plessis on August 28th, which read as follows :—

" I wish to express to the 2nd Cavalry Brigade my extreme pride and satisfaction with their conduct in the severe engagement at Audregnies on Monday, August 24th. The fight was necessary to save the 5th Division from an organised counter-attack during their retirement, and the object was achieved by the steady and gallant conduct of the Brigade. Major-General Sir Charles Fergusson, commanding the 5th Division, thanked me personally for saving his Division, adding that but for the Cavalry Brigade his Division would have been destroyed to the last man. I especially wish to commend the true cavalry spirit of the 9th Lancers in daring to charge unbroken infantry in order to save neighbouring troops, and that of the 4th Dragoon Guards in the effective support given without hesitation or thought of danger. I intend to bring to the notice of high authority how greatly I value the devotion of my Brigade. This to be read to all units on parade to-morrow."

I was first shown this order by one of the troopers of the 9th Lancers who had been with Captain Grenfell in the charge. He had become possessed of one of the original copies of the order, and proudly showed it to me as a souvenir of the event. " It was hell, that charge," he said with a grin, " but I suppose it had to be done. Anyway, to read over that order made it seem to have been worth while."

I slept in my car on Monday night, and before dawn on Tuesday, the 25th, was aroused from pleasant dreams by a sharp request to get under way. The driver who left his car opposite the door of G.H.Q.

and slumbered in his seat was apparently considered fair game for early risers. Before I was thoroughly awake I was tearing off to the north-east along the Roman road that led to Bavai. The Forest of Mormal looked cool and refreshing in the early light as we spun past it along the dusty road. I was told that General Smith-Dorrien's 2nd Corps, the 4th Division, and the 19th Brigade were to retire on Le Cateau, and General Haig's 1st Corps was to move south on the eastern side of the Forest of Mormal to a position about Landrecies and Maroilles. As we neared Bavai troops were already on the road. After delivering a message we turned and were soon back in Le Cateau.

Following the example of a couple of Tommies in the stableyard of the school, I negotiated a bath under a water-tap and treated myself to a shave. I then departed in search of breakfast. I found the Hôtels du Mouton Blanc and de France completely sold out of food, and in but little better case for drinkables. A glass of coffee and a bottle of beer were all I could forage for breakfast. The Royal Automobile Club drivers had arrived in the thick of things and been put so continuously to work that no one, they least of all, had thought of how they were to be rationed. Events of such great import were crowding so fast on one another that so trivial a matter as breakfast or dinner was not to be worried about.

The lady of the house wherein I had been billeted volunteered to wash some clothing for me. I accordingly left a goodly proportion of my wardrobe in her charge, where, so far as I know, it may be still. By eight o'clock all was bustle and movement. I drove General Henry Wilson to Sir John French's Headquarters and sat for a time listening to the German guns. British losses of the day before were reported to have been heavy—heavier than, later, they really proved to be. A staff officer told me that the Worcester regiment had been practically wiped out. A feeling of pessimism was

MONS TO YPRES.

creeping over us and becoming universal. Even General Wilson, imperturbable and invariably of good cheer, said to me, " We are not doing any too well ! " General officers, of whom there seemed to be an unusual number about, all wore a worried look on their faces.

The early morning was hot, and the sun's fierce glare promised a scorching day. The British troops, tired, had far to go, with no chance to obtain needed rest before their start. There was a general lack of understanding as to why we should be leaving the line Jenlain-Bavai-Maubeuge. Few of us were cognisant of any details of the situation. The inhabitants of Le Cateau were very badly worried. Stories became circulated throughout the countryside to the effect that the British had suffered a crushing defeat and were being driven in full flight before a remorseless enemy. Tales of Uhlan atrocities were to be heard on every side. The French folk had seen the British Army marching northward in the full pride of its strength, and had wrapped themselves in quiet satisfaction, confident that their Allies from Albion would save them from the horrors of invasion. The British retirement came to them at first as an unbelievable thing. Before midday on that Tuesday, driven by mad rumours of any and all sorts, the whole community was in full flight to the southward.

Between eight and nine o'clock Le Cateau was treated to the sight of long lines of Sordêt's French Cavalry, 14,000 of whom were moving from our right to our left rear. I was not very favourably impressed by their appearance, although I heard that in the earliest part of the campaign they had used their sinister-looking black lances to good effect. From their yellow helmets and blue tunics to their red breeches they appeared more campaign-soiled than one would have thought likely at so early a stage of the proceedings.

The Duke of Westminster drove up in his big car, and we chatted for a few moments. Interesting tales of a car-load of Germans shot to bits and a German aeroplane brought down at Dinant helped to pass a cheerful few minutes. As we stood in the headquarters yard young Robert Rothschild strolled up in the uniform of a French Staff officer. Colonel Seely, ex-Minister of War, wandered about, apparently waiting for someone, and looking lonesome.

Before ten o'clock I had a run to the village of Croix, on the Bavai road, with Lieutenant-Colonel Lord Loch of the Grenadier Guards, who was attached to Sir John French's Staff. Running along the roads in that part of the world was getting to be quite a business at this time. French cavalry, British cavalry, British infantry, and no end of supply columns monopolised every square inch of the roadway. French lines of vedettes crossing the hills stretched away to right and left. A German aeroplane sailed by us and over Le Cateau, and then sailed back again. Rifle fire from the Tommies rose and fell in waves of sound as the graceful monoplane soared high out of range in the clear sunshine.

Secker, one of my R.A.C. comrades, came into Le Cateau from Haussy, a village north of Solesmes, with the report that the Germans were there. At six o'clock in the morning he arrived in Haussy from Jenlain. He had been told to await one of the transport trains of the 19th Brigade. He found the market-place full of people who were preparing to leave the town. The Germans were reported to be four kilometres distant. A bit later someone came in with the report that the Uhlans were only two kilometres away. Finally the postmistress came to him and informed him that she had received telegraphic instructions to close her office and take her departure. Secker was inclined to disbelieve the reports as to the proximity of the Germans.

Entering an *estaminet*, he ordered a cup of coffee. The good woman of the house provided him with the coffee quickly, and then disappeared. A strange stillness seemed to settle on the village. Rising, he strolled to the door. No one was in sight. The town had been absolutely evacuated. Secker confessed to feeling a peculiar nervousness on finding himself the sole occupant of the village, and decided to take his car to the top of the hill which led away to the southward. Mounting the hill, he brought the car to rest at the top of it and dismounted. As he did so he descried a troop of Uhlans riding into the town from the other side. He jumped into his car and tore away for Solesmes, leaving the transport train of the 19th Brigade to whatever fate may have overtaken it.

Before noontide I took Lord Loch eastwarfromd Le Cateau to Reumont, the headquarters of Sir Charles Fergusson's 5th Division. The evidence of my eyes discredited the stories in which the 5th Division troops had been described to me as badly hammered. The infantry seemed in good shape, except for tired feet, and the artillery, horses and men, in fine fettle. Scars of battle were here and there apparent. Now a wounded officer would pass mounted, and now and again I saw a bandaged Tommy in the line. Battalions, regiments, and Brigades streamed by, interspersed with lorries loaded with ammunition. Long trains of motor-wagons full of provisions, sacks of flour, meal, and potatoes, boxes of biscuit, half beeves, bales of horse fodder—the food of the Army, horse and man. As I sat by the roadside one Battalion turned into a wheat field on the right of the road and another Battalion into an adjoining field on the left. The boys pulled down the shocks of wheat and made beds of the bundles. The sky had become mercifully clouded, though the day was hot and the countryside dry and dusty. Water was at a premium. I soon found that distributing a swallow of water here and there from my canteen met with great appreciation. At the further side of the field, soon spread thick with khaki-clad figures, was a farmer busy harvesting his shocks of grain on a couple of wagons. Just after noon we heard a very heavy cannonade towards Cambrai. A report reached Divisional Headquarters that the Germans had rushed the French in Cambrai and taken the town.

Many refugees mingled with the columns of troops along the road. A cartload made up of two or three families from Maubeuge told us frightened tales of German atrocities. Touring cars loaded with French staff officers tooted madly in an endeavour to pass the lines of big wagons on the narrow road. Family wagonettes filled with well-dressed people were in the line. Now and then a lady of well-to-do appearance passed, walking behind a carriage loaded with goods and chattels. At one point the road was blocked with a lorry containing printing stores, with all the presses and other accessories of a headquarters staff office. More refugees, and then more Tommies trudging along, dusty and begrimed, but all cheerful and strong ; hot and tired, but with very few stragglers in evidence.

I began to notice a striking difference between British cavalry at the halt and their French comrades. The English troopers always dismounted, and were more likely than not busy attending to some wants of their cattle. To see a French cavalryman dismounted, no matter for how long a time he might be halted, was indeed rare. French horses showed the strain, and in contrast the British horses looked in the best possible condition. Thus for an hour or so we slowly pushed our way here and there along the country roads, their fields fair with shocks of standing grain waiting for the harvest. We were doomed to spend the day in the middle of lines upon lines of troops with equally long lines of refugees filing by, and the air ever full of dust. Ox carts, horse carts, and a donkey cart with six little children in it, crawled along, then a tired mother with her three-year-old girlie on her back, some refugees with bundles, more without, all the men elderly or very young, but women of all ages and children in droves— a never-to-be-forgotten sight. Wonder, despair, patience, pain, apathy—the drifting faces made a heart-breaking picture. Now and then, but rarely, some French refugees would pass in a private motor-car, usually of ancient type. The number of mothers carrying babies through the dust and heat seemed out of all reasonable proportion to the rest.

When we returned to Le Cateau at two o'clock we found that G.H.Q. had moved back to St. Quentin. I requisitioned a half loaf of bread and a tin of bully beef from a passing supply lorry and made a splendid luncheon. A brain wave resulted in application at the chemist's shop for bottled waters. Half a dozen of Vichy were produced and at once stowed away in the car for future use, as water was precious. Aeroplanes sailed overhead and refugees drifted southwards until neither attracted further attention. Westminster told me that our soldiers brought down one of the German aeroplanes that were reconnoitring, its petrol tank punctured by a rifle bullet. The pilot and observer were shot as the machine began to descend.

A report was prevalent that the Russians had had a success, and the good news was eagerly seized upon and passed from lip to lip.

In mid-afternoon I ran to Bertry, General Smith-Dorrien's headquarters, with Lord Loch. Women, children and girls, the only inhabitants remaining, were in the streets in force and greatly excited. A Battalion of Jocks had come into the town, and every native was vastly interested and amused by the brawny kilt-clad men from the North. The local baker disposed of his stock of huge round circles of bread in as short a time as it took for him to exchange it for the modest sum it brought him. Pretty girls at the roadside with tempting pitchers of beer were catering for the wants of the soldiers. We came round a corner upon a W. and G. taxi, which brought a smile and a fleeting thought of the contrast between its former service and its present occupation. The 2nd Army Corps was well in place by evening. Some of the Brigades were in the towns, some in camp in the fields, the rest going into position along the roads as fast as they arrived. The first Battalions were divided into working parties, and while trenches were being dug, kettles were singing merrily over roadside fires.

As we returned to Le Cateau our passage was blocked by a crowd of countryfolk rotating about a German prisoner in the midst of a corporal's guard of stout Tommies. A mere lad in grey, smooth-shaven, with downcast eyes and pale face, he seemed absolutely overwhelmed by the threatening cries of the rabble that filled the road and ran alongside him screaming imprecations in a very pandemonium. If he remembered how some of his German comrades had killed our wounded as they lay on the field of battle—if such tales could be believed—I wondered whether that mild edition of the Hun was expecting a speedy execution at the hands of his captors. He certainly looked it.

At Le Cateau a staff officer told me that though some German cavalry had penetrated into Cambrai in the morning, it was still in the hands of the French in the afternoon, and that Sordêt's cavalry was not far from the town. At six o'clock a cool, refreshing rain started. This later developed into a cold drizzle, which was anything but welcome. The Le Cateau townsfolk had another spasm of excitement over a German bicycle scout who had been caught near Beauvais, a village half-way between Le Cateau and Cambrai. This German youth was thin and lantern-jawed, adorned with a straggling blonde moustache, and of most anæmic appearance. Painfully fearful of the hostile crowd, and, oh, so thankful for his round score of guards, he heaved a great sigh of relief when brought within the gateway out of the sight of the vociferous French crowd. His knees shook beneath him as he was marched off upstairs to encounter the Intelligence Officer.

At this moment Westminster was arranging a departure with a couple of staff officers for a run in his car along the front. He placed in the car a couple of rifles and a belt of ammunition taken from two of the soldiers. A very youthful Tommy, closely observant of every detail of the proceedings, connected the arrival of the spy and the arming of the car, and said to me in an awed whisper, " Where are they going to take him to shoot him ? " The youngster was almost disappointed when I explained that an enemy's scout in uniform was entitled to all the privileges of the most respected prisoner of war. " *I* would not let him go sneaking around spying. I'd shoot him," he insisted. A couple of minutes after I saw him sidle up to the German boy, who had been returned from his interview with " Intelligence," and furtively offer him a cigarette. Ten minutes later I asked the British boy if he still thought the juvenile German should be summarily executed. My Tommy grinned sheepishly and said grudgingly, as though ashamed of the sentiment expressed, " Oh, well, I suppose the poor beggar has to do just the same as we do." I found the British Tommy was more often than not annoyed when discovered at some kindly action.

That night I ran to St. Quentin. The rain had set in doggedly. Passing provision and ammunition trains, with artillery and cavalry occupying a considerable share of the roadway, the slippery *pavé* played all sorts of tricks in the way of unusual and unexpected skids. The one and a half hours of that run south seemed to occupy a much longer period. In passing a motor-cyclist at good speed, the back part of a car in front of us brushed him off his machine. He slid thirty feet, coming to rest in front of my car and in the full glare of my headlights as I skidded sideways to avoid passing over him. We picked him up, straightened his handle-bars, and bent a pedal into place. Finding him by no means incapacitated, we mounted him and started him off again. I was surprised he was able to ride. But

that was before I had come to know that the motor-
cyclists with the British Expeditionary Force bore
charmed lives.

G.H.Q. in St. Quentin was in a big barracks of a place.
When I arrived it was late and wet, and too much
bother altogether to try to get a billet, and I was too
tired to care for dinner.

At three o'clock on the morning of Wednesday,
August 26th, I was so fortunate as to encounter a staff
officer with a moment to spare, from whom I could gain
some concrete idea of the situation.

The British Expeditionary Force had been dispatched
from England with such secrecy, and I was in any case
so unfamiliar with the general make-up of the British
Army, that a careful explanation as to just what troops
composed Sir John French's command was most
welcome. It was easy for me to remember that Haig's
1st Corps was composed of the 1st and 2nd Divisions,
with the 1st, 2nd and 3rd Brigades in the 1st Division,
and the 4th, 5th and 6th Brigades in the 2nd Division.
Smith-Dorrien's second army contained the 3rd and 5th
Divisions. In the 3rd Division were Brigades 7, 8
and 9, and in the 5th Division Brigades 13, 14
and 15. The fact that General Snow's 4th Division
(10th, 11th and 12th Brigades) of the 3rd Army and
the 19th Brigade, which was not attached to any particular Division, were in evidence I knew from having
been told of their detraining when they had arrived
at Le Cateau and Valenciennes respectively. My
informant told me that General Allenby, commanding
the Cavalry Division, had under him the 1st, 2nd, 3rd,
4th and 5th Cavalry Brigades. With great patience
my mentor sat in the car and drilled into me the com-
position of first the Cavalry units and next the units
of the 2nd Corps, and finally the 1st Corps.

But my best bit of luck was to come. The fact that
my car was available at the moment a car was required
to run " up front " provided me with a journey which

The congestion of the roads by the fleeing country-folk

Belgian Refugees on the road between Mons and Bavai

Four generations of French Refugee family in one farmcart

French Refugees during the retreat on Paris

put me in much better touch with the trend of events. The morning dawned clear and cool. I was asked if I knew the road to Le Cateau. I replied that I had come over it the night before, and was quite familiar with it. Thereupon I was ordered to proceed to Le Cateau with as little delay as possible. As the sun rose it was evident that the day would be a scorcher. The air was clear after the rain of the night before, and in front of us the increasing sound of guns told of strenuous battle. I do not know the name of the officer who was my passenger, nor do I know whether he was constitutionally moody or whether some strange presentiment of the day's events came over him. In appearance he was a confirmed pessimist. I questioned him as to the general situation, and he told me that he was not clear as to what was taking place in front of us. The officer—a Major—told me Haig's Corps had been attacked in Landrecies the night before, and a severe all-night battle had resulted. The Major was under the impression that the retreat of the whole British Army, carried on with such speed on the day before, would be continued to the southward. As we drew nearer to Le Cateau our progress was rendered increasingly difficult by congestion of traffic by all manner of horse and motor transport. The battle in front of us was gradually developing, and soon the sound of guns became a continuous roar. Apparently the further retirement of Smith-Dorrien's command had been rendered impossible by an impetuous German advance.

At the edge of Le Cateau a cavalry officer told us the 19th Brigade were holding the town and General Briggs and his 1st Cavalry Brigade were at Catillon, a village four or five miles to the east of us. Briggs' force, said he, was our only protection on the right flank. He did not know where Haig might be with his 1st Corps. We told him of Haig's fight at Landrecies, and the three of us pored over my map long enough to make up our minds that somehow a gap had been left between Le Cateau and Landrecies, a matter of seven or eight miles.

We were right. That gap existed. It was through that gap that the German forces were to be poured in mass after mass that day, driving back the small cavalry force in front of them, and compelling the retirement of the right of Fergusson's 5th Division, and the consequent retreat of the whole line.

Already the air was tense with the reverberations of battle. The sound of the fighting came from in front and to the west of us.

We ran to Bertry and stopped by the railway-station. A sergeant who stood beside the car told me the Germans had the day before enfiladed a trench full of South Lancashires of the 7th Brigade and " wiped out every one of them, except one subaltern and five men, with machine-gun fire." That story was the forerunner of half a hundred similar ones I was to hear during the next few days of commands completely annihilated, or nearly so. I have often wondered if I missed any one Battalion of the 2nd Corps from out this category of disaster. If the rumours had been true, only a handful of British troops would have crossed the Marne away to the southward a few days later. As soon as the retreat was in full swing I heard the most extraordinary stories of contingents wiped out, destroyed to the last man—save always the sole survivor who told the tale. The tendency to exaggerate casualties was by no means confined to the lower ranks.

Just after seven o'clock a car drove up and General Sir Horace Smith-Dorrien alighted. He had come to the station to telephone to Sir John French, away to the south at St. Quentin. General Smith-Dorrien was as cool and self-possessed as though the battle pounding away in front of us were a sham fight.

I gathered the " situation " in Bertry as it could have been gained nowhere else that morning.

General Smith-Dorrien had under his direct command

the 2nd Corps only. The 4th Division, which was falling back from Solesmes as his 3rd and 5th Divisions retired southward, and General Allenby's Cavalry Division were under the orders of G.H.Q. With the 2nd Corps was the 19th Brigade, having on arrival at the front been pushed up hurriedly to the Condé-Mons line, and still more hurriedly pulled away from it.

Fighting rearguard actions all day long, the 2nd Corps had reached the Le Cateau position on the 25th with the idea that a stand would be made on that line. When Smith-Dorrien came into Le Cateau in the evening he found Sir John French had moved to St. Quentin. The Chief of Staff, General Murray, told Smith-Dorrien that the plans were changed. " You are not to fight. You must keep on retiring," were the instructions.

" But," said Smith-Dorrien, " I cannot retire further. My men are just coming in. They have been on their feet all day and are too tired to go on. My rearguards have been at it all day, and there is no other way out of it. I *must* fight."

Murray could only say that the orders to continue a retirement and avoid a conflict were definite and in writing. Sir John had been most explicit.

But General Murray could not change the conditions any more than he could change the orders. General Smith-Dorrien knew he could not get his men further south without some rest. Von Kluck was pressing on. Three extra corps had been swung round from the eastward to crumple and turn, if not envelop, the Allied left. A smashing blow at the advancing enemy might hold him off till nightfall of the 26th and allow retirement then. So the smashing blow was delivered.

It was two o'clock on the morning of Wednesday before Sir Horace had learned the location of the units which were to be thrown into the fight. His battle line from east to west was the 5th Division, 3rd Division, and 4th Division, with the 19th Brigade in Le Cateau on the right rear of the 5th Division. Briggs with his

1st Cavalry Brigade and a bit of another Cavalry Brigade was on the right flank, and the rest of Allenby's five Cavalry Brigades on the left rear of Snow's 4th Division. All of them were informed of the battle that was to take place and the part they were to play in it. Smith-Dorrien also sent word to General Sordêt, with his French cavalry, that the fight was toward, and any help he could give on the extreme left would be of great value. Sir John French had during the previous day (Tuesday) sent to General Sordêt more than once asking his assistance, and each time received the reply that his horses and men were so worn out that Sordêt could not come up and join issue with the enemy. General Smith-Dorrien's message to Sordêt was, " I am going to fight, and hope you can help cover my left flank."

At last, between two and three o'clock in the morning, the dispositions of the troops were made, and the tired men caught such sleep as they could before the coming of the dawn.

At break of day the conflict began. Five hundred German guns were hailing shell on that front before the day was over, and the sound of them was deafening before the morning was well advanced.

In response to a request to telephone Sir John French Sir Horace had come to the station at Bertry. He found General Henry Wilson at the other end of the wire. Wilson said, " Sir John wants you to retire at the earliest moment possible. He is anxious you shall not continue the fight a moment longer than is absolutely necessary. He is of the opinion that in not falling back you are risking a Sedan."

Smith-Dorrien explained that he could not break off the fight at any moment he might desire. " The only thing we can do is to give the Germans a smash, and we are going to do it," he said. " The men are too tired to walk further. They can't use their feet. The only thing for them to do when they can't stand is to lie down and fight. Both my flanks are in the air. I don't know where Haig is on my right. At least, I am not in touch with his left. I hope for some French support on my own left. My instructions to the Divisions are all clear, and I have arranged lines of retirement south in case we are forced back. All we can do under the circumstances is to see if we can't hold them off until dark."

Someone who heard General Wilson told me long afterwards that he said to Smith-Dorrien in conclusion, " Well, General, your voice is the only cheerful thing I've heard for three days. Give 'em hell! "

And he did.

After a short stop in Bertry I flew back to St. Quentin and G.H.Q. with my pessimistic major.

In St. Quentin I saw Toby Rawlinson, a member of our R.A.C. Corps and a brother of General Sir H. S. Rawlinson. He told me of the fight at Landrecies the night before. Haig's 1st Corps had come into position along a line from Landrecies to Maroilles about dark. They were very tired. The Germans swooped down in force through the Forest of Mormal in motor buses, and by nine o'clock were in position in front of the town of Landrecies in great numbers. Landrecies was held by the 4th Guards Brigade, consisting of two Battalions of the Coldstreams and the Irish and Grenadier Guards. The first German officers to approach our pickets were dressed in French uniforms and came in crying " *Vive l'Angleterre !* " They rushed our thin line of outposts in mass, and were actually in the streets of the town before the Guards had time to complete any brigade or even regimental formation. One Guards captain placed his men on either side of the roadway, crouching on the pavement with their backs to the houses. When the stream of Germans had filled the street between them the Guards rose with a yell and gave the enemy the cold steel. Down one street and another British machine-guns went into action and mowed down lanes in the German ranks. Rawlinson's carburettor went wrong in the dark and in the middle of the attack, and his motor-car refused to move. After the fierce German onslaught had been thrown back to the northern edge of the town with severe loss, the German field-guns poured shell into all quarters of Landrecies, setting fire to the houses. With his car pushed to the side of the pavement, in the pitch dark, a galloping battery of artillery just missing him by inches, Rawlinson took down his carburettor, effected his repair, and put it up again.

On the edge of the fierce night fight, in which the Guards lost eighty to ninety of their number killed and thirty to forty wounded, and the Germans left between 800 and 900 dead in the streets—in one place so crowded that corpses were propped against each other in a standing position—in the dark and rain, by the fitful light of bursting shells or burning houses, truly that was motor-car repair under difficulties.

Rawlinson left Landrecies at four o'clock in the morning. The fight had developed strenuously on the east towards Maroilles, but had ceased before daybreak. The German onslaught had been repulsed and the Guards enabled to get well away. Haig's retreat was continued on the main road south to Guise.

We heard but little of what was taking place at Le Cateau as the morning wore away. I was asked to take Major Thresher, the Camp Commandant, to Noyon to establish G.H.Q. there. A French major accompanied us. We ran to Noyon *via* Ham and Guiscard. At the latter town some argument between the French officer and the French reservist sentry, the former wishing to proceed without being bothered about the production of passes or other machinery for delay, resulted in our finding ourselves gazing into the muzzle of a French rifle with orders to stop until the Officer of the Guard was satisfied of our *bonâ-fides*. As I had no part in the argument, most of which I did not understand on account of the rapidity with which opinions were expressed on both sides, I felt that the sentry was

taking quite an unnecessary **view** of my importance
when he insisted upon keeping the muzzle of the rifle
pointed directly at me instead of covering the other
occupants of the car. He gave me a nervous sixty
seconds.

In Noyon the work of arranging offices for G.H.Q.
and billets for those attached to it bid fair to occupy
Major Thresher for the rest of the day, so I returned to
St. Quentin in quest of further adventure. When I
arrived most of G.H.Q. was being shifted from
St. Quentin with a considerable amount of bustle. No
effort was made to disguise the fact that the battle
along the Cambrai-Le Cateau front was going against
our 2nd Corps. There was no actual panic, but on all
sides was that obvious effort to be cool which bespeaks
strain. Running north in the direction of Le Cateau I
found the roads becoming blocked. As I turned the car
with difficulty at a point near Renancourt I realised
that to remain there would be to become involved in
the maelstrom of southbound transport. At that point
four roads in a radius of less than a kilometre debouched
from the north with but one main outlet to the southward. Running back towards St. Quentin I picked up
an Army Service Corps subaltern who was considerably
the worse for wear. He was in charge of a column of
transport on what he described as the Le Cateau-
St. Quentin road. He was moving southward with his
lorries and an escort of 150 men,who were scattered along
the train, and neither ready nor organised for attack.
As the lorries came up a hill a couple of hundred Uhlans
dashed over the top and charged the train with a rush.
The subaltern said four men and himself were all that
got away, the rest being taken or killed. He was dashed
against one of the lorries in the *mêlée* and was suffering
from a broken rib. I dropped him where headquarters
had been to report his experiences.

By evening all sorts of rumours were afloat in
St. Quentin. G.H.Q. had moved to Noyon. **My car**

was standing in front of the Mairie with two or three others when a number of officers came out, and jumping hastily into the cars, started away. It would be foolishness to allege that the general tendency was one of composure. I was the last to leave, and had not proceeded twenty feet before a rear tyre burst. The Mairie was on the north side of St. Quentin. The officers in my car left it for a passing lorry with the idea of picking up some staff car in the centre of the town. Time drags under such circumstances, and as dusk was approaching I managed in replacing the burst tyre to bungle one or two simple operations which spelled delay. A motor-cyclist stopped for a moment and told me that the road from Le Cateau would thenceforth be impassable for cars owing to the lines of troops and transport coming over it. Considering where he had been and what he had seen he was not over-pessimistic, though he was frankly of the belief that very little of Snow's 4th Division remained, if indeed much of Smith-Dorrien's army would get away. The retirement on the right he thought would result in the 4th Division on the left being surrounded and cut off.

With this unpalatable news I finally got under way for Noyon, which I reached at a late hour.

MONS TO YPRES.

CHAPTER II.

JUST before midnight as I was turning in, Borritt, the member of the R.A.C. corps who usually transmitted orders from Major Evans of G.H.Q. Staff to the R.A.C. drivers, came to my billet and told me that a volunteer was required for a precarious piece of work. Borritt's insistence that the driver must volunteer for the job, and the general air of mystery in which he wrapped it, roused my curiosity. I could only elicit from him at first that whoever drove the car which was required for the mission in hand would be called upon to dash through one or possibly more towns that were in German hands. Pressure elicited the further informa-tion that no news had come to G.H.Q. from General Smith-Dorrien during the evening, and just how much of the Left Wing of the Army remained, and where it was, was unknown. Therefore, if a message did not come from the 2nd Corps by three o'clock in the morning a staff officer was to be sent by car to establish com-munication with whatever might remain of Smith-Dorrien's Command.

When I learned that Loch was the staff officer who had been chosen for this mission I was glad to volunteer to act as his driver. I had cut away the exhaust of my car and rendered it unusually noisy. As this did not appear to be an advantage in such circumstances, I woke Jimmy Radley, an R.A.C. comrade, and obtained his permission to use his Rolls-Royce car for the journey, in case I should be called upon to make it. Before retiring I spent an hour in becoming familiar with any little eccentricities of Radley's car and putting in its tank twelve precious gallons of petrol which I had conserved in the tonneau of my car against emergency.

WITH FRENCH.

It was after one o'clock in the morning when I got to sleep, and before three Lean, a cheery young Scots subaltern attached to G.H.Q., awoke me and told me I was to dress and proceed at once to Headquarters. I lost no time in turning out, thinking I was in for an interesting experience in the way of a somewhat perilous early morning excursion. Upon reaching the street I found that news had come from the 2nd Corps, brought by General Smith-Dorrien himself. My trip with Loch was " off " and my precious twelve gallons of petrol gone.

We had news that the fight had been a severe one and that we had suffered many casualties. Our infantry had held the German advance splendidly throughout the morning. Their losses were slight compared with those of the enemy, whose attacks, hurled with persistent valour, could make no headway against our devastating fire.

With four or five German guns to our one in action our artillery had fought valiantly, but with fearful loss.

At about two o'clock in the afternoon word had come to General Smith-Dorrien from Sir Charles Fergusson that the German fire on his right flank was so hot that the men of the 5th Division were beginning to dribble away from the trenches. Investigation showed that the Germans were taking advantage of the Le Cateau-Landrecies gap and pouring through it. Nothing remained but to fall back. The order for a gradual retirement, beginning on the extreme right, was given. The troops on the left were to leave their trenches when they saw the line on their right retiring. When the 5th Division had left the line the 3rd and 4th Divisions, to the westward, were gradually to come back in turn.

Up to the time of retirement the casualties had not been great, but as the men left the cover of the trench line the German gunners peppered the fields with shell. It was marvellous that no greater casualties were inflicted. General Smith-Dorrien had worked indomi-

MONS TO YPRES.

tably to secure an orderly withdrawal from the position and prevent a rout. Had the Germans been a few hours later on our right much of our subsequent confusion might have been saved.

Fergusson's retirement commenced by 2.45 p.m., and before four o'clock the whole line was falling back.

Reaching St. Quentin at half-past eight in the evening, and finding that Sir John French and G.H.Q. had gone south to Noyon, Smith-Dorrien came on to Sir John's headquarters, after an effort to arrange for railway trains for his wounded and exhausted men, arriving between one and two o'clock in the morning.

He soon woke up his chief and reported the situation, then hurried back to the work of getting his scattered forces together again.

The need for staff officers at St. Quentin being imperative, every available man was hurried to some point where he could assist in the directing of the entangled units. A convoy of three or four cars was soon speeding away to the north, and not long after dawn had reached St. Quentin.

I suffered an annoying delay *en route*. Before leaving London I had requisitioned a couple of German-made metal-studded tyres as spares. The metal tread of one of these, which I had put on a back wheel, came adrift and fiendishly wound itself about a mudguard, so I had to chisel away the entire guard to get it loose, the metal being bent down and buried in the side of the tyre. The wheel refused to revolve until I had removed the obstruction. When one is in so great a hurry as we were that morning an operation of this kind, performed in the dark, has its disadvantages. The country of origin of that tyre was more than once casually mentioned during the stop.

The morning of Thursday, August 27th, found us in the direct path of what in the early hours of the day we believed to be but the remnant of the shattered Left of the British Army. Like the dawn of the day before, the morning broke clear and warm, promising a hot summer day. The perfect mornings on the retreat were some compensation for our short hours of rest.

St. Quentin on Thursday, August 27th, saw rare scenes and strange sights.

An orderly, well-disciplined army had been through a great fight. Its infantry, unbeaten by the infantry that opposed it, had been ordered to retire. "Gawd knows why," hundreds of Tommies were saying. The vastness of the scale of operations, the uncertainty of the General Staff itself as to just what was happening in some quarters of the field, and the universal ignorance of the rank and file as to what had happened elsewhere than in their own immediate vicinity, all tended to discouragement.

After inflicting such terrible losses as the German foot soldiers suffered at Cambrai-Le Cateau, the British Army had taken a hammering which seemed to many of them totally unnecessary.

To fight stubbornly and victoriously against an advancing enemy, hurling back his masses as fast as they are poured forward, is soul-inspiring. To leave such occupation for a scamper over a shell-swept field, comrades falling to right and left as they run, is not. Units that had just proven to themselves their invincibility were smashed and disintegrated in the very obeying of an unwelcome order to retire.

Jumbled together, inextricably mixed, each group convinced that their little remnant contained the only survivors of their individual command, confusion worse confounded was only to be expected.

The work of sorting out the men from the steady flowing stream of humanity as it moved southward, of re-forming an army that had lost most semblance of form, was the task set before the British officers in St. Quentin that morning at sun-up. It did not take them long to set about it. Stationed here and there along the main route through the town, each officer of staff became an usher, urbanely advising each little knot of stragglers where to proceed to find the nucleus of their particular unit, and obtain food, drink, and news of their comrades.

The wounded were in considerable numbers. Ambulances drew up at the railway-station and unloaded. A couple of sweet, little, old French ladies bustled about on one side of the station square, giving out tea as fast as they could make it.

Moving about St. Quentin in a motor-car that morning was slow work, as the roads were full to overflowing. Not far from the Mairie a wounded officer, his vitality all but spent, was placed in my car. I took him as quickly as possible to the station. Badly wounded in the chest, he said with a pale smile, " I've been about a hundred miles, it seems, since I was hit, and in pretty well every sort of conveyance *except* a motor-car. Two miles on a limber nearly finished me."

He looked, poor chap, as though he had reached care and attention none too soon.

For a time I was to act as usher at a point a bit north of St. Quentin. Placed on the road by a staff officer, and told where the men of the various units were to be directed, I chose to stand by a French lady, who, with her daughters, was supplying coffee, steaming hot, to the passing Tommies.

Never shall I forget that staff officer's parting instructions. " Cheer them up as you keep them on the move," he said. " They are very downhearted. Tell them anything, but cheer them up. They've got their tails down a bit, but they are really all right. No wonder they are tired ! Worn out to begin with, then fighting all day, only to come back all night—no rest, no food, no sleep—poor devils ! Yes, they are very downhearted. Tell 'em where to go, and cheer 'em up —cheer 'em up."

Of all the jobs that have ever fallen to my lot, I thought, this promises to be one of the most hopeless.

WITH FRENCH.

Cheer them up, indeed ! A fine atmosphere this, for cheer. Ragged and muddy and footsore they looked, straggling along.

The first individual who caught my attention particularly was a tall captain, an old acquaintance. He showed me his service cap, through the crown of which two neat bullet-holes had been drilled. Both of the vicious little pellets had missed their intended mark, though one had ploughed a slight furrow along his scalp, leaving an angry red welt.

No one had examined his head to find what damage had been caused, and he asked me to investigate. He bent over, and I poked my finger here and there, asking " where it hurt " and how much—in short, doing the best I could to accommodate his thirst for information.

As I was intent on my amateur probing a voice from behind commented, " A close shave the little divil made that toime, shure." Turning at the soft brogue, what was my surprise to see a Jock, in a kilt that looked as if its wearer had been rolled in the mud. Capless, his shock of red hair stood on end, and a pair of blue Irish eyes twinkled merrily. I was genuinely surprised. It was before I had learned that an Irishman in a Scotch regiment is no *rara avis*—nor a Cockney in a battalion dubbed Irish on the rolls, for the matter of that.

As if entering himself in a competition of close shaves, the Irishman held his right ear between thumb and finger. "And what do ye think o' that ? " he queried.

Right through the lobe of his ear, close to his cheek, a Mauser bullet had drilled a clean hole. " Close that, I'm thinkin'," said the proud owner of the damaged member, " and I niver knew how close me ear was to me head till that thing come along."

A burst of laughter from the group that had gathered was infectious. The boys trailed off together, chatting over further stories of close shaves, leaving me thankful the Irish lad had come by, cheered *that* lot up, and so saved me the task.

The next group to reach me contained a sergeant and a dozen or so Tommies, of most disreputable exterior.

" To what lot do you belong, sergeant ? " I asked.

" We're Riles, sir," said the sergeant.

" You're what ? "

" *Riles !* " with decided emphasis.

With a spasm, I remembered the Royal Fusiliers were in the 9th Brigade of the 3rd Division, and directed the group accordingly.

" You oughter know who *we* are," said the sergeant, somewhat haughtily. " We're the lot what was first in Mons and last out, *we* are."

" That's right," piped up a squeaky voice that came from a diminutive member of the squad ; " buck, you beggar, buck. Tell 'em the tale."

A grin on half a dozen faces told that the small one might be expected to produce some comment when occasion permitted. The sergeant turned. " What's ailin' *you*, Shorty ? " he demanded.

" Tell 'em the tale," croaked the little man. " Fust in Mons and last out. In at three miles an hour and out at eighteen. That's us, you bet," and he snorted as the squad roared in appreciative mirth.

So they drifted on, anything but downhearted, if one could judge from the running fire of banter between Shorty and his sergeant, which kept their comrades in continual chuckles as they toiled on.

Truly I thanked Shorty for his assistance in the " cheer-'em-up " department.

Detachments went past at times in step, whistling or singing. Some were obviously too footsore to walk normally, but they heroically tried to keep pace with the rest, and made a brave show of it.

One big, lantern-jawed chap, as he caught sight of me, insisted on his score of companions forming single file. They brought rifles to shoulder and stepped out in style with an indescribable swagger. The Sphinx would have broken into a smile at the sight of them. As the leader, much begrimed, came up I explained that hot coffee was to be had from jugs held by three little pig-tailed French schoolgirls under a tree hard by.

As the boys drank, the leading spirit chatted. I gathered from casual remarks, if they were to be believed, that talking was a habit with him. In fact, remarks were proffered, *sotto voce*, that he had not ceased talking, except to sleep, since leaving England. The comments of his soiled band seemed meat and drink to his soul. He fairly revelled in them.

" Pals we are, all right," he said with a grin, " though no one would think it to hear 'em, would they ? Know how to fight, they do, but can't talk—that's their drawback. Don't know no words."

A hot strong draught of good black French coffee gave him pause, but a moment later he was at it again. I told him where to go. As he tramped off he said, " Come on, you blighters ! Don't block the road. You ain't no bloomin' army now. You're a forlorn 'ope, that's what you are. Nice-lookin' lot o' beggars. 'Op it ! " And they "'opped it" to the music of his cheery abuse. God bless him !

Not long after, a very woe-begone procession hove in sight. But few were in that squad, and they seemed very worn and tired. Red-eyed from lack of sleep, barren of equipment, many a cap missing, and not a pair of sound feet in the lot. Every man had his rifle, but they looked very " done."

" Here are the pessimists at last," thought I. " It will take something to cheer *this* bunch."

I discovered their regiment and informed them of the whereabouts of their fellows. " Yes," said I, " three streets on after you get to the fountain, then to the right, and there you'll see a big building on the left— that's the one."

" We've been rearguardin'," said a cadaverous corporal

French Cavalry along the road near Meaux during the retreat

French Reservists at work on the fortifications of Paris

who acted as spokesman. " We're proper rearguards, we are. Been doin' nothin' else but rearguardin'."

" Right," said I; " don't forget. Third turning after the fountain. Plenty of food there."

" Rearguards, we are," from the lugubrious one. " Proper rearguards. Ain't done nothing else for three days."

" Cheero ! " I insisted; " three streets on after the fountain, and then——"

" *Proper* rearguards——" he started again.

" But," I interrupted in turn, " I'm telling you where there's *food*, my boy."

" And *I'm* tellin' you, sir, if you'll not mind," he continued gravely, " that we're *proper* rearguards, we are. And we 'ave learned one thing about *proper* rearguards in this 'ere war right off, and that is that rearguards ain't expected to eat. So we 'ave give it up, we 'ave. It's a bad 'abit any'ow. Ain't it, boys ? "

Off they trudged, grinning. The funereal visage of the spokesman turned and indulged in a sombre wink, whereat they laughed to a man, and I with them.

" Proper rearguards *don't* eat." He had had his joke, and played it out to his heart's content.

Ah, well, it was an experience !

I had not been long on that roadside when I realised that many of us had been labouring under a great delusion. It was not that someone was needed to cheer up the Tommy ; it was that most of us needed the Tommy to cheer *us* up.

The indomitable pluck of the soldier in the ranks and his effervescent cheeriness were to save that retreating army of Smith-Dorrien's as no staff work could have saved it had the Tommy not possessed those characteristics to such remarkable degree.

Many an officer whose hair had grown grey in the service said that day that Tommy was of finer metal than he had ever dreamed it possible of any soldier. The very air was full of unostentatious heroism.

WITH FRENCH.

One grizzled brigadier, seated on his horse, watched that straggling army pass, tears dropping now and then unheeded on his tunic, his lips pressed hard. One of his staff heard the old warrior mutter, as one detachment passed, soiled, but with bold eye and shoulders well back: " Ah! they may be able to *kill* such men, but they will never be able to *beat* them."

I began to look at the men with new eyes as the morning passed. If the thousands straggling by but continued to come, I thought, many more must have been saved than any of us imagined. Beneath the grime and dirt and weariness I saw clear eyes and firm jaws, even when men were almost too worn out to walk further. Those who appeared to be positively unable to go on were stopped at the St. Quentin station, to be sent south by rail.

I realised that in front of me was passing a pageant such as man had rarely seen in the ages. It was a pageant of the indomitable will and unconquerable power of the Anglo-Saxon.

Early in the day I was relieved and sent back to the station. Horse wagons full of wounded jostled the ambulances in the station yard. Even the motor transport lorries, as they rolled past, paused to drop off their quota of maimed and bandaged men in khaki.

One young subaltern passed, sound asleep in his saddle and unmindful of all about him, his horse following the human current.

At times a pitiable group of refugees went by, though for the most part the refugees had been crowded off the main roads by the retreating army or diverted to other routes.

A sergeant of the East Surrey regiment, of Fergusson's Division, came up. His face was haggard. He reported two hundred and fifty men, with five officers, were all that was left of that Battalion.

Standing near the bridge, close by the station, I saw General Smith-Dorrien a few feet distant. He turned,

and I caught his eye. He was speaking to a passing
officer. I hardly remember his words. Something about
plenty more of the same command being down the road
a bit, I think. It was good to see Smith-Dorrien's face
and hear his voice. I had heard much of him during
those days, and never was he spoken of save in terms of
affection. As he looked my way he smiled, with the
sort of smile that everyone within range takes to himself
as his own property. It was of inestimable value that
morning in St. Quentin—Smith-Dorrien's smile. It put
heart into many a man.

I was struck with the number of guns going by.
Battery on battery wheeled past, most of them battle-
scarred in some way. They had passed through a
rough time, our guns, and one could hardly see an
artillery unit without wanting to cheer them.

Scores of ambulances poured down from the north,
filled with exhausted men as well as wounded. The prevailing note was query as to where someone else might
be. Most men seemed to consider themselves " lost "
and utterly unaware of the whereabouts of those of whom
they were in search. The bakeries opened, and the
Tommies, all hungry, some painfully so, as more than
one had been without food for twenty-four hours,
proved good patrons. The sight of fat rings of bread
around the neck or over the arm of a passing soldier
looked peculiarly cheery.

A drowsy fit struck me. The hot sun and the
continually-moving columns affected me like an opiate.
I was roused by Lord Loch and presented to General
Smith-Dorrien, who said he had neither car nor horse with
which to get about. Loch, to my great delight, put my
car at Smith-Dorrien's disposal. It was a treat to watch
the General. Kindly and cheery, his personality pervaded
everything about him. At the station, he was much
interested in an ambulance load of wounded who had
just arrived. He spoke to many of the men personally.

Soon after I took the General to the Mairie. He was

very cordial and chatted with me *en route* just as he talked to all of us in St. Quentin that morning. Staff officers, soldiers, everyone—all were parts of the whole. It was a lesson, watching him saving the scattered pieces of his corps and welding them into a fighting force that would be all the better for the awful experience through which they had passed.

" Not very comfortable times," he said with a smile. " This part of the world as one would have seen it if touring hereabouts a month ago and the situation in which we find ourselves to-day present an immense contrast, do they not ? "

He commented on the strenuous character of my work. I remarked that the more I saw of the sort of thing we were going through, the more thankful I was to be there, if I could be of any use.

I was naturally pleased when he replied, " You gentlemen with your cars are certainly of use, of great use—of that you may be sure."

" Well, General," I said, " no able-bodied man who can get here should want to be anywhere else, if that is the case."

He laughed and added : " A man certainly wants to be able-bodied for this sort of experience."

As we crawled slowly past long lines of motor lorries, many of which had been reported lost, we chatted of the power and make of my car, and of cars in general. Smith-Dorrien not only put one perfectly at ease with himself, but acted as a tonic. One could but borrow some of his cool assurance.

A French staff officer called at the Mairie from General Sordêt.

At half-past four on the previous afternoon, when the battle was still raging in front, our rearguards fighting like mad to protect the retreating army, General Smith-Dorrien heard a furious bombardment on his extreme left. Mounting, and accompanied by one of his staff, he galloped away to the westward towards the sound of the guns. He thought the Germans had gotten round his left. Through the line of the retreating 3rd Division and on beyond them to the 4th Division he rode, only to discover that the guns were further westward than he had thought. Then he realised that the noise of battle told of Sordêt " helping cover the left flank " of his hard-pressed British Allies, in spite of the fatigue of his troops.

The French officer at the Mairie the next morning told us of a strenuous conflict in which the tired French cavalry and some French Territorials had gallantly pitched into the Germans' right with a good will, inflicting severe losses and driving back the oncoming enemy.

Corroboration of this had reached Smith-Dorrien the night before, when he had found two of his Royal Flying Corps officers in the station at St. Quentin. During the battle they had been flying over the German line in front of our left flank. Between four and five o'clock in the afternoon they flew through a veritable storm of bullets, some of which disabled their engine and forced a descent. They were able to land safely, two or three miles behind our lines, but found the aeroplane so damaged that it had to be abandoned. They procured a couple of bicycles and made their way to St. Quentin. These officers told Smith-Dorrien that, before descending, they had seen the French troops, cavalry and infantry, engaging the Germans on the extreme left.

Naturally, Smith-Dorrien expressed his thanks to Sordêt's staff officer in unmeasured terms. Asking him to convey his appreciation to General Sordêt, Sir Horace said he would there and then " make a special report on the subject to the Field-Marshal "—Sir John French.

The Frenchman, apparently the happiest man in St. Quentin that morning, after many adieus to us all, and wishes of good fortune to everyone, rode off post haste to rejoin his chief.

Later I was given a new job. I was to accompany

WITH FRENCH.

Captain Cox, of the G.H.Q. Staff, to a point to the north of St. Quentin, and there to wait with him and again direct stragglers. Cox was instructed to stay in that position as long as it was advisable for him to do so—from the standpoints of usefulness and safety. As he was the nearest Staff officer to the enemy, we judged, from what we had been told, that it was quite possible we might have to " run for it " before the day was over. We could not understand why the Germans had not followed up their victory at Cambrai-Le Cateau, and were not enveloping St. Quentin and the scattered 2nd Corps at that moment.

Cox explained to me that in case the Germans pushed ahead, and it became impossible for us to remain longer where we were, we would proceed to the square where the Mairie was located, pick up Lean, our Scot, then scoot for it to the southward, past the railway station. A subaltern named McLean, with his motor-cycle, was attached to us. I learned later that he was Marconi's secretary before the world-war. He had given the alarm of the oncoming Germans at Landrecies. We made a compact to the effect that he should be allowed to keep ahead of the car in case of a scamper, so that he could get in with us in case he fell off his " bike."

The congestion of traffic was so great along the town's main thoroughfares that I started off by myself to reconnoitre a new way round in case we wanted to get to the station in quick time. Down a side road I passed a museum which was being utilised as a hospital. A doctor asked if I would take a load of wounded men to the station. I took three Tommies, all badly wounded, into the car. Occupying the front seat with me was one of the Royal Scots, with a nasty hole in his shoulder. " We were quite all right in our trenches," he told me. " The bullets were dropping like rain, but we were keeping well out of the way of them. Then all of a sudden we got the order to retire, the Lord knows why. When we began to retire we got it very bad."

MONS TO YPRES.

That feeling seemed fairly universal.

They hated so to come back.

It was a fine thing—that splendid fighting spirit. Magnificent soldiers they were, every one of them.

I landed my trio at the station, where they all shook hands with me and wished me luck. One could not walk, and all three were in great pain, but bearing it as soldiers should, without any undue fuss.

When I got back to him Cox had his hands full. Before I rejoined him I had a cool wash in a tiny provision shop of sorts. The day was a lovely one, warm and sunny.

While I was laving myself a couple of South Lancs. men entered the shop and ordered tea and bread-and-butter. One of the pair was voluble enough for both. He was eager to explain the whole battle. He drew the 2nd Corps' position in line and placed the Germans in a half circle, the ends flanking the British right and left. " We were well entrenched," he said, " and the Germans opened on us from five hundred to six hundred yards. They fire in absolute masses. Never was anything like it heard of. One row of them lies down, behind them a row kneels, and back of them again a third row stands. You couldn't imagine such a target. It seemed *too* easy. You could just pump the bullets into 'em like smoke, and never miss a shot. You have no idea how it seemed, lying there firing into that grey bunch of men and thinking all the time what fools they were to stand there and take it. And the funny thing was that they couldn't shoot for nuts either. The standing lot didn't even raise their rifles to their shoulders, but fired from the hip. They must have sent an awful lot of pills our way, but they couldn't hit a balloon."

The quieter soldier took up the narrative. " As fast as we would knock over a German another would take his place."

That had impressed both of the South Lancs. men. They spoke of that feature of the fight with obvious respect for the men, fools and Germans though they were, who could stand such punishment.

"Our men must have hit at least ten of them to every one of us that got it," said the quiet one.

Both men were loud in the praise of our guns, the fire from which had been splendidly accurate. "But that battery back of us got it like hell afterwards."

"At one time in the forenoon we drove the Germans in front of us back quite a bit. They came on again thicker than bees. The Bedfords retired on our right not long after three o'clock, and then we were ordered back. As we went the Germans got some machine-guns up and enfiladed our trenches. When we once got out into the open the shrapnel followed us all the way. One, two, three, four in line, and then one, two, three, four in line again, further over, and so on. Lord, but we had plenty hit then ! I think their guns were mounted on motor-cars the way they got 'em about."

"Yes," chipped in the quiet one, "so do I. And as if it wasn't bad enough scampering across those fields like rabbits, our lot bunched after a bit, and then we did fair get what for ! "

And I left them to their tea, fighting the battle over again with great gusto, revelling in reminding one another of how various of their comrades had "got it."

Tired ? Well, they should have been, and no doubt they were. But in the memory of that awful battle it was easy to forget their fatigue.

I stood by Cox for a time and helped "hearten them up." One young lad from the Royal Irish Regiment was woefully tired and hungry. He was helping a comrade who had strained his knee and was in no little pain. I asked him if he thought he could get on another mile or so, and he grinned and replied, "Sure. My lot have been in action Sunday, Monday, Tuesday, and Wednesday, and after that I can do anything you like on Thursday."

MONS TO YPRES.

It was sad to see some of the lame ones come in. Now and then one would go by gingerly and slowly, every step a bit of exquisite torture.

After a number of smaller groups of stragglers, quite decent-sized detachments came through. A really very small percentage of the men were without rifles.

All were astonishingly cheerful. Many a group went by whistling in chorus. The majority of them looked full of fight, and only now and again would a broken one go by.

The French women were splendidly helpful. Steaming bowls of coffee, little boxes of food, bits of cake, pitchers of tea or jugs of milk, matches, cigarettes, anything they thought would help to cheer or comfort, they brought to the roadside for the Tommies.

A good-sized contingent swung by in step, singing. Stopping for a drink of coffee, a sergeant told me every one of them had been marching continuously all night long.

Twos and threes strolled down the road at intervals leisurely, as though interested spectators. Good-natured banter was flung from one group to another. Questions confirmed what I had been told, to the effect that most of our casualties had been from shrapnel, after the retirement had begun. Very little damage had been inflicted on our troops by the German infantry fire. All testified to that.

By noontime we wondered that we had no news of stragglers being taken up, or Uhlans cutting them off as they came ambling down the road. A subaltern told us of Renancourt. The chaos there was maddening. A battery of enemy guns or a strong force of cavalry could have piled up thousands of casualties at that point. The roads thereabouts were full of abandoned trains, and here and there an abandoned gun, he said.

But still no news of the enemy's further advance, which we had so confidently expected all the morning.

Guns could be heard to the north and to the west.

WITH FRENCH.

Sordêt's French Cavalry and our own gallant Cavalry Brigades were efficient rearguards.

A French reservist force was not far from us, to the north of St. Quentin, but in no great numbers, and not, to my mind, particularly formidable.

A German monoplane put in an appearance, but created little stir.

We began to theorise. Had Haig's lot turned, after all, and struck Von Kluck's left flank ? No, we would have heard the guns. Rumour came, too, that Haig had been fighting severe rearguard actions in front of Guise.

Had the Germans been so unmercifully hammered at Cambrai-Le Cateau that their troops were unable to follow ? Unlikely. Then, there were plenty more of 'em. That we knew.

How those German first line regiments had stood the gaff ! Losses of thirty to forty per cent. demoralise all but the finest commands, we argued. Von Kluck's stalwarts have been through the mill for days now—has our punishment stopped the rush of their onslaught at last ?

So we theorised.

And we were not far wrong, after all. Von Kluck had tried hard to smash and envelop the British Left, and had failed. He had knocked back Smith-Dorrien, in some confusion, but only after enormous losses had been inflicted on the German forces. The backbone of the movement against French, the attempt to wipe his " contemptible little army " off the map, was broken by the fight put up by the British Left that Wednesday at Cambrai-Le Cateau.

Our British Cavalry was doing wonders unbeknown to us. Briggs and de Lisle with the First and Second Cavalry Brigades were covering the 2nd Corps' retreat, and Gough and Bingham, with the Third and Fourth Cavalry Brigades, were protecting the retirement of Haig's First Corps. Chetwode, too, with the 5th Cavalry Brigade, was in front of Haig and delivering stinging blows to the German advance.

MONS TO YPRES.

By one o'clock so many of our men had passed that all thought of a demolished army had left us. Dirty, tired, and hungry though they were, they were cheery and fit. They wanted rest and, above all, food. But no one could imagine them in the least beaten. The British Tommy and his indomitable spirit had saved the day. His good temper and pluck had survived the awful experience between the commencement of the retirement from the battle line in the middle of the afternoon until dark had ended the fight. More, it had lived through the awful night of confusion and retreat with its hunger, thirst, and utter weariness. The morning had brought little respite, but the sun was shining, and with the warmth of the day Tommy came back into his own and up came his head and his heart.

He had saved himself!

Dozens of times little groups reported to us that they were " all that were left " of such and such a regiment. Almost invariably we could tell them of others of their command whom they would find further on at the point of rendezvous, where they could be sure of food and a brief rest.

Early in the afternoon word came to us from mounted scouts that the Uhlans were about three miles out and coming on in force. Cox sent me to Headquarters to see if there was any truth in the report. From what I could gather, it seemed that a Uhlan force was heading south, a bit to the east of us.

Cox considered it advisable that we should run out eastward toward Guise and search for information *re* the German advance. Accordingly we picked up Lean and with our cyclist pounded away. A mile or so out of St. Quentin we ran across the 16th Lancers, who were in Gough's 3rd Cavalry Brigade. They were dismounted in a nicely-sheltered field surrounded by trees, and were very well concealed. As Cox was talking to the Commanding Officer of the 16th a mounted scout rode up in blue overalls, old brown

43

coat, and a brown cap. Had I not heard him speak English I would have thought him of some other nationality. He reported a detachment of German cavalry just outside St. Quentin on the north. The order " Fall in in squads " was given, and the 16th mounted and started away northwards. I wondered if they would find two thousand German infantry that had been reported not long before by some French reservist scouts as coming on towards St. Quentin from the north-west.

On we ran at a good pace to the east, and before long crossed the Oise at Origny. Here we met the advance guard of Haig's 1st Corps *en route* from Guise. Haig's line of retreat was to be to the south to La Fère. Cox wanted to find Sir Douglas Haig himself, so we passed well-nigh the whole of his command to reach him. This operation, on the country road, was at times trying. Finally, not far from the village of Jonqueuse, a few kilometres west of Guise, we saw Haig on a little hilltop by the roadside, chatting with his staff and a handful of French officers, as they kept their glasses on the rolling country stretching away to the northward.

A Brigade staff officer, with whom I had a moment's talk, told me that on the previous morning two Battalions of infantry of the 1st Corps had been ineffectively picketed, with the result that the Germans had rushed them and inflicted severe damage. " Only two officers of one of the Battalions were left," he said. That was the first version I heard of the story of the Munster Fusiliers. Another staff officer told me a few minutes afterwards that the Munsters were at the rear of the Corps, and a messenger from Headquarters with orders for their retirement failed to reach them. They stayed where they were, even though attacked by overwhelming numbers, and fought until they were completely surrounded. Even then they refused to surrender until they had fired their last

round. Their losses were terrible. During the next
hour I heard the same story with half a dozen variations,
but that one appeared to be the most correct. I
climbed up alongside General Haig's staff, and stood
there for an hour or more listening to the sound of
the cannonading. North of Guise on our right and away
to the left and to the north of St. Quentin the guns
were hard at it.

Samuels, an R.A.C. driver, showed up at an opportune
moment with a Bologna sausage, a bottle of villainous
vin blanc, and some quite decent Russian cigarettes.
They disappeared instanter, to our very material benefit.

At last we started for Noyon and G.H.Q. Cox was
anxious to get there as soon as possible, so I chose a
cross-country route to La Fère down small roads
through the smiling and fertile valley of the Oise.

Even the smallest winding roads were good ones.
While still near Guise we passed a wagon-load or two
of refugees. Before we were out of earshot of the
gunning, however, the countryside took on its usual
appearance. All day long we had been in the midst of
scenes of war. Here, a very few miles away, one could
hardly imagine war existed in the same valley. Perhaps
the women and children, with an old man or two,
gathered more eagerly in the doorways of the village
houses as we dashed through, but the menfolk not at
the front were hard at work in the fields and about the
farmyards. The crops were generous and the land fairly
blossomed with plenty. A commercial traveller in his
cart was selling his wares in front of a village store as
if never a German had crossed the Rhine.

As we neared La Fère a barricade had been formed
by pulling a couple of farm carts across the road. A
trio of reservists were on guard, one armed with a nickel-
plated 38-calibre revolver of the old " bull-dog " type,
the sole visible weapon of the outpost. The sentry with
the bright bit of ordnance smilingly apologised for the
necessity of examining our passes, waving the pistol

about airily in emphasis of his urbane remarks in a manner that badly scared me. I began to get the idea that given a combination consisting of a French reservist, a firearm of sorts, and me, I would invariably be in line with the muzzle of the weapon. And I am of too nervous a temperament to enjoy that sort of thing.

La Fère was full of French troops and was the rail base of the 2nd Corps. Smith-Dorrien's headquarters, so one of our Flying Corps told us, were first located at Ham, and then moved to Guiscard. The broad road from La Fère to Chauny and thence to Noyon was soon covered. We reached G.H.Q. by dinner-time. I was thoroughly tired, so after a hurried dinner in a restaurant of sorts, was soon fast asleep in a most comfortable bed.

I was still in the arms of Morpheus on Friday morning (August 28th) when Captain Cox wakened me to borrow my map, a rather better one than those provided by G.H.Q. Cox told me I was on that day to drive Lieut.-Colonel J. S. M. Shea (35th Horse), attached to General French's staff as a liaison officer. I count the day a lucky one that I met Jimmy Shea, for he is of the salt of the earth.

After breakfast we reconnoitred the different roads through Noyon. The 2nd Corps was continuing its retreat southward. The units were still somewhat scattered and required general collecting together and organising. The Army was to drop back to the line Noyon-Chauny. We were more concerned with the 2nd Corps units which were passing through Noyon, as our own work lay with them. The 4th Division, 19th Brigade, and some of the cavalry units were also passing through our hands. Most of the morning we stood by the roadside watching provision trains, ambulances, lorries laden with ammunition, and all the transport of an Army Corps file past us. Batteries of guns and detachments of infantry all were working slowly southward. G.H.Q. had moved to Compiègne in the morning.

MONS TO YPRES.

I heard a great deal of general gossip during the fore-noon from staff officers and officers of various con-tingents that were on the road. It was fairly well known by this time that three German Army Corps had been diverted from a point further east and swung around to reinforce Von Kluck's 1st Army. We heard but little authentic news of the French, but Dame Rumour was busy with all sorts of general reports of German successes at Dinant and further east.

Once in a while a block came in the traffic, and then we had an awful job working up and down the packed lines straightening out the transport and the troops. It was a fine day and very hot. The troops were cheery and good-natured. I was particularly impressed by the kindness of the men to their horses. Not only the cavalry troopers, but the men in charge of horse transport were invariably considerate of their cattle. The roads in the vicinity of Noyon were lined with trees, the cool shade of which was most welcome. In the afternoon the 2nd Army proper began to swing through in real earnest. For three hours a steady stream of infantry in different detachments passed. All were wonderfully cheery and looked particularly well, sleepy some of them, and here and there a swollen foot gingerly treading the hard roadway. Considering the distance they had come, marvellously few of the men limped. Stragglers grew hourly fewer in number, which showed that the detachments were getting together again. Frequently a regiment came swinging along in step, singing or whistling in unison.

We had news of a peculiar order issued by G.H.Q. to the effect that the officers' kits should be taken from the wagons and destroyed, to provide accommodation for footsore infantry. The 4th Division carried out this order before it was countermanded, and eleven wagon-loads of kit were burned in huge piles by the roadside—by no means a reassuring sight.

A big Scot saw me take a letter from one of the staff

officers, and asked me if I would perform a similar service for him. No sooner had I agreed to do so than his entire regiment, which had halted for a moment, grasped the opportunity and began scribbling notes home. It was indeed touching to see these hurried missives, written on all sorts of scraps of paper. There was no chance to pick or choose as regards form. Most of the letters were to wives, and many to mothers, with now and then one to a sister or a sweetheart. The majority of them were just a line to say all was well. Few indeed could be called illiterate, and I saw none that were illegible. What most impressed me was the cheery vein that ran through them. No note of despondency crept into that wayside postbag. It was one more evidence of the stout heart of Tommy Atkins that makes him the finest soldier in the world.

Among the troops a couple of spies came, led between two French soldiers. One was short and swarthy, with coal-black moustache and hair. He looked a Greek, and was dressed as some small shopkeeper might have been on a Sunday outing. The other prisoner wore a knit cap and big khaki-coloured coat that had apparently come from our Quartermaster's Department at some time. He was tall, of light complexion, and furnished the greatest contrast possible to his companion. They both wore a look of abject misery as they trudged along in the dust to their death. Spies or suspected spies had short shrift with the French in those days.

We raised some coffee from a wayside house in the afternoon, but could get no milk. The town was thoroughly emptied of eatables, and most of the private houses were closed. Later in the afternoon we got some eggs at one house and a bit of bread-and-butter at another ; and finally found an *estaminet* where we could buy some wine. Discovering a countrywoman at a drinking hall who would cook for us, I arranged quite a dinner for Colonel Shea, Dudley Carleton, Jimmy Rothschild, who was acting as Carleton's chauffeur, and myself. After dinner Rothschild went to the post-office to send a telegram. I was sceptical about his ability to do this, for the utmost secrecy was being preserved as to our whereabouts in France. Rothschild offered to get a wire through for me. He wrote a brief message in French, addressed to my wife in England, assuring her that I was fit, well, and happy. Great was my surprise when the postmaster agreed to send it. Subsequently I was still more surprised to find that the wire had arrived in London in good time. Moreover, the telegram clearly stated that it had been despatched from Noyon on that Friday evening.

Late that night we left Noyon for Compiègne. Owing to the congested nature of the roads we lost our way and wandered in the forests of Ourscamps and Laigue till past midnight. Arriving in Compiègne, we could find no empty beds in the hotels, but finally were lucky enough to discover a couple of empty cots in a college dormitory, used as a temporary hospital.

The German pressure on our rearguards had visibly slackened on Friday, the 28th, and by night the British Expeditionary Force had made good its escape from anything in the nature of annihilation. I had seen almost all of the 1st Corps, and on the 27th and 28th had watched a large number of the 2nd Corps, 4th Division, and 19th Brigade. I had no hallucination about the Army being a beaten one. The spirit of the men alone made it impossible to describe them as beaten. The moment I realised that things were better than they had at first sight seemed, I watched eagerly for signs of a further stand. The more I saw of French's Army the more convinced I became of its invincibility, and longed for the day when we could " get some of our own back."

At an early hour on Saturday, the 29th, Colonel Shea and I proceeded to a large hotel in Compiègne and foraged for breakfast. Most of the servants had left, but resourceful Toby Rawlinson hied himself to the

E

kitchen and cooked a splendid breakfast for Shea, Jimmy Rothschild, and me.

Cox told me the Germans had left off hammering after the British Expeditionary Force, and were turning their attention to some of the French contingents on our left. I did not know at the time that General d'Amade was in touch with Von Kluck's right in the direction of Arras. French troops were east of the line between Guise and La Fère, and were engaging the attention of Von Kluck's left On that Saturday our cavalry fought a rearguard action at Ham, and subsequently a more determined one at Guiscard. After the two or three hours' fighting at Guiscard that afternoon the German advance was satisfied to draw off and leave us alone.

I spent the morning running to Noyon and back, and later took a couple of G.H.Q. staff officers to a château near Cuts, south-east of Noyon, where General Smith-Dorrien had his headquarters. Arriving at the château, which was a very handsome one, I found my car short of lubricating oil. In my endeavour to borrow some I drew an undue amount of attention to my improvised uniform, which had not improved in appearance. My efforts might have proved fruitless but for the fact that General Smith-Dorrien came out at the moment. He stepped into a big car, and was about to be driven away when he saw me. Bowing, he asked me with a smile how I was standing the campaign. Considering the circumstances under which I had met him a couple of days before, and the short time I had been in his company, I was surprised he remembered me, and naturally felt the warm and genial touch of his recognition. As he drove away, the lubricating oil which I had begged in vain before was thereafter immediately forthcoming.

On our run to Cuts, through the Forest of Laigue, we had passed many transport trains on the move to or from rail bases. Every nerve was being strained to get the 2nd Corps mobilised, rested, fed, and well supplied with ammunition at the earliest possible moment. A 2nd Corps staff officer told me that the General Orders of the Day announced that a Division or more of the enemy were advancing from St. Quentin to Noyon, and that the cavalry, which had been fighting rearguard actions since Mons, had orders once more to block the way. A subaltern in charge of an ammunition column begged for news. I asked him if he had seen anything of interest. He said : " It has been interesting enough for me. My column has had four hours' sleep in three days in addition to what they could snatch here and there on the move. No sooner had I got them to one place in response to orders which it seemed impossible to carry out, than I have been cursed for getting them there, and hurried away to some other point to find someone waiting for me there with more cuss words. I am a wandering Jew, for ever on the move, and don't ever expect to stop again as long as I live."

While at General Smith-Dorrien's headquarters I was introduced to General H. de B. de Lisle, commanding the 2nd Cavalry Brigade. General de Lisle wanted to get back to his command. He had come for a con-ference with General Smith-Dorrien. We ran to Guiscard or near it. The 2nd Cavalry Brigade had been attacked at nine o'clock in the morning at some point to the north of Guiscard. The position not being as satis-factory as desired, de Lisle had retired from Guiscard at eleven o'clock to a point about two and a half kilo-metres south of the town. There, with the support of the guns, which they had lacked in the position further north, they withstood the German attack for over two hours, and eventually compelled the Germans to retire. We passed a couple of lorry loads of wounded before reaching the 2nd Cavalry Brigade.

I had not before had an opportunity of coming into contact with the British cavalry, which had been per-forming wonderful feats of valour, and whose existence for the past week had been one continual rearguard action. I was much impressed with their splendid quality throughout. I heard that afternoon of a couple of magnificent cavalry actions of the day before by General Gough's 3rd Cavalry Brigade and General Chetwode's 5th Cavalry Brigade between St. Quentin and La Fère. They had met and routed a couple of columns of German cavalry, and demonstrated their absolute superiority as cavalry over the enemy's mounted forces. That the 2nd Cavalry Brigade should have fought so successful an action when dismounted, after the splendid mounted work that it and its fellow Brigades had been doing for days past, showed its marvellous adaptability. A staff officer came by and told us that heavy fighting had taken place on Von Kluck's right and left flanks, the French being driven back in the west and having held their own in the east.

The 2nd Cavalry Brigade was billeted that night at Ourscamps, a village a few kilometres south of Noyon. I drove General de Lisle and Captain "Rattle" Barrett (15th Hussars), who was de Lisle's staff captain, about the village and the grounds of the old château, selecting bivouacs for the three regiments of the Brigade—the 4th Dragoon Guards, the 9th Lancers, and the 18th Hussars. In the beautiful summer evening we watched a long-drawn-out fight between a German aeroplane and two British aeroplanes which were chasing it back to the north. Apparently the faster British plane was the speediest of the trio, but the German was clever in his manœuvring. We could see puffs of smoke from time to time as one or other of the airmen fired. They wheeled and dipped and dived, circling now up and now down, drawing steadily away, until they finally passed out of sight. We would have given much to have known the result of the contest.

I compared notes with one and another of the cavalry officers who had been in closest and most continuous touch with the enemy from the beginning.

Haig's 1st Corps, they agreed, had the best opportunity to get away without heavy loss, as the brunt of the German attack was further west, on Smith-Dorrien's 2nd Corps. The splendid fight put up by Smith-Dorrien's threatened left saved it from casualties to a greater extent than was yet realised.

How comparatively few casualties had been inflicted by Von Kluck's smashing attack we did not know until the official reports told us that on the retreat and the advance to the Marne the total for the three Corps and the Cavalry division was 64 officers and 212 men killed, 1,223 of all ranks wounded, and 13,643 missing, and most of them of course either killed or wounded, and not unwounded prisoners. Only 15,142 from a force of over 100,000. When one takes from that number the casualty lists of Audregnies, Landrecies, Guiscard, Néry, the fighting near Villers-Cotteret, La Ferte Jouarre, and the conflicts that took place near the Grand Morin, Petit Morin, and the Marne itself, one realises that Sir John French's Army not only escaped annihilation at Mons and Cambrai-Le Cateau, it escaped great loss, and that in the face of circumstances which made it seem impossible it could do so. At least, it seemed impossible to us, a day or so later, that it *had* done so.

Sordêt's cutting in on the left of the line at Cambrai with his guns, and letting us get away from the Cambrai-Le Cateau line, was freely commented on by the cavalry. They knew how greatly Sordêt's cavalry had helped us.

Most engrossing to me was meeting those who had been last in St. Quentin. On Wednesday, the 26th, the great battle of Cambrai-Le Cateau had been fought. Thursday I spent in St. Quentin, leaving it in the afternoon, when reports of oncoming Germans within a couple of kilometres of the town were brought in by both French and English scouts.

Friday I had spent in Noyon. The cavalry had been in and about St. Quentin most of that day. The German occupation of the town had been delayed until nearly every straggler who reached it from the north, if not all, had been gotten away.

Major Tom Bridges, of the 4th Dragoon Guards, had been sent into St. Quentin on Friday afternoon to see if more stragglers could be found. In the square near the Mairie he found a couple of hundred or more men of various detachments, who were seated on the pavement in complete exhaustion and utter resignation to what appeared their inability to rejoin the army which had retreated far to the southward.

They, too, expected the Germans momentarily. A couple of half-crazed, irresponsible chaps had preached some rot to them that made them think themselves abandoned to their fate. Bridges needed but a moment to see how far gone they were, how utterly and hopelessly fatigued. No peremptory order, no gentle request, no clever cajolery would suffice. With most of them the power to move seemed to themselves to have gone with ceaseless tramping, without food or sleep, for the thirty-six hours past.

A brilliant idea came to the big, genial major. Entering a toy shop, he bought a toy drum and a penny whistle. He strapped the little drum to his belt.

" Can you play ' The British Grenadiers ' ? " he asked his trumpeter.

" Sure, sir," was the reply.

In a twinkling the pair were marching round the square, the high treble of the tiny toy whistle rising clear and shrill. " But of all the world's brave heroes, There's none that can compare, With a tow, row, row, with a tow, row, row, To the British Grenadiers."

Round they came, the trumpeter, caught on the wings of the Major's enthusiasm, putting his very heart and soul into every inspiring note.

Bridges, supplying the comic relief with the small sticks in his big hands, banged away on the drum like mad.

They reached the recumbent group. They passed

its tired length. Now they came to the last man. Will they feel the spirit of the straining notes, rich with the tradition of the grand old air ? Will they catch the spirit of the big-hearted Major, who knows so well just how the poor lads feel, and seeks that spot of humour in Tommy's make-up that has so often proved his very salvation ?

The spark has caught ! Some with tears in their eyes, some with a roar of laughter, jump to their feet and fall in. The weary feet, sore and bruised, tramp the hard cobbles unconscious of their pain. Stiffened limbs answer to call of newly-awakened wills.

" With a tow, row, row, with a tow, row, row, to the British Grenadiers." They are singing it now, as they file in long column down the street after the big form hammering the toy drum, and his panting trumpeter " blowing his head off " beside him.

" Go on, Colonel ! We'll follow you to hell," sings out a brawny Irishman behind who can just hobble along on his torn feet.

Never a man of all the lot was left behind.

Down the road, across the bridge, mile after mile towards Roye. The trumpeter, blown, subsides for a while, then, refreshed, takes up the burden of the noble tune again.

At last Tom Bridges turned and said : " Now, boys, ahead of you is a town where you can get food and drink and a bit of rest before you go on. It isn't far. Good luck ! "

But not they. They were not going to lose their new-found patron. Clamour rose, shrill and eager. " Don't leave us, Colonel," they begged. " Don't, for God's sake, leave us ! They all left us but you. We'll follow you anywhere, but where to go when you leave we don't know at all."

So Bridges toiled on to Roye with them, got them food and billets, turned them over to someone who would see they got on to their commands in some way, and went back to duty with his regiment, arriving at two o'clock in the morning.

Big Tom Bridges! Indeed, he has more than once earned the name, but never more gallantly and wisely than on that afternoon in August in the turmoil of the great retreat.

MONS TO YPRES.

CHAPTER III.

On Sunday, the 30th, I rose early and put in a busy morning in Compiègne on messenger work, at noon time returning to G.H.Q. for further orders. The day was frightfully hot, the sky a very clear blue, quite pale in the heat. In a group under a shady tree I found Captain Kirkwood, good fellow and soldier of fortune, who had been in South Africa, big game shooting, when the war cloud gathered over Europe. Hurrying back, he reached Paris in the early days of the retreat, and after some difficulty managed, owing to the fact that he was an ex-officer of British cavalry, to get permission to report himself to Sir John French's Headquarters. At first it seemed unlikely that he would be given a chance to join up with the Expeditionary Force, but he had been told that morning that if he would report to General de Lisle he would be given work to do as a Captain of the 4th Dragoon Guards, who had lost heavily in officers. Kirkwood was in a quandary, wondering how he could obtain transportation from Sir John French's Headquarters in Compiègne to General de Lisle's Headquarters, wherever they might be. This was an undertaking that bristled with difficulties owing to the scarcity of motor-cars.

He told me his troubles, and I at once saw an opportunity to be released from more prosaic duty at Compiègne, obtain a run up to the front, and possibly see something of the rearguard fighting.

A brief explanation of the situation to Major Bartholomew, one of the officers in charge of the motor cars attached to Headquarters Staff, was sufficient to obtain permission to take Captain Kirkwood to 2nd Cavalry Brigade Headquarters. Knowing that the 2nd

WITH FRENCH.

Cavalry Brigade had billeted the night before in Ourscamps, I thought our most interesting plan would be to run to Ourscamps and then beat south along the road they had taken to reach the Compiègne-Soissons line.

I had gathered at G.H.Q. that the whole of the British Force was to fall back on the Aisne. Some rumour was about which told of a conference between General Joffre and Sir John French on the Saturday afternoon, and that the advantage gained on our right by the French 5th Army was to count for naught as the whole line was to retire not only on our immediate right, but away to the east where the German centre was dealing sledge-like blows in an effort to hammer through the French centre. Though we did not know it, that Sunday morning was to witness the German occupation of La Fère and Laon to the east of it. The retreat of the British Expeditionary Force had begun again, as had the consequent advance of the Germans. It was difficult for us, at that time, to understand the lull in the operations of the 27th and 28th of August, and the renewal of the chase on the 29th and 30th. It was long before we realised that the operations on the British front during those days were of slight importance relatively, when compared with the great battles that were taking place to the eastward. Naturally we were entirely concerned with our immediate surroundings, and the fact that the whole line to the westward had to move back to conform with the stubbornly-resisted advance of the Germans bearing down on Rheims and Châlons was as yet unknown to us.

I started off gaily for Ourscamps with Kirkwood just after midday.

Some cheerful individual had assured me that the French cavalry were still at Noyon, and I had taken his word for it with childlike simplicity.

Running to Choisy, we crossed the Oise, and, gaining

MONS TO YPRES.

its western bank, passed through Ribecourt. Pushing on with a clear road and invigorating sunshine to spur us, it would take but a few minutes to cover the eight kilometres to Noyon. The *pavé* of the main road was in such bad state of repair that a temporary path had been utilised under the trees by the roadside. It was rough, but not so bad as the *pavé*, except that here and there great ditches made one pull up rather sharply.

Groups of country folk along the highway waved us on. Once Kirkwood remarked that we had best be careful, as we were surely running very close to enemy country, but I thought we were certain to have warning from the country folk if any German had been seen in the vicinity. No sooner had I expressed an opinion to this effect, than a peasant at the roadside, a bright-eyed, bent, little old chap, indulged in a lively panto-mime in an endeavour to attract our attention. As I was running well over forty miles per hour I required a few yards for stopping, the little man in the mean-time using the fore fingers of each hand to describe as best he might above his head the appearance of the Uhlans' horned helmets, and alternating this bit of sign language with unmistakable motions indicating pointed moustaches of the Kaiser type. As we slowed down he ran to us, and in answer to Kirkwood's ques-tions, informed us that the Uhlans were just ahead of us. I suppose we looked somewhat incredulous, and the idea may have come to him that he had not suffi-ciently explained himself, for again he went through his antics, picturing the pointed moustaches and the horned Uhlan helmets. As he was somewhat inco-herent, we beckoned to another peasant, who approached and told us quietly and with great con-viction that thirty Uhlans had but a few moments before passed along the road in the direction in which we were travelling. This was alarming information If we had run sufficiently far into the German lines for Uhlan patrols to be passing along the road in both directions, there was great possibility that we would not again see Compiègne.

As an American in khaki the Huns might be expected to make short work of me if I fell into their hands. My uniform, procured at a few hours' notice from a London theatrical costumier, was of a nondescript sort, not calculated to insure my being treated by the Germans as a member in good standing of the British Army.

I had good reason, therefore, to wish to avoid capture at all costs.

The point at which we had stopped was but very few kilometres from Noyon, and at that point the road from Passel joined the main pike, giving me ample opportunity to turn the car without backing it.

While we were talking with our informants a mounted Uhlan rode out in full view in the roadway ahead of us, not more than 500 yards distant. He halted and apparently called to his companions under the trees by the roadside, for a dozen joined him immediately. For a moment they made no movement, inspecting us with the greatest interest. Kirkwood had got out of the car to have a look with his glasses and to make sure that they were foes and not friends. I swung the car around in a twinkling and Kirkwood jumped to his seat with a remark that the Uhlans were on the way.

We flew back over the road, a cloud of dust rising behind us. A few shots were fired. The car clattering over the terribly broken road made such a din one could hear little else. All sorts of possibilities passed through our minds. A puncture or a burst tyre would have meant a wheel pounded to pieces in no time: another Uhlan scouting party on either side of the road was more than probable and might have spelled disaster. All went merrily, however, and we were in Ribecourt again almost before we knew it. My forehead was covered with perspiration—in anticipation, I suppose. At Ribecourt we met a British officer in a car and a motor cyclist with him, from our Intelligence Department. They were bound for Lassigny. We warned them in due time and they proceeded cautiously by a side road, to the west of the point at which we had encountered the Uhlans.

Leaving Ribecourt we passed a British cavalry patrol of eight troopers. We again reported the presence of the Uhlan outpost on the main road. The sergeant in command of the patrol told us that in Chiry, a town between Ribecourt and Passel and only a quarter of a mile or less to the west of the main road, the Uhlans had been quartered in some strength all the morning. The patrol had been in the woods not far from Chiry watching the Uhlans for an hour or more, and in their opinion there were at least 200 of them in and about the town. That we should have thus rushed past so large a force and come back again without their intercepting us was a matter of pure luck, and turned what might have been a serious matter for us into an amusing adventure. We must have been within but a few hundred yards of them both going and coming.

We had, beyond a doubt, been well within the German advance line, and out again without being in the least the worse for it.

Crossing the Oise we ran to Le Plessis and Brion, and there encountered a party of French engineers who were waiting to blow up a line. They told us all the bridges were destroyed south of Noyon. We met one of our own engineer officers who told us that the Ourscamps bridge was blown up early that morning. If we had planned a hasty retreat by the route originally selected we would have been nicely caught in a trap.

I gained some information as to the obstacles we were putting in the way of the advancing Germans by destroying railways and bridges. Everything in the nature of a bridge which could be destroyed had been rendered impassable. This had no inconsiderable effect on checking the impetuosity of the German forward movement.

We ran to G.H.Q., and I reported the fact that the Uhlans were well south of Noyon. We again took the road for 2nd Cavalry Brigade Headquarters, planning to run through the Forest of Laigue to Tracy-le-Mont. At the fork where the roads for Noyon and Soissons branch a handsome Rolls-Royce landaulette was piled up against a telegraph pole at the side of the road; Jimmy Rothschild was standing despondently beside it. Approaching the fork, Jimmy had suddenly been confronted by a French sentry, who had emerged from the undergrowth and called upon the approaching motorist to halt, at the same time throwing his rifle to his shoulder and pointing it very directly, so Jimmy said, at the driver —who happened to be Jimmy. Realising that he must stop at all costs, he turned the car to the road-side, where the front axle struck the telegraph pole— with dire results. We took everything removable from the car, piled it into a cart, sent it to Compiègne, and, taking Rothschild in the back, we started again for Tracy-le-Mont. We were told the forest was full of Uhlan scouts, who had been seen crossing the road, but we were apparently in quite as much danger from Jimmy Rothschild's Mauser pistol, which he loaded and carried at the "ready," until both Kirkwood and I demanded that he should keep it pointed in the direction of the enemy rather than towards the back of our heads.

Down some of the long wooded aisles we could see moping horsemen in the afternoon light. If they were Uhlans they were undoubtedly quite as shy of meeting us as we were of encountering them. We passed French soldiers in trenches along the way, ready and waiting for the oncoming enemy.

Tracy was a beautiful place. There we found our

cavalry, and passed squadron after squadron and battery after battery of guns on the way southward to Attichy. From Attichy we doubled back to the village of Vieux Moulin on the south of the Aisne, where we found General de Lisle.

My run back to Compiègne was made in quick time as I had been told on leaving Headquarters that G.H.Q. was to be moved at 10 o'clock to Villers Cotteret. At 10 o'clock, however, orders were changed, and we stayed in Compiègne. Someone had annexed my room in the hotel, so I sought the cot in the college where I had slept my first night in Compiègne. I was alone in the dormitory and overslept. I turned out on the morning of Monday, the 31st, at half past seven and found everyone attached to G.H.Q. gone, except one or two tardy ones. G.H.Q. took "some watching" in those days. If one turned around it was likely to disappear to the southward. Picking up a couple of staff officers as passengers I was soon headed for Senlis, *en route* for Dammartin, the next town to which G.H.Q. was to lend the dignity of its presence. Near Senlis we went by columns of French infantry. For the first time during the campaign I saw the sturdy little French foot soldiers on the march. With a goodly interval between each company, in loose marching order they scattered all over the road. Their heavy kits included the inevitable tin pots packed on their backs. It seemed cruel to garb a soldier in such clothes on a hot day. I little realised how much I was to admire them before the end of the campaign. None of us knew what we were yet to owe to the French Army, and in what high regard we were one day to hold it. Near St. Vaast the road wound upwards through the woods. All the way up the ascent we passed the toiling legion in long blue coats over heavy red breeches, pattering along, uncomplaining, always on the move, covering the ground with most wonderful rapidity in what seemed to me a most unorthodox manner of doing so. From Senlis to Dammartin we skirted the Forest of Ermonville, running through wonderfully beautiful country. Here a silver-clad hillside, there a rare château, and by it a lovely village. Evidences of war were there, carts full of refugees generally so occupying the road that one had little space for passing. I had a fast run and arrived at Dammartin in advance of G.H.Q.

The parts of my car known to the mechanically-minded as universal joints needed grease. Nice accessible things, universal joints. Taking my car to a point on the road where I seemed sure of isolation for a time, I crawled under the brute, and with many irrelevant remarks proceeded to unlace the leather boots which covered the parts to be doctored. Plastering them with what part of the soft grease I could keep from dropping down into my eyes, I at last, sweating at every pore, and " fed up " with chauffeuring, rested, self-satisfied with my conscientious efforts. Then I tried to withdraw from beneath the car. There was the rub. I lay head down, the curb preventing escape on the lower side. I was so nice a fit between the bottom of the step and the paving-stones, that to wriggle uphill on my back was impossible. Consequently, after fruitless labours to extricate myself, I lay for half-an-hour until a couple of doughty Scots passed. When they had recovered sufficiently from the humour of the situation, they put down their rifles, and each taking firm hold of a leg hauled me forth, even more disreputable in appearance than before.

A French limousine car reached Dammartin, an object lesson for timid motor drivers thereabouts. It was riddled with bullet-holes and the seats were covered with blood. Four Frenchmen were coming from Mont-didier to Compiègne that morning and were ambushed by Uhlans along the road. The driver was shot

The wounded trumpeter of the Berlin Dragoner Garde after the charge of the 9th Lancers at Montcel

Algerian Cavalry going into action on the Vesle near Braisne

"I" Battery R.H.A. firing on the La Tretoire, which was being
attacked by the Coldstreams

through the body, but managed to keep the wheel and get the car well away to safety a mile or so further on, when he succumbed to his wounds. Beside him his brother had been shot dead. Taking the driver's place when he collapsed, one of the occupants of the car had brought it on to our Head-quarters—a gory spectacle.

An engineer officer told me of a little tragedy in his corps. Two R.E. officers and half-a-dozen men had been sent back to blow up a bridge near Compiègne. They set rapidly about their work, and were but half through it when a volley from cover near by hit the officers and five of the men, one only escaping.

Jimmy Radley, in describing what he called a " real day's work," incidentally showed of what value the motor car has become in military operations.

On the day before—Sunday—he had taken a staff officer from Compiègne to Soissons, and thence as far north as Laon. Pushing still north to Nouvion, near La Fère, they reached the Headquarters of the French General commanding the extreme French left. There they learned that the big fight at Guise had been followed by severe fighting at Renansart and Mayot, not far to the northward. In spite of the report that the Germans were even then coming into La Fère, in order to get to St. Gobain, Jimmy's staff officer dashed through Danizy and past La Fère, sighting no Germans, though evidently all but in touch with them. Next they visited Coucy-le-Château, *en route* for Soissons. At Coucy they were warned that Uhlans had been seen at Bagneux, some distance south. The Soissons road was the line of retreat of our 1st Corps, and passage of it was difficult. From Soissons, the car turned northward again, and for the second time visited Laon, soon to be evacuated in the face of the rapid German advance. The road from Soissons to Laon was full of Belgian soldiers and refugees from Namur. Leaving Laon, Radley sped south to Bourg, then through Braisnes, back to Soissons, and finally home to Compiègne, his starting-point. Truly, work enough for one day.

Some charming French folk insisted most hospitably upon my joining them at *déjeuner*, which in Dammartin was all the more a blessing as the sole village inn was unspeakably dirty and uninviting — an exceptional French hostelry.

Continuous work at high speed had depleted my stock of spare tyres. I found myself without one remaining spare cover or tube. As none were available about Headquarters nor seemed likely to be, and the Gates of Paris were less than thirty kilometres distant, I asked permission to run to Paris that evening to replenish my stock of pneumatics and return before daybreak. I was told that no official permission could be granted, but that I would not be required before morning if I chose to take upon myself the responsibility of the journey. Prince Murat, who was at that time attached as a French soldier interpreter to G.H.Q., was anxious to run into town to get his motor car, and I gladly agreed that he should bear me company. We reached Paris by dusk, passing a number of French troops scattered here and there in the towns on the way. We were frequently challenged, and, in fact, through some districts went pass in hand. At first sight, Paris seemed quite un-affected by the proximity of the fighting, but as dusk came on, and we entered the central part of the city, it assumed a very different aspect. A visit to the Invalides obtained an order for the necessary covers and tubes from the French War Office. Armed with the official order for our requirements we repaired to the Grand Palais d'Automobiles, which was the supply depôt for all motor requisites. We found the great hall full of cars, and plentiful supplies of tyres and petrol available. All was bustle and hurry, but every deference was paid to our requests, and we were soon supplied with our needs. It was dark by this time, and headlights were denied us. Paris at night in war time was no place for a motor car. A visit to Murat's flat in the Avenue de Monceau necessitated a journey that more than once nearly proved my undoing. How I escaped the excavations in the streets, which seemed for ever to be in front and upon all sides of me, I never knew. As we returned, the great semaphore arms of the searchlights on the tops of some of the buildings down town waved back and forth across the inky sky. We reached the Ritz with a sigh of relief, and sat down to a civilised dinner. Only eight or nine tables in the dining-room were occupied. The Spanish Ambassador was at one table and Sir Francis Bertie, the English Ambassador, at another. I had a chat with Sir Francis, telling him some general news of the retreat, and obtaining from him some idea of the general operations in return. He told me that the day before bombs had been dropped on Paris from German aeroplanes, and a couple of people had been reported killed thereby. At one table was a group of Americans in golf clothes.

Paris was rife with rumours. Two French staff officers told of a big engagement on that day, but they had no details. At ten o'clock I suggested returning to Dammartin, but Murat and other French friends declared that such a project would be suicidal. It was bad enough, they argued, to traverse the roads inside the fortifications in the daytime. French Reservist sentries were a bit jumpy at that season. One of my French staff officer acquaintances retailed a story of one of the Reservist sentries who had turned out a whole regiment to meet the onslaught of a German force, which proved to be an inoffensive herd of cows, two of which the sentry had accounted for before the arrival of reinforcements. Yielding to pressure of sound counsel, I ran out to Murat's flat and accepted his hospitality for the night. We would have enjoyed the picture of the continually playing search-lights but for the game of hide-and-seek between excavations and hoardings along the boulevards in the pitch darkness.

On the morning of Tuesday, September 1st, I was away with the first light. Many features of daily Parisian life were in quite normal evidence. The streets were being washed as usual, and the early morning market carts were rolling along in quite their customary leisurely fashion. Crowds of people were already surging to the railway stations. Cabs or such conveyances were notable by their absence. Sentries along the road, particularly at railway crossings or bridges, looked me over interestedly, and once or twice stopped me to afford closer inspection but peculiarly enough, I was not required to show a pass of any sort until I was quite 18 kilometres out of Paris. The 6th Corps under Maunoury was already beginning to move northward from Paris, and the road was lined with marching troops. Reservists were busy digging trenches here and there, and I heard and saw the smoke of one or two explosions where houses were being cleared away to afford a better line of fire for the guns around Paris. Further north, through towns in which French troops were garrisoned, my pass was in constant demand. In one small village I had to show it to three different sentries.

Arriving at Dammartin I found Sir John French's Headquarters were in a quaint little château faced by a circular drive lined with beds of beautiful flowers. G.H.Q. officers were located in the coachhouses and the adjoining servants' quarters of the château. Outside the gates, in a lane of truly rural appearance and dimensions, were all sorts of motor-cars. G.H.Q. was just turning out when I drove up, officers and men busying themselves with hurried toilets in whatever receptacle they could find that would hold water. All asked eagerly of news from Paris.

MONS TO YPRES.

I called at the G.H.Q. Post Office for a letter, and Major Warren, in charge of all questions relating to the post, delivered a homily on the disappointments and delays in that department. Letters had arrived the night before which had been posted in London fourteen days previously. Letters outbound from the Expeditionary Force were first carefully censored and had most of their contents deleted. Once prepared for despatch they awaited a supply train, and were then taken to our supply base, sometimes a day or two after being turned in to G.H.Q. At the supply base they were again censored, subsequently to proceed leisurely to the rail base. There they were censored once more. They were then considered ripe to be forwarded to England.

On arrival in London they were held for four or five days to ensure that any news they might contain would be sure to be stale. This procedure we accepted as a matter of course without complaint. We had little time for letter writing and little desire to transmit any information except the news as to our bodily welfare. I was not nearly so much concerned with what manner of communication I could send to England as with the failure to obtain news from London. The short notice which preceded my departure made me all the more anxious to obtain word from home, but I was destined to be a long time without it. One authentic story that I heard during the retreat, *re* the Censor, is quite worth repeating. The address which we were required to give to our friends at home was simply General Headquarters, British Expeditionary Force. If we indited this cabalistic formula on the outside of an envelope containing a letter to England the communication was instantly destroyed. If we headed a letter with this superscription it was torn off. If we embodied the address in the body of the letter, however, it was let through. One day a number of us were comparing experiences and these facts were undeniably set forth and evidence produced as to their authenticity.

We would have given much to have had the Censor present at that *séance*, and to have expressed to him, collectively and individually, our opinion as to his methods.

The early part of the morning I spent watching a never-ending stream of supply lorries and ammunition wagons. Dozens and dozens and dozens of wagons of horse transport passed through the town. For half an hour I was engrossed with the field wireless service, which was working steadily. A Scottish company was guarding a Silesian officer, who had a wound in his right arm. He was a fine-looking young fellow in a smart grey uniform and handsome grey shako.

At 10 o'clock I met an officer who wanted to obtain conveyance to Soissons to join the 3rd Cavalry Brigade. I expected to find that the Germans had crossed the Aisne and were south of Soissons, but I offered to run up that way. I was anxious to see what was happening to Haig's Corps. We ran by way of Nanteuil to Betz.

The refugees along the road were pitiable. A handsome girl, well dressed, rode by on her bicycle sobbing bitterly. Loads of women in farm carts went by crying. One mother with her baby asked anxiously for news of the Germans. When told they were undoubtedly moving southward she made a strenuous effort to be brave. The baby raised its little hand, and touched her face and cooed to her. Kissing it fondly, she burst into torrents of tears. The women had heard such stories of German atrocities that they were well-nigh frantic. There was no complaint and no reviling of the British for dropping back, but it was clear that many of the poor folk could not understand the continual retreat. There seemed no end of the refugees, cartload after cartload passing by filled with women. It was indeed rare that we saw a man among the refugees.

A light touch was given by a gracious lady and her young son, who were just about to depart from Betz in their motor-car. With true French politeness she explained to us that she wished to give her château to the British in case it would be of use to them. The likelihood that night would find the Germans in it made this seem almost a joke.

We started for Villers Cotteret for lunch, and shortly after one o'clock reached the outskirts of Ivor Heavy rifle firing could be heard in front, and the enemy was evidently well south of Villers. A bitter fight was in progress in the woods in front of us. The 4th Guards Brigade were hard at it. They suffered severe losses, although they scored off the Germans in the hand-to-hand fighting in the forest.

Giving up the idea of going to Villers, we worked southward, passing the 5th Brigade of the 2nd Division, consisting of Worcesters, Highland Light Infantry, and Connaught Rangers. It was a hot day, and the Tommies were very tired and feeling the heat. The enemy were not many kilometres behind and pressing on rapidly. We found the Germans had been in Crépy for some hours, and were moving south in considerable strength. Our rearguards were in position between Betz and Crépy.

Having delivered the officer as near to his command as possible, I called at General Haig's Headquarters at Mareuil, a town on the Ourcq, to see if I could take back a message to Dammartin. It was evening before I was again on the road. Running south on the Meaux road, I found it filled with refugees in all sorts of vehicles. Big wagons half loaded with straw and piled with country folk ambled along, pulled by four oxen. Hordes of women and children were walking, trudging along in the dust beside heavily-laden vehicles.

I arrived at Dammartin just after 7 o'clock, and while waiting outside G.H.Q. encountered Captain O'Mahoney, of the Army Service Corps. He had been captured by the Germans, and made good his escape. I gathered some of the details from him, but he was so sleepy, that to obtain a careful account of his experiences was difficult. After awakening him three or four times as he sat in my car telling me the story, I gave it up as a bad job and let him slumber in peace

The incident of O'Mahoney's escape is well worth relating. I give it just as it was told by his driver.

" One night we were poking along in a low-lying mist. The armies were retreating, and we knew we were making for the southward. I did not know where we were. I was driving the captain's car, and we had one chap in the tonneau with us. The Captain told him to keep a good look-out behind and see that the three lorries, which were following us, kept close together. We numbered about a score all told, besides the Captain. He had told me to go slow, as we were sure to butt against French or English sentries before long, and the slower we went the more likely we would be to avoid trouble. We knew the enemy were not far away, and heard all sorts of stories about their being in one town or another, close behind us or to one side. We had learned by then to disbelieve half what we heard.

" We crawled along with sidelights lit, without head lights, as we had run out of carbide days before.

" The mist grew thicker and the road blacker. Once or twice I thought I was off it altogether, but managed to save myself and the car just in time.

" Someone sang out in front of me, and as I pulled the car up I could see a sentry by the dim light of the side lamp. The radiator was almost touching him, and he was holding his rifle at the ready. The Captain rose beside me and said, 'English,' just as I heard a voice in front saying, 'Get out of that car.'

"With those five words I knew we were up against it, for they were spoken with a sure-enough German accent.

"I stood up, and the Captain dismounted from the car. He was told to unload his pistol and hand it over to a German officer who came from behind the sentry. I could see several Germans by that time. They were big chaps, and wore enormous helmets with great spikes on the top, which made them look very tall in the mist.

"I heard the engines behind us still running. The driver of one of the lorries had enough presence of mind to ditch his machine. That put it out of commission as far as the Germans were concerned, for no one could bother in that sort of a night with that sort of a road to pull the lorry out of the mud and water. The lorry behind the one that was ditched was so close to it that it had to be backed to get it round. A little ingenuity got a back wheel of that one into the ditch as well. That caused some swearing by the Germans, but they had bagged the car and one lorry and twenty-one prisoners, so I suppose they thought they had done well enough. They disarmed us all, and started us off by the road, surrounded by cavalry.

"I talked with the Captain about the fix we were in, but he saw nothing for it but to drive on as ordered. We passed at least a Division of cavalry. The Captain thought we had seen four Brigades. They were a fine-looking outfit, splendid horses, and fine-looking men.

"At daybreak we were brought before some sort of commander. The Captain was told to dismount from the car, and was taken over into the field to talk to the German chap, who gave him a cigarette as he came up. I could hear the conversation. The German spoke good enough English to pass as an Englishman.

"The first thing he said was, ' Why are you fighting us ? '

"The Captain was wise in his answer. He said, ' Because I am ordered to do so.'

" ' From where were you coming when caught ? ' " asked the German.

"The Captain threw back his shoulders, looked the big chap straight in the eye, and said : ' That is not a fair question, sir.'

" The German smiled, but his ' Perhaps not ' sounded very gruff.

" He talked a moment in German with an officer by him, and, finally, turning to the Captain, said : ' We do not want you with us. We are a flying column and cannot be bothered with you ; but we shall have to keep you with us until we can hand you over to the first supply train we meet. You will have to accept the situation, and do your best to do just as you are told, and make your movements conform with our wishes in every particular. If last night had not been an occasion for the greatest secrecy, the sentries would probably have fired upon you instead of taking you prisoner. As it is, you are an inconvenience to us, and you must bear that in mind.'

"With that, the Captain came back to the car. I could see he was downhearted. We moved along a bit further, still surrounded by plenty of cavalry, and before the sun was well up firing commenced in front. I pulled up when I heard the bullets cut their way through the trees overhead. A big mounted chap near me pointed his lance up the road and motioned to me that I had better get on. So I did. No German near us at that time spoke any English, or at least none would talk to us ; but they had no difficulty in getting me to go right on.

" The firing grew rather hot, though the bullets were going pretty high. A lane led away to the right, and we were chased down that and then sent to the left. Finally we were made to come back again, and then go still further to the left. Every little while we came into the line of fire, and more than once the bullets whistled uncomfortably close to us. The Captain said that it was becoming quite plain to him we were being purposely exposed.

" We waited about fifteen minutes at a corner, and a German officer rode up and told us in English to go on down the road. The Captain spoke up then, and said that he considered we were being put into the way of the fire of our troops with the idea of getting us shot by our own lot. The Hun officer only shrugged his shoulders and gave no answer. A moment later he rode back, and said, ' Give me that map case.'

" The Captain replied: ' I have no objection to giving up my pistol and field glasses, but when it comes to taking my map case, particularly as it is empty, it looks to me more like robbery than anything else. The map case is my private property.'

" The German officer looked very sour at this, and gave another shrug to his shoulders, and tossing up his head went away mumbling something in German.

" We were with a fine regiment for about half an hour after this, when finally the fight drifted round our way again. Someone told the Captain that the British cavalry were immediately in front. Apparently the regiment who were looking after us was not expected to make a stand, for it started away, a squadron at a time, at the gallop—a very fine sight as they tore through the woods.

" We were taken from the car and the lorry, and marched through the woods a bit, and finally put in a deep ditch in charge of an officer and twelve men. A stiff lot of rifle fire went over our heads. The officer in charge of us seemed a rather decent sort of German, and spoke a few words of English. His men were firing regularly, but were keeping down behind the top of the ditch safely, so they could not have been doing much damage. The German came over to where the Captain was lying, and sat down there for a few minutes, every little while repeating two English words, which seemed about the only thing he could produce in the way of talk. 'Very hot, very hot,' he would say, and grin.

"The attack drifted round to the left a bit and lulled down, then became more fierce again. One or two bullets began to sing down the ravine rather than across the top of it. We had all been safe enough up to this time so long as we lay low. When the firing worked round to the left, however, the officer came over to the Captain and shook hands, and said 'Goodbye.' He evidently did not intend that all his men should leave, for only two or three went with him, and then two or three more a bit later.

"The Captain got it in his head that it was more than likely we would be shot before the last of the Germans left us, and the next few minutes of waiting were mighty tough. The suspense nearly made me ill.

"At last all the Germans had gone except one evil-looking private. I never saw such a villainous face on any man. No one out of the whole German Army could have been picked for a murderer whose looks would have better fitted the part. A low forehead, narrow slits of shifty eyes, a mean thin-lipped mouth, with chin just square enough to show you that he was stubborn enough to carry through a job if it took his fancy. I shall never forget his face.

"The firing had died down again, and the stillness was awful. For the first time I counted our boys and found four were missing: there were fifteen left besides the Captain and myself, and we were all lying together in a bunch. Most of us had our eyes on the German. I could not keep my eyes away from him: the evil look on his face fairly mesmerised me. He handled his rifle in a threatening manner for a minute, and actually went so far as to finger the lock and trigger. The Captain said afterwards that it was all he could do to keep from jumping at him and downing him, but he was just far enough away for such a move to have meant a bullet, sure.

" Suddenly the firing came on again, and our guard paused for a moment as though undecided what to do. At last, with an oath he turned and bolted up the ravine in the direction in which his fellows had disappeared.

" The relief was so great when he went we almost forgot the way we were fixed. One or two of the boys jumped up and began to cheer, but this drew a storm of fire at us and over us, and the Captain's remarks were more pointed than polite. There seemed no safe way for us to attract the attention of our own troops immediately in front, so we decided to hook it. We managed to get back to the motor and lorry without getting hit, though how we did it I don't know. No Germans were in sight. We started up the machines and drove along the road to the left until we got a turning up which we could run in a general southerly direction. A mile further on we came in touch with one of our cavalry patrols, and half an hour later we were well within our lines.

" The Captain was all for going back and getting the two lorries which had been ditched, but the retreat was still on, so that was out of the question.

" Whatever happened to the four men that became separated from us I don't know, but none of the rest of us were any the worse. The Captain was a bit sore, and I think all the rest of us were, that they wouldn't let us go back after those two lorries we had lost."

Bad news came of a surprise attack by the Germans between St. Vaast and Néry at daylight that morning. Spies had apparently located the camp of the 1st Cavalry Brigade to a nicety L Battery of the

Royal Horse Artillery was attached to Briggs' Brigade and bivouacked with it.

In the mist of the grey dawn the Germans, who had brought up eight guns in the night, and numbered several thousand, opened fire at 400 yards.

In the first few minutes, so accurately did the enemy gunners have the range, three of the six guns of L Battery were smashed. Two of the battery officers were killed and three wounded. The Cavalry Brigade did not escape, the Queen's Bays, 5th Dragoon Guards and 11th Hussars suffering a number of casualties, and General Briggs' Brigade Major being killed by a shrapnel bullet.

To the hail of shells was added a storm of machine gun fire at close range. In a few minutes every officer and nearly every non-commissioned officer in L battery was wounded, and it was threatened with total annihilation. Only one of its guns remained in action and two men of its crew were all that were left to serve it.

By this time the Cavalry Brigade was engaging the Germans, and Colonel Ansell was leading a couple of squadrons of his 5th Dragoon Guards around their flank, and Colonel Tommy Pitman's 11th Hussars were fighting hard in front. Some of the Middlesex Regiment, too, of the 19th Brigade, hearing the firing, were coming up rapidly in support, as did the 4th Cavalry Brigade.

So fierce was the onslaught of the dismounted troopers, that victory was snatched from the enemy. The Germans were completely routed with considerable loss, and their eight field guns were taken. Colonel Ansell was killed and the 5th Dragoon Guards suffered heavily. L battery was, of course, the greatest victim, its losses being over eighty per cent. of its strength. The story of the capture of the German guns after so great an initial advantage had been gained by them ran over the army like wild fire, and had a most cheering effect.

MONS TO YPRES.

The following detailed account of the fighting at Néry by the 11th Hussars is taken from a diary kept by an 11th Hussar officer :—

" On August 31st, the 1st Cavalry Brigade arrived at Néry just before dark and billeted. At 4.15 a.m. on the morning of September 1st, a patrol, under Lieut Tailby, was sent out to the high ground to the north-east, and the regiment stood to arms at 4.30 a.m. The morning was misty, and it was difficult to distinguish objects at a distance of more than 150 yards. At 5.30 a.m., Lieut. Tailby galloped in carrying a German cloak, and reported that his patrol had ridden in the mist right up to a regiment of German cavalry on the ridge north-east of Néry, and had been chased back as far as the ravine.

" The squadrons were immediately placed into position, B Squadron sending one troop to the south-east corner of the village, one troop to the church overlooking the ravine to the east, one troop to the north-east corner of the village, and one troop being kept in support. C squadron defended the farm immediately to the south of the church, and A squadron was kept in reserve.

" Scarcely had these dispositions been made when an extremely heavy artillery and machine-gun fire opened from the ridge to the north-east of the church.

" As soon as the situation was clear, A squadron was placed at the disposal of the G.O.C. Brigade and sent to fill the gap between L Battery, and the right troop of B squadron, where it remained in action until the conclusion of the engagement. The German guns were in position to the south-east of the village and within 400 yards of L Battery. The wagons with their escort were left on the ridge immediately to the east of the church, but owing to the mist and a report that the French cavalry were coming up, fire was not opened on them until a dismounted patrol had been sent across the ravine to clear up the situation, and a

good opportunity was thus lost. Meanwhile the
enemy had been gradually working round to the
south and occupied the sugar factory. . . . Here
they captured the owner and his workmen, whom
they used when retiring as a screen against a party of
the Bays under Lieut. de Crespigny. Several of the
civilians were wounded, and the Germans escorting
them made off toward their own guns. These unfortunate civilians took cover in a beet field until they
were eventually rescued by us at the end of the action.
At about 8 a.m. the 4th Cavalry Brigade arrived in
support and opened a heavy artillery fire on the
German guns. The enemy then tried to man-handle
the guns out of action, but being under close range of
the Bays' machine-guns (which were most admirably
handled all through), and of the two machine-guns of
the 11th Hussars, which had been brought round to
the road at the south-east corner of the village, most
of the enemy withdrew. Eight guns were left upon
the field.

"Our infantry now arrived from the North and
passed through the village. C squadron were ordered
to mount and follow up the German retreat. They
crossed the ravine and worked round the left flank
towards the German guns; Bell-Irving's troop dismounted and opened fire on some thirty Germans
who were retiring. Norrie's troop galloped through
the German guns only to find them abandoned, and
the advanced infantry closed upon them, the squadron
pushed on to Verrines, capturing a number of prisoners
and horses, and made good a farm about a quarter of
a mile beyond that point; here they captured about
thirty led horses and more prisoners. The squadron
was recalled as the Brigade was ordered west.

"The whole action had lasted about two hours,
during which the enemy kept up a heavy fire of guns
and maxims. The regiment kept up a heavy fire
throughout, except during the short period as stated

Choisy, on the Marne

The Bridge over the Marne, Nogent

The River Aisne near Bourg

A view of the Aisne at one of the points where the British Army
crossed the river

MONS TO YPRES.

above. The casualties in the Bays, 5th Dragoon Guards and L Battery were large, owing to their position at the moment of attack. Those in L Battery were especially heavy, as they gallantly attempted to bring their guns into action under a murderous machine-gun and artillery fire at a range of 400 yards. Several of their guns succeeded in opening fire, but were inevitably silenced by the superior hostile fire. All the officers and men with the guns had been put out of action. Captain Bradbury, who died of wounds the same day, Sergeant-Major Dorrell and one other received the V.C. for their gallant conduct. There is little doubt that the attackers suffered very heavily, and the loss of their guns probably accounted for a German wireless message which was intercepted later in the day, which ran as follows :—

" 'Attacked by English at dawn, unable to fulfil mission.' The attacking force consisted of a Cavalry Division of six regiments, with machine guns and a battery of twelve guns. It looks from the above message as if they did not originally intend to attack Néry, but suddenly finding themselves in the fog within 400 yards of a British force in billets, decided to attack.

"The Brigade was ordered to join the Cavalry Division about five miles west, remained in position there about five hours, and eventually retired south to Borest.

"Sept. 2nd, 1914.

"Moved at dawn through the forest of Ermonville ; glorious weather and glad of the shade. On crossing one of the rides, came on the tracks of horses and sent a troop to follow them up. They found the ride strewn with German kit of all kinds, lame horses, etc., showing a hurried retreat. They had gone by five hours previously and turned out to be our Néry friends, the Cavalry division, who had bumped into one of our columns and retreated rapidly, leaving their four remaining guns."

At half past seven on the evening of September 1st, panic orders came for a sudden movement of G.H.Q. The driver of a car came in with word that a body of six or seven hundred Uhlans had been seen in the vicinity. A never-to-be-forgotten scene was staged in the leafy lane. The big lamps of the cars sent long shafts of light through the gathering dusk. Hurried packing was done by everybody. Groaning lorries were forced up the steep drive. A detachment of cavalry and the Bicycle Company attached to G.H.Q., some few foot soldiers, and a couple of lorry loads of Tommies hurried off together. No time was given to obtain food. Everything was helter-skelter. My car was the last out but one, and I left Dammartin with a sad realisation that my last remaining linen had been deposited that morning in Dammartin's sole laundry, and I had again left behind me goods and chattels which I was more than likely destined never to see again. I asked permission to go and retrieve my clothing, but was told that departure was a matter of the greatest urgency and I could not possibly be spared.

No one who took part in that inglorious scamper will forget it. We raced away in the night, the moonlight throwing deep shadows along the road. A few shots rang out—a dozen or so—which increased the general tension. Never was so much dust distributed over a flying column. The right side of the road was filled with slowly moving supply trains. French cavalry rode past, and French reservist infantry were occupying trenches along the roadway. A dozen aeroplanes loomed white and ghostly in a field as we swung by. Motor cyclists dashed in and out around the swiftly moving cars. We were white with dust from head to foot. G.H.Q. sped on through the night as though all the German devils were on our trail. After what seemed an interminable time we reached Lagny.

Such hurried departure from Dammartin produced confusion on our arrival at Lagny. Our entry into the town was made through lanes of cheering crowds, who were to see the Germans enter the town not many hours afterwards. No cheering then, I imagine.

At one hotel only—the Hotel de la Renaissance—food was available, and there most of us got some sort of a dinner before the night was over. I was fortunate in dining off an omelette made from the last couple of eggs at 11.30, and straightway thereafter turned in on the floor of a hairdresser's shop facing the square, in which the G.H.Q. cars were drawn up in the pale moonlight.

WITH FRENCH.

CHAPTER IV.

SLEEPING in one's clothes on the hard floor of a shop and rising to a breakfast of lukewarm coffee and dry bread, the best available breakfast, is not the primrose path to a day of light-heartedness and good humour, but, nevertheless, I have rarely enjoyed myself so much as on that Wednesday, September 2nd, in Lagny.

Sir John French's army was piling south as fast as it could come. Past the Marne and on toward the south-east of Paris it was to file in hurrying columns.

All day long my car stood in the square at Lagny, save for a short journey or two about the town.

At 8.30 in the morning a big explosion near at hand, and a huge column of black smoke, followed by another fifteen minutes later, told of the French engineers who were blowing up the bridges over the Marne. All the morning they were at work demolishing bridge after bridge in and near the town.

At an early hour I encountered an old friend or cheery personality in Colonel Reggie Ford, the Deputy-Director of Supplies, and with him General King and General Gilpin, the Director of Transport.

A pleasant chat gave me some rough idea of our lines of retreat. That both our armies and the French were falling back steadily was about all the news at that time. The front of our line was to be south of Dammartin by nightfall if all went as planned. G.H.Q. was to move southward during the day, its next stop being Melun.

The sun was scorching down on us in earnest before the morning was well advanced.

I sat in my car and gossiped. A fortunate purchase of a goodly stock of red and white wines, as well as a couple of dozen bottles of mineral water made the cool shade of my hood and the soft, comfortable seats of my car all the more a port of call. The rich orchards of the surrounding valleys were groaning with delicious fruit. A countrywoman sold me a whole basket of luscious peaches and pears for a couple of francs. Life took on a brighter hue.

Some of the stories I heard that morning at Lagny were illustrative of the little that was known of the general plan of the campaign that was proceeding. Most of the Corps commanders drove up during the day and called on Sir John French. The town was full of rumours of all sorts from every part of the line.

One G.H.Q. Staff colonel told me of one of our motor cyclists who had been found dead with lance holes in his hands and his body partially burned. I searched in vain for any corroboration of this report, though it was retailed to me in great detail and with absolute seriousness.

Another officer thought we had lost most of our guns. He could count thirty-seven to thirty-eight we had lost to his personal knowledge. One command that originally had twenty-four guns was left with but one, he said.

A General Staff officer who had been in touch with the staff of the French 5th Army on our right chatted for a long time about the disappointment of the French who had been fighting between La Fère and Guise on August 29th.

The French had a terrible hammering at Guise, he said. In spite of it they sprang a night attack on Von Kluck's left and won an unequivocal victory. Next morning they battered the Germans with 200 guns and almost had them on the run. The enemy retired, and the French were eager to follow up their advantage, sure of capturing no end of guns, which could not have been gotten away. Just then came the order to retire to Sains and Vervins. This, alas, was due to Sir John French having dropped back from Ham and Guiscard, in spite of the strong French force on his left which had come out from Amiens towards Peronne and Nesle. "All the French wanted us to do," he averred, "was to hold the centre. They begged us to do this, but back we came, and the opportunity was lost."

How bad my pessimistic friend felt and how little he knew of the great conflicts to the eastward that were preventing a stand being made in the western theatre !

Another ill-informed strategist explained that orders from Whitehall to keep a way open to the sea had forced the retreat to continue and Paris to be sacrificed. Our base at Boulogne was to be shifted to the mouth of the Loire, away to the south-west. Von Kluck was to gain his objective after all, and Paris streets would soon echo to the tramp of German legions !

Still another alarmist told strange tales of German Uhlans successful south of Dammartin and near at hand, but Borritt of the R.A.C. lot had just come from there, and declared such a rumour to be without the slightest foundation. Borritt had been compelled to leave Dammartin on the previous evening in such haste that he had no opportunity of collecting the bag containing his kit. He returned for it during the early morning. Conflicting rumours made him wary. Leaving his car south of the town he crept up the road stealthily, prepared to bolt if he saw Germans in Dammartin, as report said they were. After a careful reconnaisance he saw a khaki-clad soldier cross the road ahead of him, and on entering the town he found General Haig's Headquarters there. He told me the 4th Division and 19th Brigade had been formed into a 3rd Corps, with General Pulteney in command. They were in action, as a rearguard, on the extreme left rear of the retreating army.

Of the many stories that were rife in Lagny that day, none took account of the fact that Von Kluck would leave Paris to itself and swing to the south-east

MONS TO YPRES.

to smash the French 5th Army, as he was to endeavour to do during the next forty-eight hours. All were greatly concerned with the fate of Paris, which seemed doomed.

At noontide I was asked to take a sorry-looking German prisoner and his grimly cheerful guard, a splendid, big Cameron Highlander, to the railway station. One could hardly imagine so meek a German. Not a sound escaped him. Not a look did he give to right or left. I gave the Highlander a couple of apples from my store and he promptly handed one to the subdued Hun, who took it mechanically with not even a look of thanks. While detained at a level crossing, French soldiers, brimming over with good humour, crowded around the car to see the captive. They were kindly enough, in a rough way, and tried to cheer the poor beggar, but to no effect. Sadness radiated from him. He oozed despondency at every pore. I was glad to turn him over to the Railway Transport Officer.

The roads through Lagny were packed with fleeing refugees. White oxen in fours and fine big draught horses drew load upon load of them. Tandems of three pulled most of the great carts, and blocks in the traffic were numerous. Whole families were piled on wagons full of grain, three generations frequently in one party. Now and then a quartette of milk-white oxen lumbered along pulling a clumsy wagon crowned with a score of women and children huddled together under a dozen huge black umbrellas, an odd sight indeed.

All the afternoon tales of the fighting and explanations of and reasons for the retreat, coupled with prophecies of all sorts came from one quarter or another.

Late in the evening I had a moonlight run to Melun over a grand road. Dozens of sentries along the way stopped us and carefully examined our passes. Once we were held some time on account of our ignorance of the password, but finally allowed to proceed on the strength of my own French pass.

Refugees and columns of motor transports made slow travelling, and it was nearly midnight when we pulled up at G.H.Q. at Melun. I was not long in finding the Trois Monarques, and a drink wherewith to remove some of the dust I had been breathing for miles along the way. There I found Secker, of the R.A.C. He had lost his car when *en route* to Senlis two days before. Crushed between two lorries and towed into Senlis, he hoped to effect a repair. News of the oncoming Germans emptied the garages of the few remaining workmen on September 1st, however, and the troops evacuated the town by eleven o'clock that morning. Secker stayed until two o'clock, when the Germans were reported to be not far north, so there was nothing for it but to leave his car to the enemy and come sadly away on foot.

He was off to Paris at daybreak, he said, to purchase another car to take its place.

No room being available in the hotel, I obtained a billet in the École Jeanne d'Arc, where the motherly old sisters provided me with a clean and comfortable cot.

September 3rd saw me in a new job, which was to last me for many interesting months to come.

The French Government had the day before left Paris for Bordeaux, and Headquarters of the French Armies and the French War Office were to move to Bordeaux that day.

The capitulation of the French capital seemed to most of us to be a foregone conclusion.

General Gilpin had purchased three motor-cars, which were to be assigned to Allenby's Division for intercommunication between Cavalry Brigades. I was asked to take the trio to Allenby's headquarters at Gournay, a village on the south bank of the Marne, a few miles east of Paris.

MONS TO YPRES.

Anxious to see more of the actual fighting than I could possibly do if attached to G.H.Q., I applied to be assigned to the Brigade work for which one of the three new cars had been purchased. My request was granted, and I was off and away from Melun in short order.

The run north on the main road to Meaux found even that broad highway well-nigh impassable owing to the lines of transport and columns of refugees. The hot days and long marches were telling on the poor fleeing country folk in sad fashion. On every side were sad sights—weary mothers wheeling poor little prams ; one pathetic peasant woman seated on a bank by the roadside, rocking her dead baby and crooning over it ; aged *grandes dames* tottering on the hot way ; one well-dressed old lady, with shoes in hand, limping along, her bruised feet showing red through great holes in her thin stockings ; and more than once some worn-out women, exhausted, lying prone in the ditch in merciful insensibility.

I lost one car *en route*, the driver being delayed and separated from us by a stop for a puncture.

Turning over his fellow to Colonel Ludlow, A.A.Q.M.G. of the 1st Cavalry Division, whom I found in a fine château at Champs, I slept the night in a stable, and was off at daybreak to find the lost sheep.

It was night on Friday, September 4th, before I returned with him. Back to Melun, then to our rail bases at Mormant, Guignes, Verneuil, and Chaumes, on to General Smith-Dorrien's headquarters at Maison-celle, and at last to Sir Charles Fergusson's head-quarters at Bouleur, I ran before my mission was accomplished. A spare car was fair game for all and sundry in those days. Each headquarters would gladly annex it should opportunity present.

At Champs, Major MacAlpine-Leny, 16th Lancers, on General Allenby's Staff, had the apportioning of the cars. Learning that I was keen on being sent to General de Lisle and his 2nd Cavalry Brigade, he very kindly arranged matters thus. I found General de Lisle and his staff in a deep wood near Champs. He at once welcomed me into his mess, presenting me to the other members of it, of whom I was to see much during the weeks that followed.

Captain Hamilton-Grace, 13th Hussars, was at that time Brigade-Major of the Second. Captain "Rattle" Barrett, of the 15th Hussars, who had captained the team that brought the International Polo Cup back from the United States, was staff captain. Lieutenant Fairclough, R.F.A., was signals officer, and Lieutenant Jeff Phipps-Hornby, of the 9th Lancers, the well-known gentleman rider, and Lieutenant Pat Armstrong, 10th Hussars, were aides.

Dinner by a camp fire in the woods, surrounded by the troops of cavalry, was picturesque to a degree. Rolling ourselves in our blankets, we were not long in wooing slumber, warned of an early start on the morrow.

So thick was the foliage under which I was sleeping, that a heavy rain fell in the night without wetting or waking me.

We breakfasted by firelight soon after three o'clock on the morning of Saturday, the 5th, and were soon on the road for Limoges, eight kilometres north of Melun. The ghostly files of French and English cavalrymen had commenced their southward trek long before daybreak. The smaller roads to the west of the Forest of Armainvilliers were full of troops on troops of cavalry, so I chose a route straight south through the beautiful forest.

Each little town near the Aisne had its guard and quaint little fortifications. Here ditches, flanked by barrels of stones, there carts minus wheels and filled with bricks and cement. Now and again hastily-improvised stone walls, sometimes covered with branches, but always barricades of some sort at each entrance to each village, and all most conscientiously manned by a local guard.

The 4th Division and 19th Brigade, composing the newly formed 3rd Corps, were on the march south through the Forest. The Welsh Fusiliers and Scottish Rifles, unshaven and unshorn, tramped on in the early morning, already hot, looking fit in spite of their tattered array.

Arriving early at Limoges, I had time to run to Corbeil and back on a foraging expedition before the Brigade made an appearance. The three regiments were billeted in the farms about us, and a dear old woman in one of them cooked a splendid dinner, chiefly consisting of an omelette and a fat duck, for the headquarters' mess. Borrowing a small hand basin after dinner and repairing to a well in an orchard hard by, I indulged in a bath and general clean up.

The day was hot and clear. Most of the Brigade were engaged in cleansing the dust from themselves and their kits and accoutrements, or in taking a mid-day siesta.

Suddenly, at four o'clock, came word that the Brigade was to move at once to Chaumes, away to the eastward. We lost no time in moving. My work was to take Captain Barrett there at once to proceed with the billeting. This was concluded only to find orders were changed, and the brigade was to proceed still further eastward, through Mormant to Ozouer-le-Repos.

I slept on the grass under a great tree that threw a deep shadow in the bright moonlight. We all closed our eyes in different mood than on any night in the previous fortnight. We were moving to the east and the Germans were coming westward. At last we were advancing to meet the enemy. I felt a new life had begun. The very air seemed sweeter, the moonlight softer, the whole world a better place to live in.

WITH FRENCH.

Little, indeed, we knew, but that little was much to us.

Dawn of Sunday, the 6th of September, found me awake. The battle with the advancing enemy was to commence at last. At the breakfast table General de Lisle said to Hamilton-Grace, " See that the fighting men are in front to-day." Gastins, due east, was the first objective, and the Second Brigade was to lead the van.

That Saturday morning was to see history made. General Henderson's airmen had marked the eastward swing of Von Kluck's forces. Joffre was ready to strike, and, on Friday, had conferred with French. Maunoury was on our left, and Conneau's cavalry on our right, with d'Esperey's 5th Army east of him. At that hour the Germans—having reached the Petit Morin—were to find the river would mark the limit of their great advance.

Before the day was over Sir John French's order was to "call upon the British Army in France to show now to the enemy its power, and to push on vigorously to the attack."

The retreat was over—the advance begun.

We never doubted the outcome.

Early the order to form up was given. Through the wide village street the troopers in double column led their chargers, greeted by the rising sun.

Past the big stone barns and prosperous farm houses, past the grim old square-towered church, tramped the troopers. Now they were in saddle and in another moment away, a gallant sight indeed.

Again we had a day of dust and sweltering heat. Our line of advance was north-east, in the general direction of La Ferté Gaucher and the Petit Morin. When between Gastins and Pécy we were informed that a considerable German force was but a few miles ahead, and soon our advance guard was in touch with them.

MONS TO YPRES.

Back and forth along the roads from time to time with various officers of Staff, or standing by the General watching operations through field-glasses, new sights and scenes unfolded themselves during every hour of the day.

Regiments and batteries coming up through the fields, or pushing their way under orchard trees, bands of pickets riding in with reports and tearing away again at a gallop—all was never-ceasing movement.

While the morning was young a German shell burst in a farmyard near me, a score of geese and chickens its only victims, though it set a grain stack on fire.

The whizzy-pop of the shrapnel from the enemy's field-guns was to grow familiar before the day was over. One such shrapnel, unluckily placed, burst over a group of three officers and ten men of the 9th Lancers, hitting every one of them.

A message took me well to the front, to the gates of a big château. As we pulled away, a bang, followed by another, told of a couple of shell-bursts close behind us. A few minutes later, on another visit to the château, I saw six or eight troopers burying a still form wrapped in a rug. A quickly-dug grave by the gate was made, and the body laid in it without delay. Killed by the shells that had come as we left, they said, and killed at the very spot where the car had stood. Two wounded men, hit by the two shells, were lying near, and a sergeant showed me where a piece of shrapnel had torn away an ammunition packet on his breast, without inflicting other hurt than to bruise the skin.

Wounded came back, often supported by a comrade as the day wore on, and the fighting was sufficiently close to the point from which the General was directing operations, so that the merry popping of the rifles through the woods echoed all about us.

Scared inhabitants fled to the rear. Once or twice hysterical women in madly careering carts rushed past, threatening to smash into oncoming guns. Villagers who remained at home, old folk, looked awed and sombre on us as we passed. Colonel Seely materialized during the afternoon, and gave us news that Pulteney's 3rd Corps was fighting hard on our left, and the French on our right were fiercely engaged and forging slowly forward.

We bivouacked that night in the fields, dining in the stubble by the headlights of the car, and sleeping in the open. A chilly night after the hot day, and wet with a heavy fall of dew.

Four o'clock on the morning of Monday, the 7th, saw us up and warming ourselves by the welcome fire, over which breakfast coffee was boiling.

Moving on, the objective of our column, one of three lines of cavalry, was in the general direction of La Ferté Gaucher again, leaving Choisy on our left. Conneau's cavalry was close at hand on our right, and keeping line with us.

A wrong turning at a cross-road put me in advance of the 2nd Brigade. I ran into a bit of sniping fire, but it soon ceased as our advance guard went forward. We were in touch with the enemy every foot of the way, though we had not as yet found him in force. Seven or eight Uhlans rode from behind a cluster of stacks, less than a thousand yards from us, and galloped to the north, a handful of our troopers hot-foot after them. Then heavy rifle fire in front, and, soon after, our guns.

Oh, the fascination of it! The glory of a galloping regiment of cavalry, flowing over a green field in line of squadrons! On we pushed. Past a little village in a valley, tucked away so cleverly one came upon it unawares, then on to a rise of ground, another dip, then a steep hill, and suddenly a shell burst right in front. I pulled up short. The fascination of it was like to run away with me when our own cavalry was chasing the German cavalry. Also it was like to run away with my judgment. A car might get further forward than necessary, perhaps even further forward than was wise.

Bang! bang! Two German shrapnel. Whizz, over and beyond, with a bang behind. Crash! One fell to the right, between two squads of galloping troopers. The horses reared and shied, but not one fell. The second group rode through the white shell-cloud, and dashed on.

Rifle fire ahead, and bang came a shell, bursting over me. Bang! Much too close!

I went into the village of Montcel to seek the protection of its buildings, leaving the car.

I passed up the wide street, deserted except by a dead German officer in front of a cottage, and gained the further edge of the cluster of mean houses that composed the village.

Behind a friendly stone wall, I stopped and took out my glasses. The stubble stretched away towards a line of woods.

Diagonally, across the broad road that led north from the village, came a line of horsemen.

Magnificent in the morning sun they rode, a solid line rising and falling with regular cadence, as though mechanically propelled.

The 1st Garde Dragoner Regiment of Berlin, of the Garde Cavallerie Division of the Garde Corps, the proudest, finest cavalry of the German Army—over one hundred of them, seeming double the number to me—were charging across the fields.

On they came, like machine-made waves on a machine-made ocean.

Then from the left shot other horsemen, one well ahead, another not far back, and a scattered scurrying bunch of two score behind, riding like mad, full tilt at the ranks of German pride and might bearing down upon them.

Colonel David Campbell, of the 9th Lancers, close on his heels Captain Reynolds, his adjutant, and forty-five of his gallant regiment were charging more than double their number of the flower of the enemy's horse.

The Germans quickened appreciably, and their lances waved downwards to the rest. Their pace was slow compared with the whirlwind rush of the smaller band.

I was on the wall when the impact came. Crash! went the 9th into the Garde. Colonel Campbell and Captain Reynolds were down, and horses reared and staggered. I wondered that none of the chargers funked it. Each horse seemed imbued with the spirit of his rider. Not one charger "refused."

No sooner had the smash come than I realised the wall was no place for me, so off I dashed to my car and safety.

The 9th scored heavily off their more numerous foes. A few fell, but more than double the number of Germans bit the dust. Crack British troopers proved their undoubted superiority, man for man, by the number of German dead and wounded we found on the field. Galloping on, the 9th circled round the village and away to the rear.

The Germans stopped, and many of them dismounted. One of them went coolly through the pockets of Reynolds, lying with an aluminium lance through his side. A farrier-sergeant lay dead near a pond at the village end. The Germans knocked in his head and tossed his body into the pool.

All this happened in the twinkling of an eye. Some of the Garde penetrated the village street, but returned after a gallop down and back.

By this time Colonel Burnett, of the 18th Hussars, with a dismounted squadron, had worked round to the left with a machine-gun. When he opened on them, the Germans mounted and swung by him and into the full line of fire.

That squadron of the 18th had a splendid target.

The Black Watch crossing the Aisne at Bourg

MONS TO YPRES.

The result was a field strewn with many German dead. The rest galloped away, leaving their wounded behind them.

One of the 9th, running out from the village to pull the lance from Reynolds's side, was shot dead by a wounded German lying near.

Strange sights were seen by some of the men in that charge. A non-commissioned officer of the 9th ran his lance full through a German officer, who, thus impaled, struck at the lancer and severed his hand at the wrist. One trooper of the 9th ran his lance straight through a German till his hand touched the doomed man's breast. A German horse was seen galloping away with a corpse pinned to its back by a lance.

Colonel Campbell, who so gallantly led the charge against such odds, received a nasty lance-wound through the shoulder.

I brought my car into the village. Entering a cottage in search of a sheet to throw over the disfigured face of a dead German officer, I found two women, who had been in the house during the fighting. They told me the Germans had spent a night in the village, and had treated them quite well. The German cavalrymen had food, said the elder woman, and left money therefor. She showed me a ten-cent Netherlands piece and a ten-cent Belgian coin, with a hole in the centre, with which the Huns had paid her.

In an orchard, around which ran the stone wall on which I had stood, we found two Germans hiding. One was the trumpeter of the Dragoner Garde, with painful lance holes in both his legs. A 9th trooper gave the German a cigarette and politely struck a match for him. The other prisoner was unwounded, and had been concealed near us, loaded Mauser in hand, for an hour or more. His discovery led to the orchard being thoroughly beaten, but no more game materialised.

By 9.30 the heat was as fierce as that of the average summer noonday. The General and his Staff were scanning the country round from a stack not far in front. After I had delivered the papers taken from the prisoners found in the orchard, the General suggested I should break the lances of the dead German troopers who here and there dotted the field. I had not visited half a dozen before I found that some of the supposedly dead Germans were still alive. This necessitated a journey to advise our medical officer of quarry for him. Thereafter I mounted the stack in the heat and watched I Battery of the R.H.A. shell the wood in front of us.

A fine fight, Montcel. A fair charge, the smaller force scoring off the larger one by pure merit in handling of horses and weapons. The crack cavalry regiment of the Prussian Army met one of the best British cavalry regiments that day to the bitter cost of the former. Its casualties must have reached well-nigh one hundred all told. The Second Cavalry Brigade lost 8 killed, 22 wounded and 5 missing during the whole of the morning.

So the forenoon passed in heat and inaction after the stirring events of the earlier part of the day. G.H.Q. had sent instructions that the cavalry were, until further orders, to keep the Dagny line. French aeroplanes reported the enemy in force at Choisy. Our Brigade was to send patrols there, and to Chartronges and Leudon.

An *al fresco* luncheon, under a tree by the roadside, was interrupted by a French officer, whose motor-car panted up to us in a flurry. He brought the good news that the French were in line with us on both right and left, and that our British infantry had that morning taken Coulommiers, on the Grand Morin.

At two o'clock we were on the move. For half an hour I had the experience of being well shelled in Choisy, where a smart fight developed.

MONS TO YPRES.

Every road about us vomited infantry, horse and guns. We were hard after the right wing of Von Kluck's army, pressing on as fast as orders from G.H.Q. would permit.

That night we slept in the village of Feranbry, just south of La Ferté Gaucher, which was in the hands of our infantry.

CHAPTER V.

CLEAN straw strewn on the stone flags of a farmyard made a bed fit for the gods, and at four o'clock on the morning of Tuesday, the 8th, I was as fresh as a daisy and ready and eager for a further push to the north.

Feranbry was a woe-begone sight on that lovely September morning. The Germans had dirtied the town inconceivably, smashing and looting the little shops and the dwelling houses. Many dead horses were scattered about the town.

We were treated to a wonderful sunrise. As we started for La Ferté Gaucher the sky along the eastern horizon showed salmon pink and palest blue. The fields by the roadside were full of cavalry units and batteries of guns. Regiments advancing over the meadows in line of squadrons, an imposing array; batteries, belated, galloping into position with an inspiring rattle and bang over any and all obstructions; motor cycles dodging and panting past less swift users of the road; and even the push-bicyclists putting every ounce of energy into their pedalling—it was good to be alive that morning as the salmon in the east changed to pale gold and the blue to turquoise.

Over the brow of the steep hill leading down into La Ferté a splendid panorama was spread below. The white buildings, red-capped with roofs of tile, nestled in the valley and the rolling hills, well-wooded, rose beyond in myriad shades of green. Away to the right we could see French cavalry mounting the far rise. The morning air was heady as wine. The sun mounting upward, gathered all the rainbow hues of the sky into one great flaming ball, that gave promise of scorching heat when the delightfully cool morning breezes had left us.

MONS TO YPRES.

La Ferté was cruelly smashed ; the bridge over the Grand Morin blown up, but repaired for our passage. By the roadside at the top of the steep hill to the northward were slight trenches full of sleeping Tommies, lying rifle in hand.

Dense woods opened out into fields covered with signs of German bivouacs. Broken bottles were strewn everywhere. Dead Germans in ones and twos by the roadside, and dead horses in numbers, already fouled the pure air.

A German aeroplane soared above us. We were used enough to see enemy aircraft, but that morning the numerous troops were in the mood for action of some sort, and the appearance of the air scout was the signal for every man with a rifle to have a shot at the aerial target. The machine guns began it, and when the infantry joined in a roll of sound swelled about us like the roar of a battle. On came the aeroplane, sailing high above in apparent safety. When it came over us our troopers took up the challenge. The bugles were ordered to sound " Stop firing," but were unheard in the din. Higher and higher soared the plane, and the rifles behind us popped intermittently, then settled into a rattle and roll as ours had done.

But all to no effect, as far as one could see.

On to the north we went through Rebais, more war-scarred than any of her sister towns to the south. Houses burnt and burning on either side of the street, dead Germans and dead horses so numerous they failed to attract more than a passing glance, the marks of shell-fire here and there—Rebais had seen a hard fight and bore the traces of it.

The Germans had been in Rebais two days, the townsfolk said.

I had orders to proceed to La Tretoire, but a kilometre from the town I found the 1st reserve line of the 4th Guards Brigade lying on the grass and waiting orders to move up and join the stiff fight the Coldstreams were having in the town in front of us.

Our field-guns on left and right were in action, and German shrapnel were bursting just ahead. The 2nd Division of Haig's Corps was spread along the road from Rebais, the tired men asleep by the road-way in all postures and positions.

The wounded from the fight in La Tretoire trickled back in increasing numbers.

Clouds had gathered and the day became suddenly cool. The reserve line moved up where the rattle of small arms told of the thick of the battle and our guns hammered away like mad.

One of General Haig's staff officers told me 100,000 Russians had come through England via Archangel, and were in Ostend. The story spread like wildfire, and I heard it from a score of others before the day was over.

The 2nd Cavalry Brigade had crossed the fields to the right. Putting the car at the stubble, I left the road and followed.

Watching batteries for a time, then moving on after the advancing squadrons, I reached the tiny village of Mont Vaudron, opposite the Petit Morin from the town of Sablonnières. Leaving the car in the shelter of a stout stone house, I crept down the hill to a point of vantage from which I could see the bridge below and the town to the right across the little river.

The German shrapnel were bursting on my right and behind me. Our shells were singing overhead, and bursting on the hill across the stream.

Down the wooded hill went the 4th Dragoon Guards and into the thick foliage. For a moment they flashed into sight as they dashed across the approach to the bridge. Straight on they rode, full into and over a mud parapet that the enemy had hastily thrown up across the further end of the bridge. After them ran the kilt-clad forms of a Battalion of Jocks, who charged the town in the face of a heavy fire from in and behind the buildings. Sooner than it takes to tell it, the Scots, who, I later learned, were the Black Watch, had put to rout those of the enemy that were not killed or captured. Unable to catch more than fleeting glimpses of the fighting, I could see we had won the bridge and the town. Gaining my car, I wound down the roadway past a number of our dead, along the steep descent, and over the bridge to a group of thirty German prisoners, who had been taken in the town.

Pushing on up the long, winding, wooded hill to Hondevillers, I reached the town with our advance patrols, the last German disappearing over a farmyard wall and into the cover of the woods as we hove in sight.

Searching for General de Lisle, I ran to Le Petit Villers. There a couple of batteries of 18-pounders, soon to be reinforced by a couple more, were sending shrapnel as fast as they could fire into the retreating enemy.

A cloud of dust on the roadway on a distant hillside would tell of a line of enemy transport chased by our shells, while in the nearer distance a dozen shrapnel, well-placed in a cluster of houses, sent the Germans scurrying up the hillside like so many rabbits.

General Monro, commanding the 2nd Division, stood by the batteries, and watched the fleeting enemy with intense interest. All were engrossed with the work of the gunners, the noise being incessant and deafening. Suddenly, from a wood 800 yards to the left of us, a volley of Mauser bullets came. The Germans had crept into the edge of the trees and let fly at short range. There was a quick scamper for cover. Backing the car down the road into the protection of a wall, I found myself in a lane that had been chosen as an avenue for the battery horses and limbers.

A detachment of the Highland Light Infantry was on the double for a point where they could stop the fire on the batteries, which were spattering away merrily.

Rain started to fall. I raised my hood, getting a bullet through it a moment later. Told in strenuous language that I was in the way, I dashed down a lane that ended in a ploughed field. Fortunately it was dry, so I made my way back to Hondevillers, and from there to Basseville, our night quarters. Fairclough and I made a night journey to La Tretoire in search of our Brigade cyclists, but could not find them.

After a late and meagre dinner, I tried to sleep in the tonneau of the car, which proved cramped quarters for my somewhat ample proportions, and when called at 2.45 on the morning of Wednesday, the 9th, I woke stiff and cold. An egg, a cracker, and a cup of black coffee warmed me, and we were soon on the road in the dark, headed for the Marne.

The crossing of the River Marne promised, we thought, a hard and costly fight. The rapid retreat of the Germans, withal we were hard on their heels, was more orderly than might have been expected. Little, indeed, did they leave behind except their dead. At La Tretoire we heard that the 1st Corps had captured men and guns, but that portion of the enemy's rearguard with which the cavalry had to deal succeeded in keeping his guns well out of our grasp.

Challenged every few minutes by sentries guarding sleeping detachments along the lesser lanes, twisting here and there in a vain endeavour to find anyone who knew the general route of any particular unit save his own, I lost the 2nd Cavalry Brigade before dawn that morning. Proceeding straight where I should have turned, I pushed past regiments of slowly moving cavalry until a peremptory order to put out the side-lights of my car, accompanied by the information that not even a cigarette was allowed thereabouts, led me to ask where I was.

"On the road to Nogent, and but a short way from it," was the reply, "and not far from the head of the 1st Cavalry Brigade."

MONS TO YPRES.

Truly, thought I, a bit of luck. Briggs, I knew, had been assigned the attack on the bridge across the Marne at Nogent-l'Artaud, which lay midway between La Ferté St. Jouarre, which was to be taken by Pulteney's 3rd Corps, and Château-Thierry, where the 1st Corps was to force the passage of the river.

The line of the Marne, many of us thought, would be stubbornly held by the enemy.

Briggs, his Brigade confirmed, was to take the Nogent bridge at daybreak. We waited on the hill above, the tall trees looming taller still in the dim light of the earliest morning.

Straining our ears, we heard no sound of firing. Daybreak came and passed, and still no guns. Not even a rifle-shot sounded from the valley below us.

It was an eerie vigil. We wondered what had gone wrong, when the show would commence, and whether the enemy would shell the main road on which we were waiting, in what was no doubt fair range of his guns across the river.

A French liaison officer chatted cheerily. He told us Maunoury had a strong line from Meaux north along the Ourcq, and would soon be across it and endangering the existence of Von Kluck's right and rear. He told us, too, of a savage battle for Montmirail the night before—he had just come from somewhere down that way—and how d'Esperey had taken the town at the point of the bayonet, and was ready to push forward on our right.

As five o'clock came without noise of battle, I drove on. Just above the town of Nogent, which is on the south bank of the river, a bicycle orderly stood panting from his exertions in coaxing his machine up the hill. He was the bearer of good news. The Germans had prepared the bridge for defence in a most careful manner, and guarded it till 4.30. Some said it was mined. At all events it was well nigh impassable. At 4.30, for some inexplicable reason, the enemy evacuated the position, and fled without firing a shot, just as our advance guard reached the approach to the bridge.

I thereupon lost no time in reaching the bridge. Our troops were still crossing it. Briggs was swinging a regiment up the hill preparatory to getting our guns on the higher ground without delay.

Colonel Tommy Pitman, of the 11th Hussars, who had started for Nogent at half-past one in the morning, showed me the evidences of the thorough manner in which the enemy had blocked the way. The railway-gates at the south end of the bridge had been wound about with wire. Carts and obstructions all the way across had been woven into barricades with lengths of wire.

Colonel Pitman said his men were hard at work for three-quarters of an hour cutting their way through. And that without molestation from the Germans, the last one of whom was seen departing by motor-car in the distance, as the 11th came through Nogent. Walking over the bridge I strolled down the steep bank to the river's edge, meditating on the ease with which we had crossed the Marne, and with difficulty realising that I then stood on its northern bank.

The ground was strewn with bedding and miscellaneous loot. A mess of potatoes, pared and washed to an inviting whiteness, sat in a pot of water placed on carefully prepared twigs waiting the match. Just before daybreak, said an aged riverman, the Bosches had moved all the barges and boats from the south bank and moored them on the opposite side. A novice could see the German departure from Nogent was a surprise to the enemy rearguard.

Regaining the bridge I watched long lines of our 2nd Corps infantry file past. Guns had begun long since, away to the west, and told of an argument over the crossing of the river at La Ferté St. Jouarre. There the 3rd Corps was to fight well through the day without winning the passage of the Marne until the German defenders of the town were compelled to retire by other 3rd Corps troops, who had crossed the stream further west at Changis.

At 7.30 our guns on the hill behind us dropped a couple of shrapnel on the ridge in front. A couple of minutes later the air was full of the sound of whistling shells as they sped high above the valley, bursting over the wooded crests to the north. White clouds in miniature lined the heights.

I was admiring the picture when a horseman came down the road and up to the bridge at a gallop. It was General Briggs.

"That your car?" he questioned sharply. "Yes, sir." "Go like the devil to that battery and stop its firing. It is shelling my men."

I went up the hill road, blocked with two descending lines of ammunition trains and regiment on regiment of foot soldiers, at a speed which would have caused a Surrey magistrate to search the statute-books for the extreme penalty of the law, had I been driving at such a rate on the Brighton road.

Luckily I found General Findlay, of the Royal Artillery, without delay and delivered my message, which I was told to repeat to a Brigade C.R.A. further to the rear. That mission accomplished I proceeded more leisurely down to Nogent again, and thence to Romeny, on the Château-Thierry road, searching for news of the 2nd Cavalry Brigade.

Dippers of delicious fresh milk, proffered by charming French lassies, were ample excuse for a momentary halt. Stories of the fleeing Germans were on every lip. For two days and nights the hated invader had been pouring north in two lines through Charly and Chezy. The Germans, but few of whom passed Romeny, laughed at the villagers, they said, some of them crying out as they passed that they were *Anglais, et bon amis.* Whereat the French girls chattered their disapproval. The German smiles fell on barren soil in Romeny, where the true French hearts beat hot with hate of the Bosche, be he ever so genial to the non-combatant by the way.

"Rattle" Barrett, with an echelon of the 2nd Brigade transport, put in a welcome appearance, and suggested my looking for General de Lisle toward Chezy, to the westward. By half-past nine I had found him with General Allenby, at a farm south of Chezy. We pressed on the north, our objective being the village of Le Tholet, a few kilometres west of Château-Thierry, which had seen a stubborn fight.

The valley of the Marne afforded a beautiful view. White, fleecy cloudlets sailed lazily in a perfect blue sky. Chezy took the romance out of the panorama round about, however. Its churchyard was littered and its buildings smashed. The Germans left what had been a quaint, clean little town, dirty and foul with their passing. We climbed slowly up Mont de Bonneil after crossing the Marne. At noontide the heat was intense.

I followed Generals Allenby and de Lisle and the Divisional and Brigade Staffs across country. The dry stubble and hard meadows, free of fence or hedge, allowed ample scope for scouting a point of vantage whereby to cross the few ditches, and my progress was watched with interest by the mounted officers. A halt was made when the main Paris-Château Thierry road was reached.

News came that Baker-Carr, one of the R.A.C., leading half-a-dozen other cars, had declined the cross-country run and pushed on to Coupru. Approaching the village at a smart pace, a rifle volley stopped them short at a thousand yards. Such a competition in rapid backing and quick turning ensued as is rarely seen at the most lively gymkhana. Good luck for the little cavalcade of cars that the Germans opened fire at a distance, instead of waiting till their quarry had reached a sure range. Fortunately, none of the occupants of the cars were hit, though more than one of the vehicles bore marks of Mauser bullets.

A squadron of the 18th Hussars was sent to round up the enemy, and soon returned with a couple of dozen prisoners in tow, having killed the officer in command of the detachment and four or five of his men.

A strong, fine-looking lot, the prisoners. From Schleswig-Holstein, they said. Looked more like Danes than Germans. They were frankly glad to be out of the further fighting.

I spent the afternoon watching our gunners smash away at retreating columns of enemy transport, tearing northwards from Château-Thierry, where the 1st Corps had captured a number of prisoners, we were told, and a gun or two after a stiff fight.

Our night quarters were a near-by farm. I awoke on the morning of Thursday, September 10th, with a dawning realisation of the fact that the passage of the Marne was gained, and a great strategical victory had been won by the Allies.

We were well across the river as far east as Château-Thierry, where our right had been reached by d'Esperey's left. The news from further east was vague, but rumours of a great victory on the far right were afloat.

The Germans were on the run in earnest, and all was going well. Exactly what Maunoury on our extreme left and Foch in front of Châlons had accomplished was as yet unknown to us, but rumour was persistently cheerful.

So good was my bed of straw in the great yard of the farm that the rain at half-past two in the morning well soaked my clothing before I wakened sufficiently to realise the advisability of changing my billet for the drier, if less comfortable, shelter of the tonneau of the car.

WITH FRENCH.

There I slept so soundly that at four o'clock, when a member of the Staff called me, breakfast was over, and I was told I had best be ready to depart instanter. A good-hearted woman of the household gave me a quart or so of milk in lieu of the breakfast I had missed.

An attempt to move my car was utterly abortive. At that most inconvenient of seasons I learned much of the theory of construction of a French farmyard. Built as it was in the form of a square or quadrangle, the centre devoted to an accumulation of manure and general refuse, one was wise to keep to the stone paved roadway round the sides.

Barrett and I had arrived "home" tired out at 11.30 p.m., and I had run the car well off the firm, stone-paved portion of the farm courtyard. The morning found it a couple of feet below the surface of the surrounding fringe of roadway. I enlisted the sympathy and assistance of the farmer, and the car was brought to firm ground by a team of fine French draught horses. This badly bent the car's back axle. Later, a cyclist informed me that this was a blessing in disguise, for, if ordered to follow my car, he could always depend on marking its passage by its peculiarly unorthodox wheel tracks.

Some 1st Division troops filed through the farm while the rescue work was in progress. Proceeding to the Paris-Château Thierry road, I was ordered by General de Lisle to take charge of our two-seated brigade car, the motor cyclists and the common or garden cyclists, and keep on to the right of the Brigade, which was to proceed across country to the northward. I obeyed these orders until I was informed I was leading my mixed, if small, command over somewhat new territory in the sense that no patrols had preceded us, when I changed my plans, and returned whence I had come with all my following.

MONS TO YPRES.

Starting again, I followed the advance of the 1st Division to the left of the cavalry. Passing the long lines of infantry and many batteries was trying work. It was seven o'clock before I reached the head of the Division. Past Lucy and Torcy we went discussing at times with passing officers the wonder we felt that the retreating enemy took no advantage of such splendid positions. Just north of Torcy I reached the head of the Sussex Regiment, which was in the lead. In front was Captain Nicholson with a squadron of 15th Hussars, Divisional Cavalry to the 1st Division.

Up a long steep hill into the village of Courchamps, the Scouts informing us of Germans just ahead, and then a halt for a moment and a chat with the villagers. "For five days and nights," said a woman, who was busy filling bowls of fine, fresh milk for the soldiers without a thought of remuneration, "the Germans have hurried northwards." The bulk of the retreating invaders had passed two days before, but some infantry went by later. The German cavalry were in the village an hour and a half before us. The villagers said many guns were with the German columns.

A drizzling day. Shortly after eight o'clock we halted in front of the town of Priez. On our left a transport column of the enemy raced northward, and shortly afterwards we could see a line of motor lorries away on our right tearing along at high speed, as though belated, to a point of great danger and in full realisation of it.

A fierce cannonade on our left told us of the 3rd Corps at La Ferté-Jouarre.

General Bulfin, commanding the 1st Brigade, asked me to what I was attached. On learning I was with the cavalry he bemoaned the fact that the cavalry were not on his left, as the fast-disappearing transport of the enemy would have fallen an easy prey to one of our Cavalry Brigades on that flank.

WITH FRENCH.

Major Frazer, of General Allenby's staff, drove by at nine o'clock, and asked why I was making no progress toward joining the Cavalry Division. I explained that the only available road to the east had but recently been reached by the infantry advance, and was even then being fired over by the machine guns dinning away a few hundred yards in front of us.

Priez lay in a valley. The top of the slope beyond was plainly visible from where we stood. Bulfin's brigade was advancing up the far hillside as we chatted, and nearing the crest. An ideal spot, I thought, for a stiff German rearguard action.

Frazer suggested our proceeding as far as the village. I accompanied him, leaving my convoy of cycles behind. We dismounted from our cars in the hollow, after passing the village proper. The deployed lines—consisting of Sussex and South Hants Regiments—had reached the crown of the hill in front. Their arrival was the signal for the commencement of a very pretty little fight.

The rifle fire grew in volume until singing bullets were so frequent at the point we had chosen that I took cover in a roadside ditch. My attention was arrested by the frantic efforts of a scared woman to close the shutters of an adjacent house, the side of which was being well peppered.

Turning from my momentary aberration, I discovered that Frazer's car had returned from whence it had come. A lonesome feeling coming over me, I left the ditch and the car, and ran across the road to the shelter of a bank, behind which a number of the Sussex Regiment were taking cover. I found the detachment was A Company, Captain Bond commanding.

After a quarter of an hour of enjoyment of good shelter from the increasing Mauser pellets, an order came to A Company to advance up the hill to the firing line. They started off to the right, taking such

Melinite shrapnel bursting above the Chavonne ridge

2nd Life Guards in the straw-filled reserve trenches on the Aisne heights

A couple of Batteries of 18-pounders behind the Aisne heights cover as the low bank afforded. A disinclination to be left alone in such a warm corner led me to accompany them.

The enemy had succeeded in driving back the left of the British line, which enabled them to cover our advance up the hill from our left flank. A number of our party were hit, particularly at an open space fifty feet in extent, where the bank at the roadside was quite unnecessarily low. The two men immediately in front of me and the man just behind me were hit all three being wounded in the head.

The German guns opened on the village behind us and the slope away to the rear. Our guns replied, but their range was short, some of the shells bursting over us.

To me the situation seemed somewhat bizarre. Our enjoyment of our surroundings was by no means augmented by one of the Sussex men from the line in front, who came running back with the news of a general retirement. Rifle fire in front, rifle fire from our left, and shrapnel from both front and rear, made us wonder whether retirement was not less wise than staying where we were. But orders are orders, so we headed down the slope for the village.

Reaching the fifty-foot gap, a couple of bold ones rushed at it, only to fall before they had got across. That part of our journey must, it seemed, be taken in full sight of the enemy. While pausing and contemplating this fact, a herd of a score or more cows galloped, bellowing, down the hedge-side in the field by us. Suddenly blessed with an inspiration, we sprinted down the road in the lee of the barrier thus providentially imposed between us and our friends the enemy. " We're all right so long as the beef holds out," panted a Tommy, as the bullets went " puck-puck " into the cattle.

In a matter of seconds I had reached the car, and was mentally consigning it and its contents to the

Bosches, when a major of the Sussex battalion asked me if I would take it back with as many of the wounded as we could pack on it. I was of the belief that any occupant of a car that tried to pass through the village and up the slope in plain sight of the enemy, and in the direct path of his shrapnel, would stand little chance of escape, but the wounded were tossed into the tonneau, into the front seats, on the folded hood at the rear, and all about, wherever space could be found. I jumped into the driving seat, and backed the car to the cross-roads in the town, suffering a collision with a wall en route.

The car's steps were lined with soldiers, and one was mounted on a front wing.

" Now boys," I said, as I headed the car round for the dash up the hill, " the rise is steep, and this is no ' General ' omnibus. All that are not wounded hop off, and I'll see if I can get the rest out of it."

With a cheery word they jumped off, except one, who stood on the step at my side.

" Are you hit ? " I queried.

" No, but I'm all right. I won't fall off, guv'nor," he replied with a grin.

" If you are bound to come with us," said I, " vault up behind me and stick on."

He did so, and as I felt his hand on my shoulder I looked up at him and remarked, " I've got you between me and the Germans whatever happens."

But we found that ride no joke.

Up the hill we crawled. My load was eleven, some badly hit. Two cyclists in front gave promise of blocking the way as we gathered speed, but a shell burst over us that knocked one of the pair off his wheel. He careered into his fellow ; the pair rolled into the ditch together. Bang ! went another shell, seemingly a few feet over us. Four men from a group ahead of us were hit, so falling that they almost blocked the roadway. Bullets sang all about. Someone hanging on one of the steps was hit, and cried out as he dropped off. As the slope became less steep I overtook an ammunition limber, the team — minus driver—in full flight toward the rear. Off the road and into the dry stubble field I guided the groaning car, past the tired horses, galloping their poor best, and into the road again, urged by a quartette of shrapnel that seemed to burst—oh !—so close to us !

A mile or so in the rear, we found a hastily improvised hospital, in a field by the road, where I delivered my load. An orderly came to me as I drove up, saying laconically, " Wounded ? " " Yes," I answered, "all but one." Turning, I sought the persistent one whom I had mounted at my back.

" *I* stopped one, coming up the hill," said the object of my remark, with a grin—" I stopped one proper, I did ! " And as he disentangled his feet from those of a sadly wounded comrade on whom he had been supporting himself, he opened his tunic and showed me a blood-soaked side. " Through," he explained. " Might have got you if I hadn't been there," he added, " so maybe it was just as well. I couldn't have brought the others back in this thing." And he grinned again as I put him down where the orderlies could get him. " Good luck, son," I said, with a lump in my throat. His teeth were set as he was borne by two hospital men to where the doctors could attend to him.

As they took him down the bank the corners of his mouth twitched in another half-smile, and he said, " Thanks. Don't you worry about me ; *I*'m all right. It's nothing ! "

I have often thought of him, and hoped he came through in good shape. His spirit was so very, very fine.

Wiping some of the red off the cushions of the car, I turned it again towards Priez, and ran as far as a haystack, to the right of the road. The rain had ceased. I sat with some of the King's Royal Rifles in the lee of the stack for a time. Shrapnel was bursting near by. Two big high-explosive shells went over us, and lit not far behind. Some of General Lomax's staff and a number of 1st Division officers were in front of the stack. I joined them and distributed some chocolate I had in the car, which was very cheerily greeted. Shells came closer. As an excuse to get back for a breathing space, I picked up three or four passing wounded, to take them to the dressing station. No sooner had I started than a blinding flash in front, and a black smoke cloud in our eyes and nostrils, told of the arrival of another high-explosive shell. It had lit in the road, striking two mounted orderlies. The horses and men were literally blown to pieces, and the road scarred with a huge hole.

One poor chap in the car was so near gone when we arrived at the hospital that his chances were declared by the doctor to be one in a thousand.

Through the middle of the day and into the early afternoon our guns hammered at the enemy. Another infantry Brigade was sent up and forced the Germans to retire. The action was only a rearguard fight, but the considerable number of wounded in the dressing station, and all along the road, told of the efficiency of it. A constant procession of stretchers went past. General Findlay, seated beside the road, not far from the haystack that gave me shelter for a time, was hit by shrapnel and killed.

The Sussex Regiment lost heavily. Not only were their casualties considerable, but among the list were some of their best officers. Altogether, Priez cost us between three and four hundred killed and wounded.

Shortly after mid-day one of General Lomax's staff asked me to take a message to General Allenby.

This required my going south, and then turning east and north again. The left of d'Esperey's 5th Army was in touch with our right. Passing Grisolles and Rocourt and proceeding north toward Oulchy-le-

Château I saw many French troops, but could get no word of Allenby. I watched a couple of batteries of 75's shell Oulchy. The French officers were very friendly. As the white shell clouds burst against the dark green foliage in front we chatted of prospective victory. They were pleased when I told them that one of our Divisions, checked for a moment at Priez, had taken it and pushed on to shell Neuilly-St. Front. Soissons and Braisnes were *their* objectives, the French officers said.

I pushed on to a high point, and at last met General Allenby, whom I had almost despaired of finding. I delivered my message, and mounting a haystack watched the French infantry attack north of Oulchy, supported by French and English batteries.

In the evening, with General de Lisle, I visited Grisolles, Latilly, Nanteuil and Rozet-Ablin. These little towns in the valley of the Ourcq were charming in their simple beauty. The Germans had not stopped long nor done much damage thereabouts. The coming of the Allies had restored confidence in the twinkling of an eye. Already the peasant folk were at work digging their hidden stores of flour from out their straw stacks.

Captain Barrett and I spent most of the night searching for our Brigade transport, which had gone astray. Discovering it at last, and providing the officer in charge with a map, we ran back to our night quarters at Rozet. There we slept on couches in the partially dismantled drawing-room of a house which a villager described as the property of a French Field-Marshal. Dinner having been consumed in our absence, Barrett and I made a hearty meal off cold soup, bread and jam, and slept soundly until four o'clock the next morning.

The first hours of the next day we spent in careering about the country for news of horse transport, which had gone stubbornly astray in spite of maps and instructions. Through village after village we searched for a time to no avail. Three small detachments had spent the night in the same little village without any one of them being in the least aware of its proximity to the others. At daybreak the three had left, still unconscious that their fellows were hard by, each to go in a different direction. We found them all at last, after unravelling Gilbertian blunders on the part of thoroughly muddled " non-coms." It is easy to laugh at such "mix-ups" when they become disentangled, but truly difficult to do so until the trouble is over. Horse transport trains breed short tempers more often than not.

Our course bore eastward, and then north for Braisnes. Close to us on the right Conneau's French cavalrymen were advancing. They bore signs of campaign wear. Our appearance was far from prepossessing. A wash was a luxury and a shave unknown. Dirty as we were I think the French were dirtier. Their rusty cuirasses helped to give one such an impression, as did the once white bits of trimming on their uniforms. The Chasseurs d'Inde looked a wiry lot. Their baggy blue trousers, red jackets, and red fez on yellow turban looked still gay, though well-begrimed. Their dapper little Arabs stepped gingerly, aware all eyes were on them.

We passed several groups of German prisoners. General de Lisle told me our 1st and 2nd Divisions captured over 1,000 of the enemy the day before, and with them seven guns. Later reports swelled this to double the number of prisoners and guns, and rumour told that machine-guns and transport had also been taken.

Breakfast in an open field found us munching bully and dry bread with true ardour. For luncheon we brought similar appetites to an identical menu. Blinding downpours of rain fell for most of the afternoon. Our forward movement was curtailed by

orders from above. The 9th Lancers had pressed
well on toward Soissons. De Lisle sent me to Maast
to recall them. Major Beale-Browne, commanding
the 9th, said Lucas Tooth's squadron was beyond
Nanteuil, and well up the Soissons road. Would I
run on and pass the order to reassemble? Certainly.
Reaching them in the rain Lucas Tooth told me they
had chased the Uhlans just over a ridge beyond. One
of his troopers saw three or four of the enemy and
rode at them with a yell. They dashed back and
soon overtook seventy of their comrades. Catching
sight of the larger body the 9th trooper turned and
galloped for assistance. The Uhlans came on slowly
behind him. Gathering together the troop of which
he was a member, the handful started full tilt for the
enemy. The moment the troop came over the brow
of a rolling hill, and in sight of the Germans, the
latter, disregarding their greatly superior numbers,
turned and fled. Our cavalry was gaining a sinister
reputation.

We spent the night of Saturday, the 11th, in Arcy,
where a good dinner cheered us all. A hot bath in a
wash-tub, and a blanket-bed on the clean tiles, made
for solid comfort.

On the morning of Sunday, the 12th, a French
officer told us how well the Allied Forces were
succeeding. Foch had pressed on and might soon
be at Rheims, he said.

I was with the extreme advance during the forenoon. Rifle shots close at hand; pools of fresh blood
in the roadway; dead horses, not yet cold, and scared
peasants, all told of cavalry patrols in collision at
daybreak. We stopped on a line of hills. Down the
slopes in front lay Braisnes and the crossing of the
Vesle. We were afforded a splendid view of the field-
gun battle for the river. The horizon in front and
away to the right, as far as the eye could reach, was
one long line of black or white shell-clouds. Dozens,

scores, hundreds of cloudlets, ever changing, new ones born with every second, yet no two alike in form. Before eleven we lunched. A big round loaf of bread, to obtain which a kindly native walked two miles, a tin of sardines, two tins of bully beef, a tin of marmalade and a tot all round of wonderful Army rum, provided a hearty meal, not only for our own staff but for General Allenby and many of the Divisional Staff as well. Rain fell in sheets while we were lunching, our dining-room being the shelter, more imaginary than real, of a small haystack. The fight for Braisnes was within earshot. The Germans had barricaded the bridge and the main street of the town, and were putting up a strong rearguard action.

Some of the 3rd Division Infantry Battalions trudged by at a good pace unmindful of the downpour or the mud underfoot. Many of the Tommies had ponchos, some had overcoats, and here and there a blanket or brown gun-cover kept off the wet. Only a few of them were without protection of a sort. By noon-time the bridge was taken, and a couple of hours after we moved up. The Queen's Bays had been in the lime-light, and greatly distinguished themselves. From the winding wooded road down into the valley the hills across the river loomed grey-green in a rain-mist. On the bank by the way lay the dead body of Bertram Stewart of the Intelligence, who had taken a rifle and gone down to lend a hand. Beyond him a wounded trooper sat propped against a milestone gasping with pain. Across the bridge we came upon a broken bit of loop-holed wall, then a barricade of sand-bags in the street, a score or more of German prisoners, a crowded ambulance, and behind it an old rickety one-horse landau, creeping slowly so as not to jar the wounded soldier stretched on a door laid crosswise over the carriage superstructure. The main thorough-fare was full of infantry. The 1st Cavalry Brigade that had taken Braisnes was on ahead, winning the

MONS TO YPRES.

German positions on the slopes beyond the town. Shops were emptied in short order of what little the Germans had left untouched. A dear old Sister of Mercy, not five feet tall, found me endeavouring to make a purchase of viands of some sort and took me under her wing. Calls on storekeepers proving futile, she guided me to a pretentious dwelling. Here we found an old lady who gave me a half a loaf of bread, a small pat of butter, and a bottle of wine for our mess. She could not be induced to take any remuneration. A shell hole had ruined the grass plot in the centre of her dainty garden, having first passed through her bedroom. The Germans had demanded her keys at the point of a pistol and had well ransacked her house, she said. She was a sweet old lady. How a human being could maltreat her I could not imagine.

The fight for the hill north of Braisnes was not over, but after half-an-hour's wait behind a haystack outside the town I was allowed to proceed. At the base of the hill our shrapnel had played on the roadway with deadly accuracy. The ditches were full of dead and wounded Germans. The steep slopes were lined with well-made trenches one above another. On up the winding road that mounted the slope we toiled, three lines abreast, squadrons of cavalry, lines of ammunition wagons, motor-cars and horse-guns all together. The rifle and rapid gun-fire from the crown of the hill was still telling of the stubborn fight while we were crawling round the lower curves of the ascent. As I gained the crest I saw a group of over 100 German prisoners and piles of broken German rifles by the road. Still more lines of trenches disfigured the fields on either side.

Our billet for the night was the quaint village of Longueval, less than two miles from the Aisne. I was alone in the car with General de Lisle when we entered the village. We were well ahead of our troops. Personally, I felt some qualms at such a reconnaissance, but we found no Germans thereabouts. The people were most cordial in their welcome, and told us the enemy's troops had been billeted on them for the past ten days. A big stone farm with an ample yard housed the headquarters' contingent. After dinner, I took Raymond Hamilton-Grace to General Allenby's headquarters for orders. That run in the dark, rain, wind and mud, was a veritable nightmare. Several times carefully-followed instructions as to the localisation of Divisional Headquarters were proved to have been utterly wrong. Once we went past our last outpost and into the light of the still burning ruins of farms beyond it. When we at last located the head of the Division, we found it planted in an awful hole, approachable only through a sea of mud. Our quest for orders was in vain, as no orders had yet been issued. I had hoped for a letter from home, as not one line from London had reached me since my departure nearly a month before. But no letter awaited me. It was late when we returned to Longueval, and a bundle of straw on a stone floor made a tempting bed.

MONS TO YPRES.

CHAPTER VI

On the morning of Sunday, the 13th, no less an undertaking than the crossing of the Aisne was to fall to the lot of the cavalry. Orders had come for a general advance. The 1st and 2nd Cavalry Brigades were to move north. The 2nd Cavalry Brigade was to reconnoitre the river crossings from Villers to Pont-Arcy.

The item of the greatest interest to me in the daily orders was the point given as the general objective of the Brigade. No matter how impossible for motor cars the country which de Lisle would traverse with his troopers, if I knew the objective, I would be there before his arrival, or close after it. The point given as the 2nd Cavalry Brigade objective that 13th of September, was Chamouille, a village some ten kilometres due north from Bourg, on the road to Laon. Night did not find us at Chamouille. True, we were to cross the Aisne on that day, and to do so in unexpectedly good time. Chamouille, however, we were not to see that day, nor the next. Nor have English or French troops set foot in that village yet, though another 13th September has come and gone.

At 4.30 a sergeant came in with the report that the bridge across the Aisne at Villers had been found destroyed, and a pontoon bridge had been constructed within fifty yards of it. A bit later came a report from Bourg. The bridge there also was destroyed, but a nearer bridge over a canal that ran parallel to and south of the river had been left intact. More important, a third bridge in the vicinity, by which an aqueduct was carried over the main stream of the river, was still standing. If that bridge could be rushed, the passage of the Aisne would be secured and a way made for the advance of the troops of the 1st Infantry Division behind us.

Daylight struggled through the haze just before five o'clock, and showed us a lowering sky. A sharp burst of heavy rain fell.

The 9th Lancers and the 4th Dragoon Guards were ordered to take the Bourg bridge at five o'clock, and effect a crossing of the river.

Why we were allowed to get over the Aisne with so comparatively little opposition at Bourg will probably never be known. Some German had blundered, and blundered badly. A couple of batteries of our field-guns gave the town a sound shelling, and the dismounted troopers surged across the canal bridge. At the far side the damaged river bridge gaped before them. On their left was the aqueduct bridge. Behind its embankment were German infantry with a machine-gun. Their position rendered them safe from our shells, and gave them opportunity to pour a fire into the flank of our attack, almost into its rear. Nothing remained but to rush the enemy, which was done most gallantly, and with gratifying success. The 4th D.G.'s lost Captain Fitzgerald and four or five men killed at the bridge, and the 9th Lancers suffered some casualties, but, considering the advantage gained and the importance of the crossing, the resistance was absurdly slight. When the aqueduct bridge was finally won, and the Germans who defended it dislodged or killed, great was our amazement at the weakness of the force which had been left to guard it. The German guns from the heights north of the river began shelling Bourg as soon as we had taken it, but for the most part they were busy protecting the broken bridge at Pont-Arcy and the pontoons at Chavonne, both to our left. At these points the 2nd Infantry Division met stubborn resistance, but eventually won their way across the river.

MONS TO YPRES.

Showers came and went. The roads were deep with mud. I crossed after the guns. The main bridge over the river being impassable, my only alternative was the aqueduct bridge. The half towpath, half lane beyond was not meant for car traffic. The artillery had ploughed through, however, so on I went. Axle-deep in thick mud, slipping, sliding, skidding slowly forward, I at last came to the point where the guns had made a path up the steep bank to the main roadway beyond. No choice remained but to charge it at such speed as one could muster. Near the top the whirring wheels refused to bite, and back the car slid towards the river. At the edge of the bank the driving wheels luckily encountered some obstacle that gave them a grip, and the straining, striving car slowly crawled upwards, eventually to force its way, back wheels revolving at full speed in the ooze, up to and over the crest of the bank and on to safety beyond.

The 2nd Cavalry Brigade advanced north towards the town of Vendresse, three to four miles distant. The 1st Infantry Division tramped along in their wake.

Towards noon I encountered an orderly who said General de Lisle wanted me to come up front and bring the luncheon basket, to carry which had now become a daily duty. As I passed detachments of cavalry on the Vendresse road I asked if the General had gone on in the direction I was pursuing, and invariably was answered in the affirmative.

As the road became free of lines of Tommies and ammunition waggons I quickened my pace. At the side of the road the 4th Dragoon Guards stood, dismounted. Someone at the head of the column waved as I sped by, and gave a friendly shout. I waved in return, slowing to pass a squadron of that regiment proceeding in column of twos towards Vendresse. I had lowered the hood, encouraged by a glimpse of the sun, but as I reached a sharp bend in the road not far

125

from the town a sudden shower pattered down, the big drops promising a quick drenching. Mindful of the lunch in the tonneau I stopped the car and jumped out to raise the hood. Before I had done so the squadron overtook me and passed on the trot. First I was tempted to hasten and precede them, but a refractory nut delayed me, so I let them pass, tailing an affable sergeant at the rear, who threw me a cheery word as he jogged by.

A moment later a sharp rattle of fire directly in front, and the whirr of bullets all about, made me pull up in record time, throw in the reverse, and back frantically for the shelter of the bank around the turn. The scattering shots became an angry roar, and a storm of whistling missiles sped overhead. The horsemen left the road at the first volley, and disappeared into the scrub on the left, some of their number falling before they could escape from the path of the fusilade. A bullet tore through the canvas of the hood and gave one of the sticks a nasty smack, but in less time than it takes to tell it I was out of harm's way behind the shoulder of the hill. Backing to the 4th D. G.'s, Colonel Mullens greeted me with a sarcastic question as to whether I was trying to get killed. "Playing at advance guard with a car," he termed it. What I had taken as a friendly wave in passing had been an effort on his part to stop me, as General de Lisle had left the road at that point, and climbed a hill to the left. The fire grew hot again in front, and stray pellets spattered round, so I turned the car in the narrow road and ran further to the rear. Our batteries began the game of dislodging the enemy from Vendresse and the slopes beyond.

An officer from G.H.Q. drove up and chatted for a time. We were not the only part of the Army across the Aisne, he said. The passage of the river had been won by the 3rd Corps to our left and by the 2nd Corps beyond them. All along the seventeen miles allotted to the British front the north bank of the stream was ours save at points of exceptional strength, such as Condé, which was, it proved later, to remain in German hands for many a long month. He told me the sum total of official casualties to that date. Out of 15,800, the number of killed, wounded, and missing, 12,500 were missing, most of the latter being killed or wounded of course. This intimated a sad jumble of reports due to the confusion of the retreat.

By two o'clock I found the Chief and his Staff, who welcomed the luncheon-basket. Before our repast was over the German shells were searching thereabouts, two disquieting visitors coming close over us. Orders came to move back. As I had headed the car forward I was told to turn again and make for a safer position. As I backed to do so two more shells fell in the road not far distant. My consequent effort to rush matters resulted in my back wheels becoming embedded to the hubs in soft earth at the roadside. Whizzy-bang went two more big ugly fellows just beyond. No one was in sight along the way. What to do I did not know. Reckless efforts to jerk the poor car out by its own power drove the rear wheels deeper in their soft bed.

Bang—bang—bang—bang !

Four shrapnel burst over the trees across from me and rattled and crashed through the branches with a terrifying din. I was at a loss for a solution of my difficulty, and became apprehensive of results.

Down the road from the rear came a two-seated car. The driver pulled up, took in the situation at a glance, dismounted, and producing a stout rope, tied it to my car, and coolly towed it on to the roadway. No sooner had he done so than a very rain of shells fell over the road fifty yards ahead.

Thanking him and admiring his coolness, I explained that the headquarters of which he was in search was further to the rear, and we pulled out without delay to a safer locality. I never learned the name of my benefactor. His pluck saved me. The next day I examined the spot and found two good-sized shell-holes had been made in the road not ten yards from where I had been so ignominiously stuck.

The Brigade went to the high ground between the Bourg-Vendresse road and Verneuil. A battery was shelling the Germans from that position, and soon the German guns replied. The 9th Lancers suffered on the ridge, losing Captain Lucas Tooth, a splendid cavalry officer. Before dark we were relieved by the Rifle Brigade, and our troops went into billets at Oeuilly. A château there had been left in a filthy state by the Germans, but piles of clean straw in the ransacked drawing-room made a comfortable resting-place.

On Monday, September 14th, I was called at a quarter-past two in the morning, and asked to be ready to start at 3.30. We were still inclined to wonder by what good fortune we had been allowed to force a way across the Aisne at Bourg, the day previously, with such great success and so few casualties.

Our passage of the Aisne and our pressing forward to Vendresse and up to the Chemin des Dames, a great east-and-west highway beyond, was so important a move, and bore such prospect of result, that it was but natural we should be in ardent expectation of a sight of the Rhine within the near future.

The winning of Bourg, and the consequent following up by Haig's 1st Division of the advantage thus gained, gave Sir John French an opportunity to quickly develop the situation by a general push along our whole front on that Monday morning. We learned that Maunoury, with his French Sixth Army, had crossed the Aisne between Compiègne and Soissons. We knew the French were across the Aisne on our right and we were expected to advance to a new line from Laon, due north from Bourg, to Fresnes, which lies practically due north from Soissons.

MONS TO YPRES.

The 2nd Cavalry Brigade was ordered to move off at once *via* Troyon and Courtecon. Our route from Oeuilly led to Bourg, then north. Between Bourg and the Chemin des Dames the road lay through beautiful country. Well-wooded heights rose on the left, and the way ran along a deep valley until reaching Vendresse, then wound upward past the little village of Troyon. Just before it reached the Chemin des Dames the road passed a large sugar mill. The town of Courtecon, our objective for that day, lay beyond. Courtecon was at that time, and has always been since, in German hands.

We started full of hope of pressing on to further success, the battle of the Marne fresh in our minds.

In the dark and the rain, without any lights, the road full of cavalry regiments and attendant batteries of artillery, progress was slow. Ahead of the Brigade, I found a detachment of infantry, which challenged in the dark in so truculent a manner that I decided to wait and allow some of our own command to precede me. I brought the car to rest at a point where the road from Bourg forked, one branch leading to Vendresse, the other to Moulins. As I waited in the rain a single shot rang out on the ridge, the dark woods of which towered above. The Brigade advance guard came up, de Lisle and his staff close behind. The General directed me to follow after him, preceding the advance squadron of the 9th Lancers, which was under command of Captain "Rivy" Grenfell. Passing through the dark gorge before the road curved round to the right and left as it entered the first scattered houses of the village of Vendresse, I lost touch with the advance party and the General. Slowing down, I had a chat with Captain Grenfell. I told him that my orders were to push on, but that I thought it would be wiser for me to keep out of the way of his advance squadron and follow behind it. I was not sure of the road, had lost the advance guard, and manœuvring the car without lights, with no one preceding me in the roadway, might cause some delay and confusion. Grenfell agreed that I should be less in the way if I would follow his squadron. This decision undoubtedly saved my life.

We toiled along in the dark, when suddenly from the front came the rattle of machine-gun fire and a storm of bullets. The road was sufficiently wide for me to turn the car. I sped away towards the other squadrons of the 9th Lancers, which were coming up. The leading squadron, behind which I had been crawling, scattered off the road when the machine guns in front opened fire. The first volley shot Captain " Rivy " Grenfell dead, a bullet striking him in the forehead as he was riding up the road.

The Germans were bent on holding the crest of the hill. General Bulfin's 2nd Brigade, the Sussex, the Northamptons, and 60th Rifles, were on our left front. The 4th Guards Brigade were further to the left, but what troops, if any, were on our right I could not discover. The machine-gun and rifle fire grew increasingly heavy in front. The enemy were in greater strength than we had anticipated. For a time I sat in the valley with but little information. Stories were told me of Captain Grenfell's squadron, one being that the Germans had allowed our advance guard to pass through their lines before opening fire. Later we learned that the advance guard had left the road, and Grenfell's squadron was acting as the point.

A motor cyclist was sent up to get information of the situation on the crest. On his return he reported that our Brigade was well under cover, and we were holding our position but not advancing. Later an orderly from the front, with a moment to spare, told me our troops were no further forward than the point we had reached the day before. A captain who had a scouting party along the crest during the night joined our conversation. He said he saw no Germans above Vendresse, evidence that some of the enemy had advanced at dawn. Some Scots Guards came down the hill wounded, and reported that the fire from the enemy in the vicinity of the sugar-mill was very heavy.

It was a rainy, dreary morning. By seven o'clock a number of wounded had come to the dressing station at the foot of the hill. Our batteries had begun firing, but so far no enemy shells had disturbed us. Another of our batteries dashed up towards Vendresse, a most inspiring sight. Major Beale Brown, of the 9th Lancers, told me more of Captain Grenfell's death. His squadron had proceeded under the impression that they were following the advance guard, and bumped right into the German picket. Captain Grenfell was the fifteenth officer of the 9th Lancers killed during the campaign. The 18th Hussars and a battery went by. Our field-guns opened with increasing frequency in positions to the right and left. The Welsh Regiment and the Gloucesters passed, the former followed by its handsome white goat. Stout chaps the infantry men, bearded like a pard, except for sundry hairless youths. Their firm step in the muddy road as they swung along at a good four miles an hour was evidence of their fitness and the spirit that was in them. Their faces showed great contrast, and I was struck by the youthful ones among them. In the dull, lowering, apprehensive weather, swinging forward grimly in the drizzle to face the German machine-guns on the crest, one could well be proud to be fighting under the same flag. A short mile away many of them were to meet their death. They were not going towards it carelessly, or thoughtlessly, but were pressing forward with the eagerness of splendid fighting stock, when the battle is within sight and hearing. A heavier roll of rifle fire, or an increase in the staccato of the rapid fire guns, seemed a signal for a quickening of their step. I never saw finer soldiers.

General de Lisle took me down to the headquarters

of the 1st Division at the cross-roads outside Vendresse, where we learned that the infantry had definitely captured the ridge, and on the right were through Paissy, which was taken the day before, and had got well beyond it. The numbers of wounded increased every minute. Batteries continued to be sent up the hill and off to the right. The German shells came closer to us. Three shells fell on the roadway not far ahead of a dozen couples of stretcher-bearers, who had started for the front. They trudged on stolidly. Our guns behind us, right and left, were hammering away so pertinaciously that it was likely we would soon come in for a severe return fire. A heavy infantry engagement commenced in front of Paissy. The shots echoed down the glen in an increasing din. The General returned to the 2nd Cavalry Brigade headquarters. We passed the North Lancashires on their way to the firing line.

De Lisle's formula when starting on our little expeditions by car was, " I would like to go on now, President, if you do not mind going under fire again." " President " was my nickname, bestowed to mark my nationality. De Lisle was always cheerful. He had an increasing amount of enjoyment that morning watching my nervous jumps when the " Black Maria " shells exploded in our vicinity. The big howitzer shells caused me an unusual amount of nervousness. Just before ten o'clock a couple of messages were passed by word of mouth down the troops along the roadway. The first one, thrown from detachment to detachment, was, " Pass the word back that no notice is to be taken of the white flag." Sinister message that, telling its own story. Someone had trusted the white flag as a signal of surrender, to his cost.

The next few days were replete with such instances, but the first of such stories that came to our ears made the greatest impression.

MONS TO YPRES.

The next message said, " Pass the word that German prisoners are going by." Fast on its heels, as we looked up the road in anticipation, came another message, " Pass the word back that no rude remarks are to be made as they go by." How many budding gems of scorn were nipped by that last order !

Prisoners drifted past, half a hundred of them, dejected in appearance, but sturdy and well-fed. They looked little like members of an army that had been pressed so hard in retreat as had Von Kluck's. At ten o'clock we ran up a cross-road, a mere lane, to Moulins, and climbed the steep hill to Paissy, a mountain village. Its cave dwellings and its one roadway nestling in the shelter of the high cliff side were full of picturesque Algerians and Zouaves. Leaving the car we walked to the top of the cliff, and were afforded a wonderful view. English cavalry of another Brigade galloped by on the skyline. We could see but few troops, but the General explained that in front of us some of the 1st Corps infantry were getting into touch with our 2nd Cavalry Brigade. As we stood at the top of the ridge it was most inspiring to feel that one of the greatest battles of the world's history was in progress in front of us. No one was at so good a point of vantage as we were to witness it. Yet we could see but little of it. If our First Army and d'Esperey's French troops on our right could succeed in forcing a way through the German line, and drive a wedge separating the seven Corps in front of us, a great victory might result. French motor-cars filled with eager officers had been pushing about all morning in search of our Divisional generals. Events seemed to be marching rapidly towards the consummation of our desires.

Once let us break through and pivot the line on our left, swinging our right up the road to Laon, great things might be expected. Our anticipation of success in this huge battle for position between armies of somewhat equal numbers, and our enjoyment of the magnificent view of the high hills and deep valleys, were interrupted by the continual searching in our vicinity of the German high-explosive shells. Their increasing frequency made me wish to cut short our visit to Paissy, in spite of the vantage afforded, for the longer we stayed the closer they came. Running down the hill and to Moulins, I turned up a cross-road when the engine of the car began to miss fire, and finally stopped. Of all the positions in which I had been during the morning, that was the most awkward in which to repair a balky car. A battery was stationed forty yards distant in a field. It was firing steadily, and the German guns were returning the compliment with equal persistency.

I detached the pipe leading to the carburettor, and blew out the petrol line with the aid of the tyre pump. To hurry the operation was impossible. A couple of shells dropped in the field at my side, and made me bungle the work. The banging of our guns, the smash of the German high-explosive shells near-by, the rattle of the rapid-firers and the roll of the rifles all round us as the great fight drifted to the left, made the air seem charged with electricity. I steadied myself, made a careful examination of the petrol line, and at last got it cleared. The General had walked on. I lost no time in leaving that unpleasant position. Passing over the same road a few days later, I marvelled to see the holes on either side and on the edge of it, where hundreds of German shells had fallen that morning

We returned to our wayside headquarters and made a good lunch of bully beef and bread and butter. General Bulfin's 2nd Brigade had been held up at the sugar mill, and the North Lancashires had been sent up through Vendresse in support. The 4th Guards Brigade, advancing in front of Chavonne and Soupir, with Ostel as their objective, had experienced wicked fighting, but reached the Ostel ridge. The struggle for the sugar factory and the Chemin des Dames position was still proceeding. Our troops that had passed Paissy had not yet reached the Chemin des Dames on their side. The Moroccan troops, on the right of the British line, had not brought their line far forward.

We received a report that the French had taken Craonne, further to the right. We were destined to receive numerous reports to that effect within the next few days.

That lunch was the first meal I had eaten to the sound of heavy artillery fire in close proximity. I have breakfasted in a boiler factory, and dined to the accompaniment of an equatorial thunderstorm. That luncheon had elements of both. I went with General de Lisle to Major-General Lomax's headquarters and heard our batteries sent up the hill to assist the attack on our left front. I was sent to move back our transport, as the 2nd Cavalry Brigade had been ordered to the left. The counter-attack of the Germans to the west of the 4th Guards Brigade had threatened to drive back the 3rd Division, who were in front of Vailly. A staff officer told me that the 3rd Division had been unable to reach Aizy, and that the enemy counter-attack in that quarter might turn our left flank.

After I had delivered my message to our transport I waited at a fork in the road, watching 300 German prisoners, including four officers. Nearly double this number of prisoners were taken that morning. The 300 gathered at that point had been captured in the trenches above Troyon by the Sussex Battalion, in a direct charge, in which Lieutenant-Colonel Montresor, of that regiment, was killed.

By noon the German counter-attack in front of Chivy, north of Verneuil, developed strongly. Half an hour later, the fight still drifting westward, the 2nd Cavalry Brigade left the road to mount the hill toward Verneuil, winding up the steep ascent in column of twos. Squadron after squadron and regiment after regiment disappeared in the undergrowth at the top of the rise. A lame horse left behind refused to be abandoned, and hobbled along in the rear of his regiment in pathetic testimony to his willingness to go with the others, no matter where they were bound. The rain ceased and the sky cleared, a fresh wind springing up to dry the muddy road. I walked up the slope, and, gaining a good point of observation, lay and watched the artillery duel on the far hillside. Clouds of black smoke and white bursts of shrapnel against the varying green of the thick foliage made a fascinating picture. A despatch rider showed me a message from General de Lisle to General Lomax stating that I Battery was in action one mile north-west of Bourg, that the shelled Germans were running from their trenches, and that our 1st Division troops could be seen advancing. Red Cross attendants, doctors and ammunition supply passed frequently. At 3.45 I ran to General Lomax's headquarters to enquire which road I should take to rejoin General de Lisle. I was told to go to Verneuil, and there ask for information. Returning to Bourg, which I found full of 1st Division wounded, I passed on to Verneuil, the streets of which were littered with dead horses and men. I counted thirty-five dead horses from where I stopped. I was told General de Lisle was further to the right, but the shell-fire was so continuous over the road that I returned to a point near Bourg. High explosive shells fell before me, behind me, and on both sides of me, as I made the return journey. At times I ran through clouds of black smoke from the big howitzer shells. In front of Bourg a battery of our 60-pounders was in action, and I stopped by them some little time. Fifteen empty ambulances passed en route for Verneuil, and shortly afterwards another dozen followed. One of the hospital men told me three hundred of our wounded were in the town.

A German aeroplane hovered over a battery of our

guns to the left of Verneuil for a moment. Immediately afterwards a very tornado of the enemy's shells were hurled at the battery. We expected to see it put out of action, but, to our surprise, it continued firing.

Seeing the cavalry moving west across country, I drove to Soupir, and from there to Chavonne. On reaching Chavonne I found that the General had gone up the steep road to the heights north of the town, where the Coldstreams and the Guards had entrenched themselves on the crest. Shells were dropping with monotonous regularity between Chavonne and Soupir.

At lunch we had discussed the desirability of annexing something in the nature of drinkables. Lieutenant Rex Benson, of the 9th Lancers, told me that in the quaint hill town of Pargnan, not far from Oeuilly, I would find a woman at a tiny hotel, from whom I might obtain a bottle or two of wine. I left word that I would return before dark, and drove hurriedly to Oeuilly and up the winding ascent to Pargnan. The proprietress of the hotel was most hospitable. She could let me have two bottles of wine at one franc each, she said. The production of a twenty-franc note and a request for a good supply led to a journey with Madame, an old retainer, an emaciated youth and a pair of infants. Down the cellar stairs we went, moved a pile of large empty casks from a further corner, then down a black hole, stooping low and stumbling against each other in the darkness. At the end of the passage a candle showed we were in a good sized cave in the hillside, with low ceiling of damp rock and floor of soft sand. A walk into the further blackness, and the boy was told to dig. The woman had buried her wine to keep it away from the Germans. Dig the lad did most valiantly for some time, but in vain. One of the toddlers was despatched for a larger shovel. After its arrival, by dint of our combined exertions, we exhumed four bottles of champagne and fourteen of a very passable red wine, which had been buried four feet below the surface. My offer of twenty-five francs for the lot was eagerly accepted.

I arrived at Soupir after dark, finding our headquarters in a small tumbledown barn at the corner of the grounds of a château which had belonged to Calmette, the editor of the *Figaro*, not long before shot by Madame Caillaux. General de Lisle ran to the château, where we found General Briggs' headquarters. After a consultation, we returned to our humble quarters and turned in for the night. I was so tired I went to sleep in the car. The firing in front of us began vigorously in the early part of the night. Another message to Briggs became necessary. Captain Barrett wakened me, and asked me to run to General Briggs' headquarters. There was a strict order against any car lights. The road was in a frightfully slippery condition and deeply ditched on either side. So it seemed better policy to walk. As I had been the only one to accompany the General on his previous visit, Barrett asked me to act as guide. Cavalry and artillery filled the beautiful parks. The dull light of the camp fires showed picturesque groups here and there under the trees. We were challenged several times. More than once the challenge was accompanied by the ominous click of a bolt, always disconcerting when the challenging sentry is so close to the line. One never knows just how jumpy sentries may be under the stress of circumstances.

We found General Briggs seated on the steps of the château. He explained the situation carefully. The left of the cavalry was to rest on the river, its right to be in touch with the left of the Guards. We returned to our own headquarters by eleven o'clock to find that the mess wagon had come up. A slice of ham and a piece of bread made a good dinner, and I immediately afterwards " turned in " on a blanket spread beside the car. Firing became incessant towards midnight, but I slept soundly until a sharp rain storm drove me under shelter. I tried the floor of the barn. The General was sleeping in the manger. The staff were spread about here and there on the earthen floor. I chose several positions in turn, all of them being impossible from the standpoint of comfort. Hummocks and hollows of exasperating shapes seemed to protrude themselves upon me wherever I might lie. Withal, I spent one of the most uncomfortable nights of the campaign.

So the day ended, with our hopes of piercing the German line shattered, and with the dawning realisation that we were facing a splendidly prepared and dangerously strong position. It began to filter into our minds that the German retreat was over and that we had best prepare ourselves for fierce counter-attacks to hold the lines we had gained. We were well across the Aisne. We heard that Maunoury at Vic had done well and was not unsuccessful at Soissons. Our 3rd Corps were reported to have a strong position in the direction of Chivres and Vrigny. The 3rd Division was still in Vailly. Our Chavonne-Soupir line leading away north of Verneuil and on to Troyon, thence to a point north of Paissy had been maintained, if not advanced materially. Good news came from the French in front of Craonne, and again we heard they had taken that town, although subsequent reports invariably came after news of Craonne's capture to tell us that the Germans still held it.

Promise of a hard fight to maintain our positions was sure on the morrow. Sleep was of inestimable value, so we slept as best we could.

WITH FRENCH.

CHAPTER VII.

Typed reports from G.H.Q. began to bear universal interest about this time. One that reached us during our first days on the Aisne collected evidences of German discomfiture, due to the pressure we had given their hurried retreat. Enemy shells were thrown into the Vesle at Braisnes. We captured German cavalry orders crying for aid to their infantry, admitting that their horses were worn out and the roads so congested they could not get their transport away. Some half-starved Huns were taken prisoners, and others found who were nearly dead of fatigue and exhaustion. Diaries from the bodies of enemy dead testified to the horror of our continual shrapnel fire. A bomb that one of our airmen dropped on a party of Uhlans killed fifteen of their number.

We called these reports the " Cheer-up Journal."

The Chavonne-Soupir ridge was definitely ours by dawn on Tuesday, the 15th. Earliest light was the signal for the enemy to commence shelling our hard-won positions. A blue-grey smoke pall hung over the woods on the crest in front of us all the morning. The air was rent with the sound of continuous battle, in which all arms, from rifles to big howitzers, played their part.

No morning ablutions these days. We were an unwashed, unshaven lot.

German gun-fire meant business on the Aisne. Shrapnel was hurled at the hill-tops by scores. I spent some time watching the shell-bursts twenty to thirty at once. Salvoes of sixes and dozens burst together in the tree-tops. Thick clouds of greenish-yellow massed and drifted in the clear light. The early sun, fighting through hazy clouds, painted the floating smoke-balls a pale heliotrope.

The General took me to Soupir, and up the steep mountain road toward the trenches. Our shells screamed over our heads, and enemy shells as well, the latter bursting in all directions, in front of us, behind us, on every side. As the road changed to a mere track, de Lisle left the car and proceeded on foot. A wounded Tommy sauntering past volunteered the information that the wood near by was full of dead Germans. In a cottage beside me was a dressing-station—a sad sight. Worn-out men, bandaged, were sitting about it, heads drooping, broken, weary, many in awful pain, yet not a word of complaint. Cold-streams, Irish Guards, and Connaught Rangers were among the wounded. The Irish Guards suffered heavily in taking the woods. Four of their captains were killed, one wounded, and a subaltern wounded as well. Lord Arthur Guernsey and Lord Arthur Hay were among their dead.

Someone had noted a couple of officers shot from behind. One of the wounds was in the back of the neck, the bullet ranging down the spine. A search resulted in the discovery of German sharpshooters hidden in the thick foliage of tree-tops in the rear.

One of our gallant officers stooped to give a wounded Prussian officer a drink. The shattered German looked up, recognised that the would-be Samaritan was one of the hated enemy, and shot him dead.

A group of Germans in the wood surrendered, waving a couple of white flags in token of their submission. As our men ran out to take their arms, another enemy detachment, coming suddenly upon the scene, opened on friend and foe alike, and mowed down scores.

Returning to our barn near the Calmette Château, we were stunned by the shock of two big howitzer shells, one fair on the roadway beyond us and the other close beside it. Pushing on, we found one of the two had killed nine battery horses and five men, wounding fourteen of their comrades. One horse had fallen across the road, and had to be moved to allow our passage.

Before we left the vicinity of that château, Black Marias and dead horses became so common as to fail to excite remark.

After a run to General Allenby's headquarters, we again climbed the Soupir ridge. The cottage that had been a dressing station a couple of hours before had been found to be too directly in the line of fire, and the wounded had been moved to some point below. As we went past, shells were bursting close to us, several landing less than one hundred yards distant. Down the road trickled a procession of wounded, an unusual percentage of them hit in the face and head.

A pathetic little sight came under my eye as a quartette of shattered soldiers—two British Tommies and two Germans—walking abreast and evidently communicating with each other with difficulty, came to a halt. They turned, each German extending a hand, and each Tommy grasping it. After a moment's handclasp, they plodded their bandaged way, one limping badly. Stretcher parties were numerous.

A message to the headquarters of General Monro, commanding the 2nd Division, took me from Soupir to Moussy-sur-Aisne. Dozens of dead horses lined the road and the town was full of them. Moussy proved a veritable shambles. Blood had been spattered everywhere. General Monro's headquarters were beside a haystack outside the town.

Before noon, while I was resting on the Chavonne road, Major Hugh Dawnay and Westminster drove up, asking for the Guards Brigade. As they left for Soupir, four high-explosive devils lit a couple of hundred yards away with a crash. Then four more, only little beyond us. Westminster and Dawnay returned a few minutes later

" Pretty hot in Chavonne, isn't it ? " said one of

MONS TO YPRES.

them. "Two shells lit in the trees just above our heads as we started back."

The sky-line was white with shrapnel. Someone joked about a recent G.H.Q. report that told of a shortage of German ammunition. It seemed the enemy must stop searching in our vicinity for batteries or the General must move headquarters, at least, if he wished to have any Staff left to him. But close as the shells came not one of us was hit. We even became in a measure accustomed to them as the day wore on. I lay in a ditch and took snapshots of the bursting shells above me.

After lunch I strolled past the imposing gates of the Calmette Château and through the beautiful grounds. A fairy lake, covered with pond lilies and lined with a rare rockery, was tucked away in a bower of trees. The clear, cool water provided a refreshing bath.

At General Haig's headquarters in Bourg, later in the day, Hugh Dawnay outlined the strategic situation to me most lucidly. He gave me a simple explanation of Von Kluck's plans and the state of affairs generally. I jotted it down and retailed it to more than one interested listener during the next week. No one would imagine how little regimental officers, or Brigade commanders, for that matter, knew of the broad plan of operations at that time. The fact that the line of the French 5th Army on our left stretched from Noyon to Soissons was news to us. To the east the French held from our British right at Paissy to Rheims, thence to St. Menehould, and on to Verdun and beyond. Dawnay gave me my first definite news of Foch's great victory on the advance north, when the enemy left 9,000 dead on one battle-field. "The French," said Dawnay, "ever thorough in all matters of scientific detail, have made post-mortems on dead German soldiers. The data thus obtained confirms the report of the Intelligence Department that the invaders are subsisting off the country."

WITH FRENCH.

Our night stop was Oeuilly, and for the second time we were sheltered in the ravished château.

Rain set in—the sort of rain that soaks into one's system—and by the time we reached Oeuilly we were thoroughly wet.

Wednesday bade fair to be one continual drizzle. Our brigade was ordered into the trenches on the Chavonne ridge. I ran the car to the very top. As the road wound above the village the ascent became quite steep. The valley of the Aisne stretched away in panorama below. Cave dwellings lined the way at frequent intervals. The inevitable convoy of stretchers met us as we mounted upward, many of the wounded pale and drawn from hours of suffering while waiting for daylight to permit their being moved. The path was in no condition for night traffic. At the top of the hill were our trenches, and those of the enemy in plain view a few hundred yards in front of us.

The 4th D. G.'s, 9th Lancers and 18th Hussars spent the morning "taking over" from the Queen's Bays, 5th D. G.'s and 11th Hussars. As the men came out of the trenches they looked tired and worn but splendidly fit.

Brigade headquarters were located in a house on the hill, a poor place, but affording shelter.

Just after noon we sat down to lunch. Hardly had we done so when word came that the enemy was advancing all along the line. At the same moment news reached us that the German shells had rendered Bourg uninhabitable, and Haig had found it advisable to move his headquarters.

Increasing shrapnel fire in front made the echoes resound. We were off through Chavonne and up the road that led to the trenches. A Battalion of Jocks had made a wall of good-sized stones which barred the way. A few moments' work by a score of them cleared a path. While we were waiting shells burst near, and hot bits of shrapnel fell in the car. On we

The famous Sugar Mill trench above Troyon

Hiding chargers behind the road bank from the enemy observers

Colonel Steele's Headquarters (Coldstream) above Vendresse

Colonel Serrocold's Headquarters (60th Rifles) on the Aisne

climbed. As we passed a cottage a shell hit it and tiles showered down in armfuls, some of them rattling against the metal panels of the car. Horse ambulances had found their way up and down from the valley to the crest during the morning, and had made the road so slippery that de Lisle left the car in the shelter of a bank and trudged on afoot. The 2nd Life Guards came up and occupied the shallow straw-filled reserve trenches beside me. Our guns took a hand with increasing fury. I began to like the sound of our own shells on their flight overhead—a song I was to learn one day to love.

An hour passed. The General came down from the line and told me our batteries had smashed the enemy attack in splendid style.

I took Hamilton-Grace to Haig to report. As we left our headquarters a shell struck it, but only tore off a bit of roof and hurt no one. Before we had gone one hundred yards a big black chap smashed a tree in the road in front of us. Soon after we passed another one fell in almost the same place. " Close work," said Grace with a laugh.

Beside the wall of the Calmette Château we sped, mindful that we were traversing an unhealthy locality. The 1st Brigade were along the roadway, the 11th Hussars at the further end of the wall. A German aeroplane was overhead. As he watched it Grace saw it drop a glistening signal. I was compelled to slow down, the road at that point being full of cavalry horses and ammunition wagons. The ditch was lined with resting troopers. Rumph! Umph! A Black Maria fell close on our left, its sinister pall of smoke drifting almost on to us. "Get on, old chap," said Grace. I "got." Down went my foot on the accelerator pedal. The car leaped forward. I narrowly missed a horse and swung away at full speed. Crash! went a shell where we had been a second or two before. It seemed as if fear lent the old car wings. Grace looked back and remarked, "If I'm not mistaken that one hit some of the fellows we came past a moment ago."

Not long after, having bumped over the pontoon bridge at Bourg and back again, we returned over the road past the château.

As we drew near, a wounded black mare, her side covered with mud, galloped madly past. A scared group of transport drivers were huddled behind a stone cairn by the roadside. We came to a pile of accoutrements, then a dead horse in the road. Reaching the wall we found the ditch piled full of dead horses and men. Two dismembered horses lay in the way, other dead horses were piled in the field, and stretcher bearers were picking up still forms in khaki from under the trees.

Fifteen horses and a dozen men was the toll taken by that shell. It burst just by the roadside two or three seconds after we had sped past.

I was kept busy, up the hill and down again time after time, till late in the evening. Cold bully beef was the *pièce de résistance* of our dinner that night, a dish of which I think I could never tire.

For the next two days we "hung on" in the trenches on the ridge. Most of the time we were under shell-fire. The weather was damp and cold, the rain making the trench-life miserable enough. The cavalry had seen the last of open mounted fighting. An officer of the 18th Hussars made an interesting reconnaissance with a squad of men, crawling close to the German trenches. Captain Kirkwood, of the 4th D.G.'s, did a "stalk" on the following night, returning with useful information as to the enemy's position. For the most part we could see the German lines in the daytime quite clearly, but the night adventures put us in close touch with the parts of their line that lay out of our sight.

One or two incipient German attacks were reported, causing headquarters to rush to the trench-line, but nothing serious materialised. Once an officer sent word that the enemy were advancing in force, and he could not hold his position unless reinforced. Upon the anticipated attack proving a false alarm this officer was interviewed by the chief. After this interview he heartily wished the Germans *had* come

A battery commander was ordered to move his guns to another position and go into action at once. On the arrival of the gun horses the battery was heavily shelled. Back the horses were rushed under cover. Again they were ordered up and again the Germans commenced to shell them. After a wait of twenty minutes the horses were brought up for the third time, only to be shelled and driven back as before. This puzzled the gunner commanding the battery. Our troops held the ridge above him, and no enemy position was in sight from the spot occupied by the guns. A village lay on the hillside. Taking a couple of men he searched the houses, and in a cottage far up the rise found a strapping chap in peasant garb who proved to be a German guardsman. In a stack beside the hovel the spy had concealed himself for days, lying at the end of a telephone wire which led over the hill, past or under our front line and into the German trenches. The gun horses had been brought up in front of his very eyes. When he gave the word by telephone to his own guns they banged away until he told them the target was withdrawn.

To execute the spy and shift the battery was but a matter of moments. The guns were moved not a second too soon, for before they were far away a battery of German howitzers was turned on the field they had left, and in a short time had torn the surface with great rents into which one could put a gun-team.

The Germans did not always have such fine targets for their gunners. One morning a sudden burst of sun from behind a bank of cloud found a couple of officers on the ridge just back of a line of trenches, lying on the grass enjoying a respite from the usual sodden weather and overcast skies. Together they gazed on the panorama together. The Valley of the Aisne was an entrancing sight. Here lay this town and there that, some smashed by shells, some practically unharmed.

As they looked down the wooded hillsides into the lower land toward the river, one of them called out, " Look ! a helio'."

From under a hedge back of Moussy came the flash, flash, flash, in regular intervals. A junior signals officer tried to read the message. Once, he said, he caught a word, but for the most part it was Greek to him. " Must be some fool sort of code," he confessed. " I never saw anything like it before."

As they watched it, the Germans saw it, too. Bang went a big black Jack Johnson not far from the spot. Smash ! came another. Still the flashes twinkled from the surrounding green.

The first two shells were the forerunners of dozens that crashed through the hedge and into the turf all about the tiny centre of light.

Black shell-clouds showed all round that field and the next. Soon the sun crept behind a cloud, as if intent on protecting the object of the Huns' iron wrath.

Next morning a brief ten minutes of sun caused eyes on the ridge to wander valleywards again. Sure enough, a couple of flashes, intermittent and apparently quite without coherence, came from the spot at the hedgeside.

Soon the enemy howitzers played on the vicinity, fiercer than the day before.

After the sun had gone from sight, they kept up their bombardment of the unfortunate spot for half an hour. Dozens of shells fell thereabouts, then scores on scores.

A signals officer on the crest, watching the play murmured : " What idiots our helio' lot are to choose a spot in plain sight of those Germans on the far ridge."

That afternoon a cavalry officer had a journey to make which took him to General Monro's headquarters near Moussy. His work done, he continued a few hundred yards, and sought the spot that had suffered the awful shelling.

It was not hard to find. The hedge was smashed in places. A tall tree was knocked down near by. Great black holes were torn in the green fields. On one side of the hedge lay a dead cow. No sign could be seen of the helio' party. This was hardly surprising, as for over half an hour shells had fallen all about the flickering light until it seemed no man could live thereabouts.

The staff officer strolled over to a battery position not far distant, and asked for news of the signallers. The gunners had wondered at the heavy shelling not many hundred yards from their funk-holes, but had seen no human beings near the hedge, before or after the bitter bombardment.

Nonplussed, the officer walked back to the devastated area, and, just as he was leaving, discovered the cause of all the trouble.

There, caught on a twig of the hedge, swinging lazily in the wind, was a bright-bottomed empty sardine tin, thrown carelessly aside by some satiated luncher.

The sun, catching the bright bit of moving tin, had made of it a tiny reflector.

Surely, never had so insignificant an object or one so intrinsically worthless caused the Huns so great an expenditure of costly ammunition.

A detachment of 18th Hussars were bringing about 150 led horses from Bourg to Chavonne over a road that was within telescopic range of the Huns.

Two or three Black Marias in the midst of the column made a scatterment thereabouts, and for the rest of the afternoon the new mounts were careering all over the surrounding country. A few horses and two men were killed, and many of the horses slightly wounded. All but eight were recovered by nightfall.

The same day the German look-outs must have taken a herd of a couple of dozen cows for some of our horses. A battery of howitzers opened on the inoffensive cattle, driving them from one corner of a large field to another. For quite half an hour the enemy guns pounded away at the herd. It seemed odd that any of the poor beasts were left alive, but only five were killed—in spite of the tons of metal embedded in their pasture by the Bosche gunners.

The effective strength of most of the commands on the Aisne was low. That of the 2nd Cavalry Brigade was but fifty per cent. of its full complement. The Brigade had, since leaving England, lost twenty-five killed, 120 wounded, and 220 missing—some 365 casualties all told — over one-third of its original strength.

On the afternoon of Friday, the 18th, unable to catch forty winks owing to the banging of a dozen 18-pounders just below our house, de Lisle gave me permission to walk up to the trenches and watch the shelling. A short cut through the woods was the route advised. As I got well in among the trees the enemy began to shell them. No troops were in the wood, but every day the Germans seemed to deem it necessary to visit a certain amount of iron wrath upon it.

The crashing and splintering of the branches, and the ripping of bits of shell through the thick foliage overhead, were among the most thoroughly unpleasant sounds I have ever heard. A feeling that I might be wounded and lie helpless in the undergrowth, to die of starvation or thirst before being discovered, entered my mind. A quartette of particularly vociferous shells burst above, a splinter striking the good-sized tree trunk behind which I was endeavouring to compress myself into as small a space as possible.

MONS TO YPRES.

That settled it. No route was too far round if it obviated the necessity of traversing that dreadful wood. I incontinently fled downhill, and after a long detour reached the crest by the main path up the slope. A natural tunnel ran through the rock at the summit. Twenty to thirty feet from its outer end were our trenches. The Coldstreams were in occupation, " well dug in," and quite happy. In front, the ground sloped away for a thousand yards, then dipped gently. A further slope was not so far distant, but that I could see German reserves coming over it toward the enemy trench-line that faced us.

At the time I arrived, the German gunners were shelling our trenches 100 to 300 yards to the right of the tunnel's mouth. One or two landed, now and again so close as seventy or eighty yards from me. Most of the shells hit the ground a few hundred feet short of our trenches. Many burst in the air at close range. Not a few went over and exploded close behind. The men in the part of the line in which I sat were utterly careless of the bombardment of the bit of trenches so close beside them. They had an air of absolute detachment, as if it had nothing to do with them. Comment and criticism followed each new arrival. A few Tommies had mounted the trench parapet, and sat coolly in the open as though ticket holders and entitled to good front seats.

" What if those devils start on this bit of trench ? " I asked a captain, whose dug-out I was sharing. " Oh, the men would get down quickly enough if the shells start this way," was his reply.

The space between the lines had widened. At least 1,300 yards separated the entrenched armies on that immediate front. Now and then a German walked across the skyline, 1,400 to 1,500 yards away. Both sides were beginning to learn the value of deep, well-made trenches, and the comparative safety such shelter gave from shrapnel fire. Hundreds of shells burst over the crest and left hardly a single casualty to record.

That night I tried sleeping in the open ; but, as usual, a nocturnal rain-storm came up and drove me to the shelter of the hood of the car. A bitterly cold night it proved to be. A bad night for the many gun crews that had to sleep on the ground beside their batteries. The men in the trenches had made nests of straw which were much warmer than might have been expected, though the persistent rain eventually soaked through such make-shift shelters. One gun crew near me were drowned out of their "funk-holes," and gathered round a somewhat discouraged fire till morning. At daybreak I met troopers from the front trench-line who for hours had been standing in a foot of water.

Saturday, the 19th, was a rest day in which our brigade retired to billets at Longueval, south of the Aisne, and thoroughly dried out. I ran to G.H.Q. at Fère-en-Tardenoise, where Ted Howard, an R.A.C. member driving the Provost Marshal, had boasted a comfortable lodging. He was out and his little billet empty, so I took possession and managed a bath under the water tap in his kitchen sink. A tedious process and fraught with some general saturation of the entire culinary domain, but it served.

MONS TO YPRES.

CHAPTER VIII.

THE Sunday was an eventful one for me.

General de Lisle was up at three o'clock and away half an hour later. The Brigade was ordered to Paissy. A couple of squadrons of the 18th Hussars were to go into the trenches close to the firing line while the remainder of the command was to act in reserve.

I crossed the river on the pontoon bridge at Villers, the water almost covering the boards.

Paissy was built half in and half out of the rock of the hill proper. Some houses were so constructed that part of the rooms were mere caves in the cliff. The farms all boasted a cave in the wall side, convenient for storage of such rude property as implements of toil and carts or the stabling of live-stock.

We arrived at five o'clock. The General left the car and went on mounted. On the left the cliff ran sheer to a point above the highest building in the town. To the right of the roadway the ground dropped away into a miniature crater, the bottom of which was mapped with tiny squares of growing crops of green pasture, low hedges marking their boundaries. The cliff side ran round the valley in the form of a horseshoe. At the far end a steep wide path led to the summit.

The Germans were firing regularly, the shrapnel bursting a couple of hundred yards from us. A Sussex supply column was busy harnessing its horses in the farmyard I chose for shelter, so I backed the car under the outside wall. The shrapnel began singing over my head. I sat on the step of the car and watched a robust French farmer try to drive three huge white oxen into the gate. Swinging their heads

153

low as if feeling their way with their great branching horns, their mild eyes opened wide in astonishment at the noise of the bursting shells.

A Sussex Tommy begged a drop of petrol to fill an automatic cigarette lighter. Around the corner came a line of wounded Algerians, some supported by comrades and one swarthy fellow carried by his companions. They seemed to have suffered a bad mauling. The dazed look of mute questioning, a failure to understand, was on their faces. From red fez to blue putties, their uniforms were a riot of colour. Blue capes over light blue jackets trimmed in yellow and red, once white trousers, unusually baggy, with here and there a head-dress of odd hue, they presented a variegated but woe-begone appearance. They might have been part of a pageant which had started out gaily enough only to meet catastrophe. Some of them were almost white. Some were quite black. One was grinning. From another a sharp cry of pain caused his bearers to let him gently down for a moment in the roadway.

A loud explosion came so close at hand that it ripped the air apart. The shock struck me like a blow in the face. Bricks, stones, bits of *débris*, and shrapnel fell in every direction. A rush of fumes and smoke came through the gateway from a German shell which had burst inside. The farmer shot through the air, falling on his back in the roadway by me. After an effort to raise himself, he fell back with a shudder, and lay twitching convulsively. A couple of horses and two forms in khaki were piled together against the cliff side. One of the big white oxen lay a few feet away, his snowy side turning crimson. *Débris* of all sorts rained down, the heavier bits with a sharp staccato as they struck the *pavé* roadway.

The impulse to leave the spot where a shell has fallen is overpowering. I gained the shelter of a further wall, when a shell burst behind me in the

pathway that led from the crest. It lit among the
fleeing Algerians. Numbers of them were hurled
aside. Loud cries told of pain and terror. A great
black fellow came down the hill screaming shrilly,
dashed round the corner and sped away, lurching and
straining as he ran. Down the road came a flash and
a milky shrapnel cloud over the roadway. A shell
had toppled the big Algerian over in full flight.

Under a wooden gate, torn from its hinges, I cuddled
close under the wall of a house. Shell after shell
burst over the roadway. Huddled groups of Algerians
still came down the path. They had no idea of how
to seek cover. The wounded lay thick on all sides.

A tiny man, his ebony face distorted into a ghastly
grin, struggled under an enormous comrade limp as a
sack of meal. Through that hell of shell-fire the little
Algerian made his way slowly, stepping gingerly over
the dead and skirting shell-holes with the greatest
care. At last he reached one of the hillside caves, and
deposited his load at the feet of one of our brigade
doctors, who was busy dressing a most heterogeneous
collection of wounded.

No sooner had the little man got clear of the
roadway than a shell burst over it. Involuntarily
ducking at the force of the explosion, I felt a sharp
blow in the ribs. It literally " knocked the wind out
of me." At the moment I was afraid to feel my side,
apprehensive of a nasty wound. A glance showed me
a large brick had struck me, hurled as though shied
from a catapult. My ribs were sore for days afterwards.

I fled a few yards further, keeping close to the wall.
I stopped by Captain Algy Court, of the 9th Lancers.
Court was standing beside his horse in such shelter as
the wall afforded, waiting orders to move his squadron
up the hill. We tried to talk to each other, but
bursting shells rendered conversation impossible. A
piece of shell struck Court's charger in the chest. The

blood spurted in a stream. The captain led him inside the gateway. I followed. As I came past, the poor animal fell backwards and all but pinned me against the cliff side.

An English soldier and an Algerian were brought into an adjacent cave. A couple of old peasants looked on sympathetically while our doctor dressed both wounds with equal care. The doctor asked me to accompany him to a larger cave, where several of our wounded were reported to be.

There we found forty or fifty cases, mostly Algerians. Standing in the doorway of the cave, the shell-fire seemed louder, but I was in comparative safety. A passing officer advised me to get my car away if it was still runnable. It was covered with *débris*, but no beams or large pieces of wreckage had fallen on it. It was by that time but six o'clock, though it seemed as if hours had passed. I crept along the wall towards the car, when the noise of a passing shell sent me back to the cave mouth. A pale little French soldier, with spare black beard, was brought in wounded — a splendid, plucky little chap.

A high explosive terror burst in the road in front of the gate of our adopted dressing station. Then for twenty minutes the din of exploding shells was without a break. Most of them burst just above the roadway. Now one would light on the crest above the cave mouth, and shower mud, stones, and pieces of shell over us.

The yard was full of harnessed teams. The effect of the shell-fire on the horses was interesting. Some were apathetic; others were nervous and jumpy; most of them took it quietly.

A woman came from a house, leading a four-year-old child. She was making for the safe retreat of the cave. The little girl was wonderingly interested, but not in the least afraid. She prattled incessant questions to her mother as they hurried to shelter.

MONS TO YPRES.

Well up the steep path that led to the crest, I could see the wide, low mouth of a cave that faced the direction from which the enemy's shells were coming. A dozen Algerians with their horses were gathered there. I watched them as they stood near the opening. Then came a flash and a red smudge right over the cave mouth. Black smoke poured out in dense masses. A Black Maria had exploded inside the cave. Not a man nor a horse of the group escaped instant death.

An hour later a lull in the shelling induced me to walk forward and look at the car. It was intact, though covered with still more masonry and *débris*. A piece of shell hit the road in front of me, and threw the mud in a conical little spurt, whereupon I lost no time in regaining the mouth of the cave.

The General was in the firing line somewhere ahead.

A battery of 18-pounders on the crest had been "answering" at times during the morning, but had been unable to "find" the enemy's howitzers.

At last came a full five minutes' lull in the firing. Its effect on the artillery drivers and reserves standing near was electrical. The men walked across the yard and into the road quite as unconcernedly as though a truce had been declared. To judge from their demeanour the danger was over. A German aeroplane sailing high above slowly turned and circled over us. German aeroplanes spelt trouble. We had not long to wait for it to materialise.

Just as I had planned to remove the car the shell-fire began again, to last for another half-hour. In the lull which followed I dug the car from under the *débris* which covered it and moved it to a point of greater safety. Pieces of shrapnel had left their mark on its sides and made a hole through one of the mud guards. One of the panels was spattered with blood.

In a house selected for our headquarters I found a kitchen fire, which was most welcome, as a chill rain was falling. All forenoon the shelling continued at intervals, until my head rang with it.

The line in front of us was held by the newly arrived 18th Brigade of the 6th Division. This Brigade, under General Congreve, consisted of the 1st West Yorks, 1st East Yorks, 2nd Notts and Derby and 2nd Durham Light Infantry. The extreme right of the line was in the hands of the West Yorks, a green regiment so far as German tricks were concerned.

The Algerians had been driven from their position on the far left of the French line. Three trenches in echelon, facing north-east, we hoped they would hold, for their retirement from those trenches uncovered our right flank. As a precaution de Lisle ordered Colonel Burnett, of the 18th Hussars, to prepare and occupy a couple of trenches between the right of the West Yorks and the left of the Algerians to protect any possible gap.

Still the fire rained on Paissy. One shell in the roadway killed a lieutenant and four men of the 18th. The roof of our headquarters house was continually peppered with hot splinters. The Sussex Battalion (1st Division) were in Paissy. I saw a message from General Lomax to the Sussex, saying that the 2nd Cavalry Brigade were to support the right of the West Yorks during the day, and rest in Paissy that night, to be on hand in case the French on the east of us were compelled to fall back. The Sussex were "resting." I had a good laugh with their Commanding Officer at the idea of "resting" anywhere near Paissy that day.

The Commanding Officer of the West Yorks called. He was very nervous about his right, but de Lisle reassured him. Personally I thought there was altogether too much talk of the precariousness of the situation. Such a thing exists as unnecessary apprehension.

MONS TO YPRES.

The General suggested a visit to Divisional headquarters after the West Yorks Colonel had departed. As I lowered the hood a shell burst across the road twenty feet distant, and dirt and stones showered over me. I felt myself well over to be sure I was not hit. A piece of another shell hit a tree on the opposite side, and a shrapnel burst over the yard behind. How delighted I was to clear out of the place, if only for a short time! At General Allenby's headquarters, by a haystack above Tour de Paissy, a heavy shower gave me a thorough drenching. When the rain ceased we had a fine view of the country round. The French trenches and those of our troops could be seen with the naked eye.

Standing at a safe distance, watching the enemy shrapnel over our trenches or seeing clusters of four or eight burst over Paissy, with a Black Maria in frequent interlude, was a very different matter from being under the bursting shells.

On the way back to our own headquarters we had to wait outside Moulins until the enemy gunfire, covering the road ahead of us, had died down. One of the recently-arrived 60-pounder batteries, cleverly concealed, was thundering as we sped by its hiding-place.

At headquarters I felt drowsy and tried to sleep, but found it impossible. The German 8-inch howitzer shells were coming at regular intervals, their explosions rattling the panes and jarring the very foundations. The patter of *débris* on the roof, the sharp slap of a bit of shell or a shrapnel bullet in the yard, and the screams and moans of passing missiles, put my nerves on edge.

The General and Phipps-Hornby rode out to keep an eye on the trench positions. The hammering, hammering, hammering was growing painfully monotonous. The hopelessness of escape from it was galling.

Like a bolt from the blue came a West Yorks

officer with news that the Germans had once again attacked the Zouaves on our right and pushed them back, getting in on the West Yorks' right flank. The Huns had taken some of the West Yorks' trenches, and driven back the line. Two companies of the Yorks Battalion had been captured. No sooner had he told his tale than Phipps-Hornby galloped up. General de Lisle, he said, was trying to get a company of the Yorks together, and wished all available troops sent up at once to reinforce him. All was bustle. The 4th Dragoon Guards were off instanter, the 9th Lancers hard on their heels, with the Sussex not far behind.

A real breach in the line and Paissy lost meant serious business. The muddy roads and the narrow pontoon bridges over the Aisne would not allow a thought of retirement. Nothing remained but to regain the ground that had been lost.

I was ordered off post haste to 1st Division headquarters, and then to General Allenby to bear messages explaining what had transpired. Speeding over the greasy road I soon reached General Lomax, and a few moments later was at 1st Cavalry Division headquarters. The fight was in plain view. The Germans were coming over the brow of the hill. A couple of hundred dismounted 4th Dragoon Guards, the first line of the counter-attack, under Major Tom Bridges, could be seen climbing the stubble-covered hillside, dotted with still forms in khaki, and crowned by the lost trench.

Batteries—French, British, and German—sent round after round as fast as the men could serve the guns.

Still up the stubble crept the thin line, Bridges' tall form in the lead. The support, eager to have a hand in the game, pressed on in haste, but could not overtake the invincible Dragoon Guards, who swept away the Germans in their vastly superior numbers as if endowed with some superhuman power.

They gave the Huns no rest. Pouring a deadly

A cave Headquarters above the Pargnan

General FitzClarence's cave Headquarters (18th Brigade) on the Aisne

Eighteen-pounder hit by a "Black Maria."

and accurate fire into the blue-grey ranks as they came on, Bridges and his 200 reached the front trench at last under a very heavy canopy of whizzing bullets. With a wild cheer, they leapt at the Germans, and threw them back from the trenches. The fierceness of the onslaught could no more be withstood than one could stem a cyclone.

The lost position regained, the big major leaped ahead, and again his men poured on after him. The enemy was not only to lose what he had won, but more. Before the 4th Dragoon Guards stopped, they had taken the Chemin des Dames, three or four hundreds yards ahead of our original position. There we stuck and held on against counter-attack on counter-attack—our line to be kept without losing an inch of it during assaults that for the next few weeks were to leave pile on pile of German dead as an earnest of their stubborn refusal to admit the ground for ever lost.

A splendid charge was that at Paissy. A triumph of individual leadership and splendid quality in a handful of men. To watch it made the blood run hot and fast. To have taken part in it was worth a lifetime of mere ordinary existence.

Running back through Pargnan, the roads and fields were full of the battered Algerians. Out of 6,000 of them only 2,000 were left after five days' hard fighting

I was under shell-fire a number of times during the remainder of the day. At dusk the Staff was in the road under the brow of the Paissy hill when shells fell closer than usual. Captain Hamilton-Grace suggested I should back the car further round a turn, under shelter of the height of ground. I was too tired to bother, but at his second suggestion I backed for some fifty feet to please him. The moment I brought the car to rest in its new position, a shell lit on the spot from which I had moved it. I voted Grace's foresight little short of uncanny.

WITH FRENCH.

To cap the climax, the French won back their original positions on the right, and night closed with the line in better position than dawn had found it.

We seemed firmly installed in our billets in Longueval. The men were very comfortable in the picturesque stone-built village nestling low between the steep hill sides. The village folk were exceptionally friendly. A little bakery did the trade of its lifetime. A dry, warm billet at night makes a vast difference to the efficiency of a command, and for a fortnight the 2nd Cavalry Brigade waxed fat in Longueval, in spite of sundry days spent in the ever-shelled Paissy.

On Monday, following the Sunday fight in front of the Chemin des Dames, the Brigade was ordered to rest and refit. The line was comparatively quiet, save for the inevitable intermittent shell-fire. The weather was exasperating. A flash of real warm sunshine at times gave hope of a change, but the hope always vanished in cold, dispiriting rain. General de Lisle made a tour of divisional and corps headquarters that put us in accurate touch with the march of events. At Braisnes we found General Gough, in command of the newly formed 2nd Cavalry Division, consisting of the 3rd and 5th Cavalry Brigades. General Smith-Dorrien's headquarters were in a great medieval château at Muret, a picturesque spot.

The universal feeling was that the new form of warfare, the trench fighting, might prove a tedious business. In spite of the arrival from England of half a dozen batteries of 60-pounders, the Germans were able to fire thirty shells to our one. Their preponderance in machine-guns was also marked. But few days of the trench war had passed before the machine-gun had come into its own. Officers who had given but little thought to the intricate mechanism of the death-dealing quick-firers could be heard cursing administrations of all sorts because of the obvious shortage of rapid-fire guns in the British Army.

MONS TO YPRES.

A well-informed gunner gave the following twist to one such conversation : " I know of reports impressing the necessity of an increase of machine-guns and machine-gunners that for years went annually into the War Office. Why was nothing done ? Because no money was forthcoming, that's why. The taxpayer wouldn't stand it. No unlimited amount for army expenditure has ever been available, and rapid-fire guns are costly things. Reduction of army appropriation, not increase of its ordnance, is what a politician preached if he wanted to court popularity. Machine-guns, indeed ! It's a wonder we have *any* guns !" Point of view differs, does it not ?

Hard on the heels of Monday's peace came Tuesday's disquiet. It was Paissy again for the day. A jaunt to the reserve trenches and over the ground of Sunday's battle was interesting until the German gunners commenced shelling that part of the field. At the first quartette of shrapnel I decamped. Rifles, coats, kits, and all manner of personal property were thrown about the trench where the fiercest part of the action had taken place. Bibles, note-books, match-boxes, bits of clothing, knives—the jumble of oddments contained everything a soldier ever carried and many things one would never associate with Tommy or his German prototype. In a little rain-washed gully a miniature case lay half-covered in the mud. Inside it was the work of an artist of ability, a lovely face painted deftly on ivory, the sort of face possessing a sweetness of expression that makes one wonder where one has seen the original.

A transcription from my diary pictures life in Paissy.

" 11.30 a.m. Have been sitting on a rock under the lee wall of a house we are using as headquarters. The shelling of this town has gotten to be a German habit. As I sit I face a narrow path from the opposite edge of which the ground drops away to the valley below. Big shells and little shells are going over and around me. Now and again they explode behind my back with a concussion that is nerve racking. White clouds for shrapnel and big black clouds for Jack Johnsons follow the explosions in front after the shriek of the shells in passing. Those which strike near by frequently send a jagged piece of projectile hurtling through the air with a peculiar demoniacal wail of its own. The shells which land behind jar the whole hill. The house wall at my back trembles with the explosion. When the big black melinite ones land in front, if they are anything less than seventy-five to a hundred yards distant, I feel the concussion. If they are closer, there is a real physical shock when they explode. Down the road, tree branches fallen, great holes torn in the side of the roadway, and a pile of dead horses are evidences that yesterday's shell-fire was effective. In front, and a bit to the right, half-a-dozen troopers are sorting out a pile of rifles and ammunition which have been brought back from the scene of the battle.

" 11.50 a.m. Four came close all at once. Could almost feel one of them. It seemed just overhead. Major Frazer has called, and with Captain Hamilton-Grace has climbed a winding path which leads to an old stone church on the top of the hill. The tower of this church is an artillery observation post, and the boys have gone up to have a look.

" 12.5. Fairclough asked if I would like to go up into the church tower and have a look. Quaint old place. I climbed the narrow winding stairway, the stone steps worn down six to eight inches, and then a rickety ladder to the bell loft. We had a fine view of our trenches, and high in the sky, on the right, was a German war balloon—a 'sausage,' as the men call it. A lot of shells came near the tower while we were in it. They whirr past in a weird way when one is far up. When I came back down to this back-to-wall position, a Sussex officer and a sergeant were looking over my car. They told me they thought it must have been hit by a shell that came a moment ago, but they could find no new shell marks on it. It was well I put the car in the shelter of the wall. While I was in the church tower, I am told, a shell burst on the other side of the wall, wounded six troopers in the yard, and one of the party who were sorting the ammunition under the big tree. His companions had left that job for the moment!

" 12.10. An orderly holding a couple of chargers is sharing my wall. One of the horses is very restless under this cannonade, and jumps nervously when a shell bursts near us. The other horse seems to be watching the lower levels where the green fields are cut with dozens of big black holes, close together, in even circles, which show where the big melinite chaps have burst. I wonder if he is deprecating the spoiling of that fine pasture-land ?

" 12.15. A dozen shrapnel came over at the same time bursting in such close succession I could not count the separate explosions. All but one or two of them went off over and a little back of me. There is a nasty, singing, twanging sound to those that burst behind as the contents of the projectile and pieces of it whirr over. The nervous horse nearly walked on me. Shells cannot come any closer and not score a hit. The troopers have stopped running out and picking up hot pieces of shell. A while ago they thought that good fun. I can't understand it. For my part such keepsakes never interest me. I am far too likely to be taking away a piece of shell as an internal souvenir, without troubling to fill my pockets with similar keepsakes. Our guns across the valley are replying now, and their shells sing over our heads on their way to the enemy trenches. Major Frazer came up and asked if I was writing home and telling how much I am enjoying myself! The nervous horse belongs to him. He and his orderly mounted and rode away during a lull in the shelling. I wish him luck getting down that road.

"12.25.—Another bunch of shrapnel all in a heap. Six or eight bursting at once make a din. Now the great melinite fellows are coming again. A couple of enormous black clouds from the ravine tell where they struck. There go two just behind on the cliff. They left their cards in the form of scattered bits which fell on the pathway in front of me, not more than four or five feet distant. Close work. Too close for comfort. A piece of shell about four inches long and sharply pointed has stuck right into the gravel path about thirty inches from my foot.

"12.30.—Five or six more, all high explosives. The air in the valley is black with smoke. Two of the last lot went through the trees a few feet away. If one of them hit the tree trunk and exploded it would be nasty here. Immediately afterwards a dozen or more shrapnel, again in a group, went through the same trees. Leaves and branches fell in showers. An absolute rain of shells now for five minutes. I dislike most the ones that burst behind me. The noise of the whirring pieces is trying.

"1 p.m.—Still steady firing. Our batteries have taken a hand in the noise production at the rate of thirty to forty shots to the minute. There is nothing to do but sit here and hope I shall get a run out of it before long. It is better here than up on the crest, for I am, I suppose, quite safe under the cliff side behind the wall.

"2 p.m.—The General is going now to pay a visit to another part of the line. I am not sorry, for three hours of this sort of thing are quite enough for one day."

By General Allenby's haystack at Tour-de-Paissy was a big telescope mounted on a tripod. It was in disgrace. It served the Divisional Staff soberly and well until the very moment of the German attack on

MONS TO YPRES.

the West Yorks' trenches. Seeing men coming over the ridge, Colonel Home, General Allenby's G.S.O. 1, declared his field-glasses made him think them Germans. To make sure, the big telescope was turned on the ridge. For the first time in its history a moist film formed over the inner lens. A line of grey smudges was all that could be made out through its formerly far-seeing eye. When later events proved that Home was right, and the men in sight were Germans, moments precious to the guns had been for ever lost. Had the telescope possessed a soul it would have shrivelled in the heat of some of the remarks caused by that unlucky atmospheric visitation.

Not far from the haystack beside a muddy lane rose a knoll. Under a small tree a couple of gunners were on observation post. By the tree stood a wayside shrine, on its pedestal the inscription, in French, " Jesus is the way, the truth and the life." Flanked by trenches, the guns of two Christian nations hurling death from so little a distance that the mound trembled with each discharge, the shell-fire of a third we once thought Christian searching every foot of ground about it in frenzy to kill, I was struck by the numbers of passers-by whose eyes were caught by the familiar words, their faces softened as by a memory of other days.

Fitting it should be so. The Englishmen who were shedding their blood on those hillsides were battling for the Cross as surely as those of their forebears who followed Richard and the Crusades. It is modern to be cynical and hard, but the old faith has deep root in most of us, after all. We Anglo-Saxons should be proud of such a heritage.

The 2nd Notts and Derby came in for an awful hammering during the afternoon. Battery after battery of the enemy's guns were turned on the trenches above Paissy, but our men stuck to their line

in spite of the inferno the howitzers made of it. The
men reported seeing many Germans in front of them
in British caps and tunics. The Hun trenches were
400 yards from ours, and the desire of the German
soldiers to show themselves in their newly captured
khaki outfits was overpowering until the Notts and
Derby sharpshooters convinced them of the foolhardi-
ness of so doing.

A sight that attracted daily attention on the Aisne
was the appearance of German aeroplanes, which
dropped signals to their guns, and thereupon were
shelled violently by our field batteries. Lines of tiny
white shell clouds, in long arcs across the sky as the fire
followed one of our airmen, told of enemy anti-aircraft
guns, the criticism or praise of whose marksmanship
aroused continual controversies among the Tommies.

At dusk General de Lisle suggested scouting a new
route around the Paissy crater. An army map showed
a road none of us had thus far found. To pass through
Paissy was an unpleasant experience. At a corner,
dead horses were piled high, and, in the vernacular,
" stunk horrid." A hole, three feet deep and six wide,
had been torn in the centre of the road since I had
made an earlier run over the same route. In the dusk,
I landed the car with a smash and a jar plump in the
middle of it. With badly bent front axle we pushed
on, wondering at being able to do so. Over piles of
débris from shattered dwellings, and past felled trees
we crawled, then circled another shell-hole in the
road so wide that one side of the car dipped into it at
a dangerous angle in passing. The road became a
mere lane, then a grassy, slippery track along the edge
of the precipice. A drop meant a fall of eighty feet.
Struggling up sharp ascents with wheels skidding in
the mud, at last we came to the end of the path. We
kept on a few hundred yards over the long grass,
negotiating one stretch with the car canted at an angle
of forty-five degrees.

MONS TO YPRES.

We mounted a short, stiff gradient, and before us lay a black abyss, trackless and sinister, obviously too steep to allow of safe descent.

Turning the car on the edge of that drop, the grass slippery from the early dew, no light permissible to aid us, was at last safely accomplished. We retraced our way, and took the usual route to Longueval, having thoroughly proved the unreliability of the map.

The bent axle necessitated a run to the G.H.Q. repair shops at Fère-en-Tardenois. "Rattle" Barrett and I borrowed a car there from Westminster, who had two, as we had an errand for de Lisle which took us to Sablonnières, where one of the General's horses had been wounded and left to convalesce.

At Fère-en-Tardenois I received my first letter from London since my departure, thirty-three days before.

French Divisions were moving to the north-west and had been doing so for days. Joffre had started de Castelnau's 7th Army and Maud'huy's 10th Army toward Maunoury's left. The flanking movement to turn Von Kluck's right had begun. De Castelnau was to reach from Roye northward to Chaulnes, and Maud'huy from north of the Somme near Albert to Arras and beyond.

On September 24th we were up at three o'clock, and once more made our way from Longueval to Paissy, where the Brigade was to "stand by" in support. From Paissy I took the General to Troyon by way of Moulins and Vendresse.

German shrapnel were paying the customary attention to the road from Paissy. We waited by a farm for a moment watching the shells burst ahead. "Go slow," came the order. I crawled. De Lisle, who was seated beside me, turned and looked sharply at me. "Go! Go!" he cried. I had misunderstood him. "Now, go!" he had said; not "Go slow!" I pushed on as fast as the car could gather speed. But the momentary delay had upset the General's nicely turned calculations. Before we had crossed the open plain, Bang! came the first shell; and Bang, bang, bang!—three others, just above us.

The slivers rattled on the metal panels. A shrapnel bullet made a clean round bed in the top of the radiator, and a good-sized splinter cut a deep incision in a front wing. The door panel alongside de Lisle was scraped by a sharp bit that buried in the step. A piece the size of a pea struck the chief on the nose, and a similar one gave me a stinging blow on the shoulder. The floor of the car held half a dozen fragments as we pulled up and took stock beyond. Our luck had held, and we were none the worse.

A bright, pretty day for a change, made our visit to the "sugar mill trenches" above Troyon all the more enjoyable. The men of the 18th Brigade were burrowed in the high road bank. Tiny cave-like shelters, canopied with branches or straw, made snug quarters, safe, under the brow of the hill, from the everlasting shell-fire. A subaltern of the East Yorks said his lot had three killed and eighteen wounded by high explosives in the front line the day before. The same regiment, he said, lost eight officers and seventy-three men when the Germans attacked so strenuously on the previous Sunday. Two companies of the enemy had come straight on, that day, in close formation, and suffered such casualties from the East Yorks' fire that they had to retire in confusion.

A persistent rumour had spread that the Canadians were "out." "They won't be worth much until they have had some of this sitting under Black Marias. The best troops on earth would have to take a day or so to break into it," sagely remarked a beardless junior subaltern. His Division had arrived on the scene but few days before, but he looked with the eyes of a veteran on all newcomers.

Real quiet rarely visited the Troyon ridge. Our

shells howled over, and the German shells screamed back. Rifle-fire rose and fell in spasmodic waves of sound. The evenly-punctuated barking of the machine-guns echoed across the gorge.

On our way back to Paissy two new shell-holes showed where eight-inch projectiles had dropped since we had passed over the road. Once a howitzer shell burst so near we ran through its smoke-cloud—an ill-smelling mess.

All wished to take advantage of the rare opportunity of a warm sun-bath. We lined the wall, all the staff lying sleeping or reading as the afternoon wore on. I slept soundly. An overwhelming crash awakened me. A wicked high-explosive chap had burst above the headquarters yard. My eyes and mouth were full of dust and evil-tasting smoke. I could not see a foot in front. As the smoke-cloud cleared I saw Barrett swaying, and thought him wounded. He had merely stumbled in rising. Not one of us had been hit, though pieces of shell had rained down. We scampered through the gate and into the cave in the cliff. For an hour or more Paissy underwent a bombardment that eclipsed anything in that line with which it had been visited formerly. Venturing to sit on an overturned bucket at the cave's mouth, I was toppled back by a brick, which took me fair in the middle. Thereafter I was content to keep well inside the cave until the Hun-hate had been somewhat appeased, and the shelling died down.

WITH FRENCH.

CHAPTER IX.

The Germans pounded our troops well during those first weeks on the Aisne. Their shell fire scored until our positions were strengthened and the shelter from bombardment improved. Day by day this work went on, the continual shelling taking less toll of men as time passed.

We had our " days." A fresh Division of the enemy, brought by train from St. Quentin to a point fifteen miles from our lines, were seen at daybreak one Saturday in front of Troyon. Our first sight of them was when they marched in column of fours over the brow of a hill not 400 yards from our advance trenches. At their head strode a tall Hun bearing a white flag tied to a long stick. The first rows of men behind him were dressed in khaki. An interesting procession. Over the crest of the hill they came, every second bringing more of them to their certain fate. To those who were watching it seemed the enemy could not know the position of our lines. The strain was too great for a sergeant behind one of our machine-guns, and he " let go." His officers nearly wept with rage. The forepart of the German column shrivelled under the stream of bullets from the quick-firers and rifles. Our whole line was ablaze in a moment. Many huddled forms lay in plain sight of our trenches as the light grew, but most of the Germans had safely reached the cover of their front trench, from which they kept up an incessant and perfectly harmless fire for more than an hour.

" If that blessed sergeant had been a bit patient," said his company officer to me that morning, "we would have jolly well bagged the lot."

The same officer was gazing idly toward the front

during the late afternoon. His glance rested on the still bundles of grey lying between the lines. Storms of bullets from both sides had swept over the dead all day long. A thought came to his mind. What a crowning horror it would be to find that some of the fallen were merely wounded. As he watched, little bits of earth were kicked up here and there by bullets that fell short and cut the soil of no-man's land. Shell fire had ploughed furrows in it at frequent intervals. Shrapnel bullets were sown broadcast over it.

Suddenly, as if in answer to his soliloquy, one of the inanimate bundles seemed to come to life. It rolled over. The man inside the grey coat leaped to his feet. Hands held high in air, he ran like mad for our trench line. Over the parapet he tumbled, crashing on his head in the soft earth. Gaining his knees, hands still held above him, a beatific grin spread over his decidedly Teutonic features.

He spoke English quite well. " I shall to England be sent, no ? " he queried. " It was too long, the time I lay out there. At first, I would to stay till dark come. But my nervous, it was finished. I could no longer quiet keep, no ? " And the cheerful Hun, happy as a clam, was marched off under guard, to be turned over to the London Scottish, who were guarding lines of communication, and entrained for the South.

General Allenby and his headquarters staff lived at Villers, south of the Aisne. A trooper was pulling bundles of grain from a stack near Villers when he found a man covered in the straw. Jerked from his hiding-place, a tall young German Guardsman in uniform stood before his captor. Examination led to the alarming discovery that the German had been lying at one end of a wire that tapped a telegraph line from divisional headquarters. For thirteen days, possibly, the messages over that wire had been heard by ears for which they were by no means intended.

General admiration for the German's pluck was heard

on all sides. To have stayed so long hidden so far within his enemy's lines required coolness and bravery.

Many were the conjectures as to how the information which he gained was transmitted to his own army. No other wire leading from the stack could be found. Careful search of the vicinity resulted in no enlightenment. At points the Aisne was dragged with long rakes by energetic signallers, but all in vain. The news of the capture was made a secret, and night after night a vigil kept to intercept possible callers laden with food for the German or in search of messages from him. No result was forthcoming, save that the watchers caught one another one night, and the next night caught cold, and the solution of the puzzle remained a mystery.

Periodical visits to the trenches made me sure that one day a fat howitzer shell would land in the wrong place for me. The enemy made some roads impassable, but we always found another way round.

Colonel Steele of the Coldstreams showed us a souvenir one day in the form of a ruined poncho. His shelter above Vendresse was a short way back of the trenches on the crest. Lying on his back, his legs spread out, and his poncho so arranged that it served for bed and coverlet, he dropped off to sleep. He was awakened by one of our own 18-pounder shrapnel, fired from somewhere in the valley below, which fell short. The misguided shell went directly between Steele's knees, ripping two gaping holes in his poncho and burying itself, unexploded, in the bank on which he was lying.

Tom Bridges was promoted Colonel of the 4th Hussars, but four days after he had assumed command of the regiment a motor-car from G.H.Q. called for him and hurried him off to Antwerp, for service with King Albert and his Belgians.

Major Budworth and H Battery of the Royal Horse Artillery came from England and joined the 2nd Cavalry Brigade while we were in Longueval. At dinner on the night of Budworth's arrival General de Lisle said that he, the Major, Captain Skinner of H Battery, and I would next morning take " a run around," visit our gun positions past and present, and " show the Major what German shell fire was like." From experience I knew that meant we would more than likely go " looking for trouble."

Heavy cannonading continued throughout the night. " Promiscous " one of the troopers called it. Seemed wasteful, but at the end of two weeks of it the British Army had suffered over 3,000 casualties from the shell fire alone.

Our men were learning to keep to cover, and our batteries had learned to disguise themselves well. Miniature groves would spring up over the guns in a night. The " heavies," what few we had of them, were made to look like sheds or haystacks when conceal-ment of the battery was impossible. These tricks our gunners learnt from the enemy, who was a past master at such contrivances.

After doing the rounds of the guns our party visited the trenches above Troyon. Serrocold's Battalion of the 60th Rifles and Steele's Coldstreams were in front that day.

The Sugar-Mill Position, so called from the huge mill above Troyon, since destroyed, that had been taken and retaken a dozen times and had afforded the Lancashires a chance to gain fine laurels, was our nearest point of vantage in one sector of the line.

There our barricade was one hundred yards south of the summit of the ridge, and the German trenches but eighty yards to the north of it. The Sugar-Mill barri-cade had seen heavy fighting, but was comparatively quiet at the time of our visit, though sniper bullets occasionally sang overhead and shrapnel came past at intervals.

Tucked under the brow of the hill, not far from the front line, were Colonel Serrocold's headquarters. A mutual friend had a few days before sent by me a case of most welcome provender to Serrocold's mess, and in consequence I called to sample the goods.

"We will get out of this to-day, sure," said the Colonel.

"I think not, sir," I replied. "I have heard nothing of a change so far this morning. Why do you think you are to move?"

"Because we have just finished the construction of the first good dry shelter we have had for some days," was the answer. "I'm sure this is so perfect a spot now that we are doomed to be sent elsewhere, and others will spend a comfortable night in our snug quarters."

I laughed at his mock pessimism, and had another laugh the next day when I learned that sure enough the 60th had been shifted late in the afternoon. Serrocold's prophecy had come true most unexpectedly, and his palatial quarters had to be turned over to his successors.

We visited General FitzClarence and his staff in a typical cave Brigade headquarters under the brow of the Aisne Heights. Well inside the cave the Brigade staff work could be done without fear of interruption.

These cave headquarters were quite "comfy." But any spot in those days might be a headquarters. I remember one that consisted of the body of a defunct W. and G. taxicab.

In Vendresse half an hour later we were treated to some fairly close shelling, the first projectile landing on the other side of a high stone wall as we passed. A run to Paissy and a view from the church tower concluded our tour of sightseeing. We returned to Longueval for luncheon. We had taken Budworth under rifle and shell fire and shown him heaps of German dead a few yards distant from our trenches. As we pulled up, one of the party made a comment on the quiet and security of quaint Longueval, far from scenes of violence which had become the daily round in such towns as we had visited that morning.

But Longueval had proved less safe, in spite of its dis-

A temporary Headquarters on the Aisne

London Scottish in guard of German prisoners at Fére-en-Tardenois

Moroccans at Tour de Paissy (Aisne)

tance from the firing line, than the trenches and the hill towns close behind. Half an hour before our return five great howitzer shells from long-range guns had crashed into the village. One struck the centre of the stone-paved yard of a farm where a squadron of 9th Lancers was billeted. Lieutenant Whitehead was directing the cleaning of an open space between the barns. He and eleven of his men were killed and thirteen wounded. Among the killed was the sergeant-major of the 9th and two sergeants. Five horses were killed, and others wounded so badly it was necessary to destroy them.

The General was of opinion that the few shells had come that way as a chance bit of itinerant bombardment, to which most of the Aisne towns within range of the German guns would be subjected at one time or another. At two o'clock five more Black Marias fell near Longueval, but did no more damage than to rip up the field in which they fell.

After luncheon I ran to Rheims with the General to see the ravaged cathedral. The stately Gothic pile was reported to be a heap of ruins. It was hardly that, but nevertheless had been cruelly knocked about. Streets near by were choked lanes between rows of desolate monuments to the German love of wanton destruction.

Back in Longueval late in the afternoon we found the Brigade saddled and ready to move from the village. Less than an hour from the time of the General's departure a dozen high explosive shells had been hurled into the little town. One lit in a narrow street outside the door of our headquarters, killing a man who was standing in the doorway and four other troopers who were grouped near by, and wounding twelve who were passing. My bedroom had been used as an emergency dressing station, and my bed as an operating table. The place was soaked in blood. As in the morning, the 9th Lancers had been the regiment to suffer. Of the two dozen killed and nearly as many wounded that day in Longueval all but one or two were 9th Lancers.

WITH FRENCH.

An explanation of the shelling was at last forthcoming. A supply train had been halted by an injudicious Army Service Corps subaltern on the brow of the hill above the village and in plain sight of the enemy's observation posts on the heights across the Aisne. The lorries on the skyline had caught the attention of our gunners on slopes far in front. Word was sent at once that such advertisement of our billeting centres would bear sinister result, but the message came too late.

I spent the night on a bundle of straw in the open. My only warm blanket had disappeared in the *mêlée* attending the hurried dressing of the wounded and their prompt dispatch to the hospital at Villers. In consequence I woke on the morning of Wednesday, September 30th, with a decided chill. The Brigade moved at daybreak to St. Thibaut, a village on the Vesle between Braisnes and Fismes. I had planned a joy ride to Rheims. With Major Solly Flood of the 4th Dragoon Guards, Osborn, the 4th Dragoon Guards' sawbones, and Fairclough, I paid a second visit to the cathedral.

The fields and roadways near Rheims were full of townsfolk driven from their homes by the German shells.

A high fever induced me to take a couple of hours' rest between clean sheets at the Lion d'Or, across from the great church. Not even the novelty of a cool white bed lowered my temperature, which had so mounted by afternoon that Osborn bade me spend the night in Rheims, while he and the others went back without me. From three to five o'clock, and again at seven in the evening, German shells were poured into the town, one striking the hotel. It was by no means the first that had done so. The sole remaining chambermaid apprised me at night that at one time during the afternoon I had been the only occupant of the hotel who had not taken refuge in the cellar. This was due largely to the fact that I was sound asleep during the hottest part of the show. Twice, she said, she had run upstairs to see if I was still whole and sound, to find me pouring forth scornful snores to the accompaniment of the frequent crashes of the howitzer shells.

The next day I sallied forth, very shaky on my pins, but comparatively free from fever. My old friend Frank Hedges Butler was in Rheims, braving the bombardment to procure the pick of the vintages. With him I visited the Pommery and Greno caves and those of G. H. Mumm. Crowds hung about the entrances waiting to rush inside the moment further shelling began. The Pommery château was demolished by the scores of Black Marias that had sought it out. The champagne had been but little disturbed, and most of it lay safe and snug in the miles of subterranean passages that honeycomb underground Rheims. Mumm, a German, was a prisoner in French hands. Robinet, his French partner, was delightfully cordial.

" The day the Germans came into Rheims a colonel stamped his way into my house," said Robinet, " and told me abruptly I was to prepare immediately fifty beds for German wounded. I replied in his own tongue that fifty beds I could not possibly arrange, but would be glad to provide ten if he would give me sufficient time to do so. The colonel was very brutal. He left the house swearing he would return in an hour's time. If I failed to produce the fifty beds demanded I would, he said, be shot forthwith.

" An hour later a thin young German officer came in, a couple of bottles of champagne in one hand. Depositing the wine tenderly in a corner, he asked to see what accommodation I had provided for the wounded. I showed him the ten beds, which were being got ready as rapidly as possible. ' This one,' said the young German, ' I wish to have reserved for a member of my staff who has been severely wounded. See that it is kept for him, please.'

" Something in his tone and manner made me look closer at this officer, and suddenly it flashed over me that it must be the Crown Prince. As he left the house, after carefully turning over the two bottles of champagne to one of his staff officers who had appeared on the scene, I asked if he was the Prince, and found my conjecture was correct. He called several times thereafter, evincing the greatest interest in the welfare of the wounded member of his staff until the latter was sent back to Germany.

"The colonel who had threatened me with death as a punishment for not acceding to his demand for fifty beds called the same night and very elaborately apologised. He told me he had been wounded, and for four days his wound had been undressed. For three days he had hardly tasted food. ' To go so long with no time for eating or sleeping,' he said, ' and with the irritation of constant pain, made me inexcusably uncivil. I wish to be pardoned.' He was so punctilious about it that the following day he asked me to step down to his headquarters, where he called in several officers, some of whom had witnessed his abusive conduct of the day before, and again apologised in their presence. He was decidedly thorough about it, once he took it into his head to make amends.

"One of the Crown Prince's staff said to me, ' Why do your Parisian papers lie so ? They say the British force is here or there, as if they do not know that French's army is either killed or captured to a man. I can assure you,' he continued most vehemently, ' on my word as a gentleman, the British Army no longer exists. It is finished absolutely.' He was equally dogmatic in his assertion that the German army would enter Paris in three days' time."

Eight hundred wounded Germans were cared for in Rheims. Some were there still at the time of my visit.

An early start after a second night's rest at the Lion d'Or landed me at St. Thibaut for breakfast.

The day before, an officer from G.H.Q. whom I had met in Rheims had told me of the prospective change of area of operations of the British Force. Antwerp was

like to fall, he said, and the Huns to press on towards
the Channel with their eyes on Calais, Boulogne, and
even Havre. Joffre's movement on the left to outflank
Von Kluck's right was being met by a German offensive
in the same area that had not proved altogether unsuccessful. To move the British Force west and north
would put it in direct touch with the seacoast and the
British Fleet, and free it from the inconvenience of
having its line of supply crossed by those of the
French 6th, 7th and 10th Armies to the westward.
Besides, he argued, the trench warfare on our front
had degenerated into a stalemate. To hold the line
along the Aisne much less seasoned troops could with
advantage be employed, and French's men, already
veterans, released for more important and exacting
work in the northern theatre. West Flanders, he
opined, would see some stiff fighting. All this was
secret and much of it left to implication, to be pieced
together as the next days passed. That but few had
an inkling of the prospect of such change I am sure.
It was not anticipated in our own command, or if it
was, not a soul breathed a word of it.

On the morning of Friday, October 2nd, the 2nd
Cavalry Brigade left its billets at St. Thibaut and
moved up to Chassemy, in front of the enemy's
stubborn position at Condé. The next day Gough's
2nd Cavalry Division moved west *en route* for the
Allied left flank. Allenby's 1st Cavalry Division, of
which our Brigade was a part, followed on the night of
Sunday the 4th.

The Condé salient had proved a strong one. We
flanked it on right and left, but the German batteries
on the heights dominated the level ground to the south
of the Aisne in and about Chassemy. Taking General
de Lisle and our three regimental commanders, Colonel
Mullens, Colonel Burnett, and Major Beale-Browne, to
Chassemy from Braisnes, our route lay over a road where
a crawl at intervals was enjoined, as the smallest dust

cloud meant a rain of German shrapnel. Chassemy was battered and the road from that town to Condé a mass of shell holes. Leaving the car in the shelter of a house, a walk along the edge of the forest in front, the Bois Morin, gave a good view of the German position. One hundred yards beyond the Condé bridge a German outpost was securely dug in on the hillside, ready to sweep the causeway with machine-gun fire. By the bridge lay the bodies of Captain Henderson of G.H.Q. and his chauffeur, alongside their riddled car. Henderson was thought to have lost his way about September 20th, and run into the Condé outpost by mistake.

Dodging in and out of the forest edge, keeping well out of sight of the enemy to avoid attracting his ever-ready shells, blazed trees told us the safe path. Now we passed a battery of guns, now a reserve of machine-guns protected from the searching shrapnel fire. Splintered trees and fallen branches showed that the German artillery had played frequently on the wood.

In Braisnes I chatted with a guard of London Scottish at the railway crossing. They had been " out " for a fortnight, they said, but, as a fine-looking sergeant disgustedly informed me, " had seen nothing as yet." The day was to come when he would have no complaint on that score, and, little as I imagined it then, I was to be with him.

Our forty-eight hours in that part of the line was uneventful, and on Sunday night, when the darkness had closed in sufficiently to veil our movements, the Brigade started off to the westward.

The Aisne we had reached with such sanguine hopes twenty-one days before was still the high-water mark of our advance. The three weeks' fighting had cost the British Army in France nearly 600 officers and 13,000 men. We had learned much of warfare, and were off to green fields and pastures new to further our education.

MONS TO YPRES.

CHAPTER X.

THE march of the 1st Cavalry Division from the Aisne to the zone of operations in West Flanders occupied a week.

Until clear of the Aisne country our marches were made at night. In the daytime the troops were kept under cover in order that enemy aircraft should be able to collect as little information as possible.

An airman told me the secreting of troops from air scouts was much more of an art than most folk might imagine. " The Germans," he said, " are adepts at hiding their guns, but not so good at concealing moving troops. They were very much ahead of our people at covering traces of their ordnance, and are still so, though not to such degree as formerly. I have seen some of our batteries that were well protected from the front, but perfectly visible when viewed from the rear. The Germans cover the wheel tracks when they take their guns from the road and across the soft earth of the fields. I have noted the position of one of our batteries, splendidly hidden as far as the actual field pieces were concerned, which I could " spot " with the greatest ease from the marks left by the wheels as the guns were brought into position.

" A French Zouave was taken prisoner and escaped, making his way back to Rheims. He reported a German battery at a certain point which neither we nor the French airmen could locate. Questioned, he described the enemy guns as being so hidden that only the muzzles protruded from elaborate shelters built around them in the form of low sheds. We were then able to find the exact spot, and not long after our howitzers blew those fake sheds to pieces, scoring at least one, if not two, direct hits on the enemy's guns."

WITH FRENCH.

On the night of Sunday, October 4th, we made Hartennes, south of Soissons, by bright moonlight, and there spent the following day. The change from the pestilential Braisnes district to the quiet country was delightful. The gently rolling hills, well-cultivated, seemed far indeed from scenes of war and pillage, though Soissons was less than ten miles from us.

My work for the week's trek was to push on ahead, reconnoitre the roads, and wait to guide detachments at points where errors in direction might be made. Taking the billeting officers from the column to the area of the next stop also fell to my lot. Last, but not least, I kept touch with the General, ready to carry messages for him or take him for a frequent journey.

The G.H.Q. printing office was productive of pages of extracts from diaries and letters found on the enemy. All the ills that flesh is heir to had been absorbed by the pessimistic writers whose quotations adorned those sheets. One read depression and despair in every line. The prevailing tone was in sharp contrast to the inevitable grousing good-nature of Thomas Atkins.

"Information about Engagements with the Enemy" was another cheery publication which told of doughty deeds of never varying success. The editor of these effusions at times waxed solemnly humorous, as the following paragraph bears witness :—

"It is reported on reliable authority that on one occasion when the opposing trenches were within seventy yards of each other, our men made frequent attempts to tempt the enemy to come out by gentle badinage. All efforts were unavailing until someone shouted in a peremptory tone, 'Waiter!' when no less than twenty-three heads appeared."

Our objectives on Monday night were three villages not far west of Villers-Cotteret. I landed Bernard Neame, of the 18th Hussars, and Algy Court, of the 9th Lancers, in the billeting area in good time, after passing battery on battery of French guns *en route* for the north-west.

MONS TO YPRES.

Largny, one of our villages, was found filled to over-flowing, in possession of two battalions of the 13th Infantry Brigade. The Colonel of the West Kents said he had received orders to move, but before he could do so the orders were countermanded. Two other Brigades held Vez, our second village, and Haramont, our third, was providing standing room for the greater part of six or seven hundred French infantrymen. The arrival of "Rattle" Barrett and Solly Flood, the other billeting officers, cast but little light on the situation. A bivouac for the brigade in the thick woods was planned, but about midnight further instructions reached us that three other adjacent villages had been assigned us. The wild hunt in the dark, past batteries of guns, troops of cavalry, hordes of French infantry, and all manner and condition of Allied supply trains, was temper-trying, but we won through at last.

The château at Coyelles, the second station of our journey, had been robbed by the Germans of every bottle of wine in its cellars. Big wagons were sent, the caretaker said, to cart away the loot. Yet the Germans had left the house otherwise unrifled. The cabinets were full of silver, rare ornaments littered the tables, and old tapestries hung on the walls. The many bedrooms each held a complement of French officers, so most of our staff reposed on the polished floor of the drawing-rooms. Beautiful rugs and embroidered draperies, carefully folded, were piled high on the centre tables. Without damage to them or inconvenience to their owners, we rearranged them in such wise that they made a softer couch than the hard boards, and slept the sleep of the justly weary.

In passing through Villers-Cotteret I saw Langton, the secretary of the Paris Travellers' Club, who told me that for seventy-two hours a continual stream of troops had been pouring through the city day and night.

On Tuesday the Brigade did not wait for nightfall to resume its pilgrimage, but were under way about noon.

WITH FRENCH.

Short of petrol that morning, I begged some from an obliging French airman. Quite a collection of French monoplanes, covered in their nighties of canvas, cuddled around a quartette of stacks away from the road. At a short distance one could hardly distinguish them from innocent farm machinery, put aside, carefully swathed, till harvest time. No more friendly men live than the French airmen. I was never in want of anything they could supply for longer than it took to tell them my needs, in whatever part of the line I might be.

Reconnoitring routes on the edge of the Forest of Compiègne was fascinating work. At level crossings trainload after trainload of infantry and guns, mostly of Smith-Dorrien's 2nd Corps, sped by. We passed the town which had been occupied by General Smith-Dorrien himself the night before, and learned that he, too, had been hurried north by rail that morning. Huge pontoons across the Oise marked the change of our direction from westward to a more northerly course, rounding a corner close to Compiègne, and then heading for Montdidier. Remy was our night stop, a village missed by the Germans when Von Kluck pushed south towards Paris. The rich farm country gave us of its best. We revelled in incomparable produce, fresh as morning dew, and a great treat to our unaccustomed palates.

A still earlier start was made on Wednesday. I had suggested a quick dash in and out of Compiègne to purchase certain necessities. De Lisle said, " No, not this morning. Keep in touch with the Brigade. We are concentrating to-day, and may possibly go into action before night." By early afternoon we passed through Montdidier and turned towards the east.

Captain Baron le Jeune, of the Cuirassiers, a French liaison officer attached to the 2nd Cavalry Brigade, ran with me ahead of our column into Montdidier.

A French staff officer who knew Le Jeune told us of de Castelnau's push forward to Noyon in September,

MONS TO YPRES.

and the awful conflict that resulted in the Germans forcing the French line back from Noyon and Lassigny. Maud'huy, he said, had come into position north of de Castelnau, and hoped to envelop the enemy's right in the direction of Cambrai and Valenciennes. But Maud'huy had well-nigh been enveloped himself and thrust back to Arras and beyond it. News had come on that October 6th that Maud'huy had retired to the high ground west of Arras, though not giving up the town, while Lille, defended by a French Territorial Division only, was sore pressed.

A French medical officer on duty at the Montdidier railway station joined in the conversation. Over ten thousand French wounded, he told us, had been through his hands during the previous eight days.

The reason for the diversion of our 1st Cavalry Division to the support of the French forces fighting in front of Roye was a superhuman effort by the enemy the day before. Roye had been evacuated by the French, and the fiercest of the conflict was already a few miles to the west of it. Naturally, as the Division was passing the very point of danger, the French asked that it should be held in the vicinity for twenty-four hours in case of need. We were taken up within sight of the shells and sound of the battle, but the French line held to the satisfaction of its commanders, so by nightfall we pushed on to the north. We slept at Aubvillers, *en route* to Amiens, and the next day passed through that thriving metropolis to Villers-Bocage, where we spent Thursday night.

At daybreak on Friday, the 9th, we were awakened by interminable lines of troop-laden motor lorries and convoys of armoured cars. French troops were being poured north at breakneck speed. The race for the sea was daily becoming more exciting. The collision of the hurrying armies was to make a bloody meeting-place of Flanders one day soon. By night we had passed Doullens and were to the west of Arras.

WITH FRENCH.

The following morning an early start found us proceeding eastward, the sound of the guns hourly growing louder and louder. Arras was being shelled by the Germans, and conflicting stories as to operations thereabouts were afoot. I was alone, with orders that allowed considerable latitude as to route. Reaching Aubigny, I turned towards Arras, and was soon on the outskirts of the city. Parks were full of French transport, villages and towns were crowded with French troops in reserve, and refugees were swarming along the broad highway. The entire population of Arras seemed tramping that road. Dozens toiling towards the town met scores hurrying away from it. Acquaintances bound in opposite directions met and argued the wisest procedure. Every hamlet within miles was full to overflowing. The merits of a roof over one's head in the path of the shells were weighed against a night spent in the open fields out of range of the guns.

I met two residents of Arras, apparently men of substance, both well along in years. " Two days ago," said one of them, " the Germans demanded the surrender of Arras. The General in command sent back word that the city would never surrender, but would be defended to the last man. Every pick and shovel was in use day and night to entrench our soldiers. After a vicious bombardment the enemy attacked in mass. The Germans came on well within the suburbs to the south-east of the city, between our trenches, cleverly concealed, that commanded the line of their advance from two sides. When at last the waiting defenders opened fire the carnage was awful. Back the Germans were driven, and still back, to a point a good five kilometres to the south-east. Seven thousand dead and wounded Germans were picked up in Arras, and two thousand more behind a sugar factory outside the city, from the shelter of which the fleeing Germans were driven like sheep by the glorious ' *soixante-quinze.*' "

It was thrilling to hear the recital of it. The good

man's tally of the casualties may have been high, but the pride of French achievement that vibrated through his story dwarfed detail.

His white-haired companion told me the whole of Arras was destroyed by German shells, but he who had recounted the tale of the fighting shook his head. " No," he said, " not all destroyed. Hurt, but not so greatly. My friend's house was hit by two shells and lies a mass of ruins. To him, indeed, little of Arras remains. It is natural, is it not ? " He smiled sadly, but his eyes lit up as we parted, and he said, " They came on between the two lines, and when the fire leaped at them they were mown down like corn. Arras is not in German hands, nor will be." He strode on with thin shoulders thrown boldly back, full of that wonderful fighting spirit that has fallen over France and enveloped the race—man, woman, and child of every age and calling.

That afternoon we learned of the evacuation of Lille by the French Territorials and the screen of German cavalry, reported to be seven Divisions or more, thrown out to the westward. Villers-Brulin, a village west of Lens, was our halting-place on Friday night. We were within a day's march of where Smith-Dorrien's 2nd Corps was being hurried, some Brigades on foot and some by columns of light French motor lorries. The 2nd Corps had detrained at Abbeville and the 3rd Corps at St. Omer. We were drawing near to the fighting zone. A Frenchwoman was brought to our headquarters that night who had seen French infantry and cavalry retiring in our direction during the afternoon through Bruay. Country folk there told her of German troops in Vermelles and Mazingarbe, not far south-east of Bethune, and less than a dozen miles from our billets.

So Sunday, October 11th, found us at the end of our peaceful trek from the Aisne. By night we were launched into the fight in an area that was to see the troops of the British Expeditionary Force for weeks that were to lengthen into months, and months that bid fair to lengthen into years in turn.

Our first objective was a village close to Bethune. During the early morning our way led through France's Black Country. Crowds of people poured from the big factory and mining towns to watch our passing. Chocques, Gonneheim, Robecq, and St. Venant were on our line of march. Names strange to us then, but to grow in time as familiar as names of Midland towns at home. At Chocques a long column of 2nd Corps infantry was trudging eastward, to be thrown into the battle line the next morning.

Firing had been heavy to the east of us as we had pushed on northward, the roll of the rifles sounding clear in the near distance. As we lunched word came that the enemy were hammering hard to force our infantry from Vieille Chapelle, and Conneau's French cavalry were prosecuting a vigorous attack in the direction of Laventie. Gough's 2nd Cavalry Division had been fighting in front of us.

By dusk the 2nd Cavalry Brigade had reached the outskirts of Merville. Our orders were to press on through the Forest of Nieppe, holding through the night a line on the eastern edge of the forest.

I covered many miles that day. I was rarely without a message to deliver to Divisional headquarters or one to take back to de Lisle. Colonel David Campbell, of the 9th Lancers, arrived from England with his wounds healed. I took him from Merville to General Allenby's headquarters at St. Venant. Returning, we sought to follow the road Hamilton-Grace had carefully marked on my map, as the Brigade had moved on into the forest.

The French soldiers lowered the drawbridge and we ran through Merville, the streets full of Briggs' 1st Brigade, troops of French cavalry and French Territorials. A barricade had been thrown across the road by which we sought to leave the town. Long argument preceded its removal to allow our passage. A few yards further a second obstruction had been placed at the edge of a canal and the drawbridge opened. No pleading could move the French non-commissioned officer in charge. His orders were to allow no one to pass. Besides, he said, the Germans were just beyond. Incidentally, he remarked that should he allow his barricade to be pulled down the bridge had been so wedged as to prevent its spanning the canal until some missing parts had been replaced. Nothing remained but to retrace our steps, again derange the first barricade to allow our return to Merville, and make a detour.

Next day we learned that had we crossed the canal we would have encountered German cavalry outposts and our own, an almost equally hazardous proceeding in the dark. One of the 9th Lancers was shot by a patrol of the 4th Dragoon Guards that night along the same road, and not far away Lieutenant Montefiore, leading the advance squadron of 9th Lancers, came upon a German outpost, whose discovery at eight to ten yards distance led to a sharp exchange of fire, in which a trooper was killed and Montefiore received two bullets through his arm. Withal I was quite pleased the road had been so well blocked.

The night in the wood was cold and damp. The Headquarters Staff was housed in a rude *estaminet.* We slept on bundles of straw spread about the floor.

Before the thick mist had risen from the long lanes through the forest I was off with the General to visit the outposts. A dead German charger nearly blocked the road beyond La Motte du Bois, and the villagers tried to stop us to present us with the saddle. On our return our appetites for a waiting breakfast were not augmented by the sight of peasants taking steaks from the dead horse. The fighting started early, and desultory actions took place all morning, the enemy gradually failing back before us.

The formation of a Cavalry Corps, with General

Allenby in command, was announced. General de Lisle succeeded to the 1st Cavalry Division and assumed his new duties at once. He kindly asked me to accompany him to the Divisional Staff. I had become a genuine admirer of de Lisle as a soldier, and we had grown to be fast friends. Nevertheless, it was with not a little regret that I changed the blue Brigade flags on my car for red Divisional ones. Never had I met, nor shall I ever meet, a finer body of soldiers than were in the 2nd Cavalry Brigade.

11th Hussars on the march from the Aisne to Flanders

A wayside lunch; General de Lisle and the Staff of the
2nd Cavalry Brigade

A British Gun on the Lys firing.

MONS TO YPRES.

CHAPTER XI.

The 1st Cavalry Division saw hard fighting soon after its arrival in Flanders. On October 12th, Smith-Dorrien started an action with his 2nd Corps which had for its objective the capture of La Bassée and the occupation of Lille. For five days the fight raged. A frontal attack on La Bassée was early found to be abortive. The Germans at that point occupied the strongest natural defensive position in the whole northern area. Consequently Smith-Dorrien attempted a swinging movement to the north of La Bassée, to get astride the road to Lille, and attack the La Bassée position from the rear. It so far succeeded, after strenuous work, that the Lille road was almost in sight. Then it stopped, hard against the main position of a heavily reinforced enemy.

While Smith-Dorrien's 2nd Corps was winning ground, step by step, between Laventie and La Bassée, and pushing as far eastwards as Aubers and Herlies, Pulteney's 3rd Corps was sweeping eastward to Armentières. Disentraining at St. Omer and hurriedly marching to Hazebrouck, a sharp engagement took place at Meteren. Bailleul and Armentières were occupied with but little effort, and by the night of October 17th Pulteney faced a strong German line to the east of the River Lys.

Allenby's Cavalry Corps, the 1st and 2nd Cavalry Divisions, was on the left front of Pulteney's advance, and Conneau's French Cavalry on his right, the latter coupling the 3rd Corps with the left of the 2nd Corps. To Allenby fell the forcing of the Lys from the left of the 3rd Corps near Armentières to Warneton, a task which was quickly proven to be beyond the powers of the small force at his command. The Cavalry Corps then became the connecting link between Rawlinson's 4th Corps in front of Ypres and Pulteney's 3rd Corps in front of Armentières. The thin line of troopers held on gallantly in the centre of the British line, though overwhelmingly outnumbered by the enemy, while the German attacks on Haig and Rawlinson at Ypres and on Smith-Dorrien at La Bassée surged forward and back in the bloodiest fighting of the war.

Our knowledge of the situation in Belgium was slight. We knew Antwerp had fallen on October 9th, and that Rawlinson's 4th Corps, consisting of Capper's 7th Division and Byng's 3rd Cavalry Division, having landed at Zeebrugge two or three days before, were covering the retirement of the shattered Belgian Army westward along the coast, but that was all.

The night of October 12th found us in possession of Vieux Berquin and Strazeele after an afternoon of desultory fighting. Gough's 2nd Cavalry Division on our left had pushed north through Caestre and Flêtre, and reported the Germans in Meteren.

In mid-afternoon the 9th Lancers moved from Strazeele towards Merris and came under the enemy's shrapnel fire. Budworth was sent post-haste to Strazeele with two guns of H Battery to draw the attention of the German gunners from the 9th. He had to guess at the position of the enemy's guns. The H Battery field pieces went into action at the edge of the town. No sooner had they done so than the Germans opened on them, and after the first few rounds got the range to perfection. Budworth directed operations from behind a tree close by. The shrapnel burst all about the guns. Of sixteen men serving them seven were hit. Still they replied, keeping hard at it until dusk. The 9th Lancers took Merris, though they retired in the evening to the line at Strazeele.

That night an ambulance arrived to remove the wounded H Battery gunners. Budworth went into a house, the only building in the vicinity that was not on fire, to say good-bye to five of his wounded men before they were taken back. The doctor said one of the five, though a piece of shell had torn away part of his head, would, he thought, pull through safely. Of the recovery of the other four he was very doubtful. Two of them he considered hopeless. One had lost both hands.

A lump in his throat, Budworth passed from one to another with such words of cheer as he could muster. Each of the four who could speak—the poor fellow whose hands had been shot away was half-unconscious—eagerly pressed upon their chief but one request. Every man was concerned with the paramount idea that he must get fit again as soon as possible and return to duty with his battery. " Promise, sir, that I can come back to H Battery when I am right," was the one thing they had to ask, the one desire of their hearts. Such is the morale of the men of the Royal Horse Artillery. In spite of the severity of their wounds, each one of the four pulled through, and every man of them lived to see the day when he was back in France and again serving with his beloved battery.

Early on the morning of Tuesday, the 13th, after a comfortable night in the ample La Motte château in the Bois de Nieppe, we ran to Strazeele, then on at noon to Flêtre. General Keir was at Strazeele, and his 6th Division, the 16th, 17th and 18th Brigades, was pushing the German rearguard to the east while the cavalry circled round the left flank of the advance. Gough's Brigades were on the extreme left and swept over the picturesque Mont des Cats, rising like an artificial mound from the level plain and crowned with its quaint monastery. Boeschepe and Berthen were in Gough's hands, and his troopers were feeling their way across the frontier line of Belgium.

Prince Max of Hesse was badly wounded, left behind in a village by his men, and soon died of his wounds.

The broad road, poplar-lined, that covered the two miles from Flêtre to Meteren ran straight as a die.

From Flêtre, the Meteren church spire marked the exact centre of the end of the path between the tall trees. The infantry attack on Meteren, planned for one o'clock, was delayed until three. By that time a drizzle which had set in early in the afternoon had become a steady downpour. Our headquarters were in an inn bearing the imposing name of the Estaminet de Rouckelooshile. The dame who dispensed such cheer as could therein be obtained was busy. Black coffee and cognac of sorts were not to be despised as the cold mist settled down on the damp countryside. Bustling about, she made no bones of disturbing a conference of general officers, pushing a map away to reach a cupboard as she sought a relay of tumblers wherewith to meet the exceptional demand. Her shrill voice rose high in an altercation over change of English coin, drowning the low-toned words in an ante-room that were outlining plans of battle. Unconscious of her, the stern group of officers merely raised their voices to carry above the din, thoroughly engrossed in the grim business of war, but no more so than the old virago in her pursuit of nimble coppers.

Keen to see an infantry charge at close quarters, I walked on towards Meteren. The rifle and machine-gun fire made one long roll ahead. Wounded men passing rearwards in search of a dressing-station told of a very hell of a hollow where the German quick-firers swept the ground clean. Our guns had been firing earlier in the day, but the mist closed in and stopped their further participation in the fight. The enemy in Meteren seemed to have no guns. At least no shrapnel came our way. I reached a reserve position as the troops were moving up, the bullets singing overhead in swarms. Rain and mist made it impossible to see far enough ahead to get a view of what was going on, so I ploughed back to headquarters through the mud.

The enemy had placed machine-guns in the roofs of houses, removing a few tiles to allow just sufficient aperture through which to fire. These quick-firers accounted for most of our casualties at Meteren, which totalled some two hundred odd. The town was taken at the point of the bayonet, and the Germans in the houses captured while still serving the machine-guns.

Nearing the *estaminet* I passed a horseman in the dim light whose face gave me a shock. I would have sworn him to be Captain " Rivy " Grenfell, of the 9th Lancers, killed at Vendresse on the Aisne. Involuntarily I gasped out " ' Rivy ' Grenfell ! " A closer look confirmed the uncanny feeling that I was faced by a man I knew was in a soldier's grave far to the southward. The uniform was that of a captain, and the regimental insignia of the 9th was plain on the collar of his tunic.

" Not ' Rivy,' but Grenfell," said a grave but pleasant voice, which went on to explain that the officer I had taken for the gallant captain killed some weeks before was his twin brother, Captain Francis Grenfell, also of the 9th Lancers, who had recovered from the wounds he had received at Audregnies in August, at which time I had had a brief word with him. He had been awarded one of the first V.C.'s of the great war. The likeness between the two brothers was perfect. I became great friends with Francis Grenfell, whom I was afterwards to see carried back wounded from Messines, again to recover and return to France. Months after that I was to look on his face for the last time as he was prepared for burial after his third wound, a fatal one received while distinguishing himself by gallant work in the trenches of the Ypres salient.

Fine men of noble character, the Grenfells. Surely the monarch responsible for a war that mows down the flower of the world's manhood in the fullness of its youth must one day answer for his crime, in this world or the next.

In the farm where we spent the night food was given us which the day before had been ordered by the Germans. Hardly had the good woman of the house started to comply with the Huns' demands when the cry was raised that the British cavalry was approaching, and her enforced guests stood not on the order of their going.

General de Lisle's Divisional Mess was formed that night. It consisted of the General ; Colonel " Sally " Home, of the 11th Hussars, G.S.O. 1 ; Major Percy Hambro, of the 15th Hussars, G.S.O. 2 ; Captain Cecil Howard, of the 16th Lancers, G.S.O. 3 ; Colonel Drake, of the Artillery ; Captain " Mouse " Tompkinson, of the Royals, well known as a polo-player and gentleman rider, Assistant Provost Marshal of the Division ; " Pat " Armstrong, of the 10th Hussars, the General's aide-de-camp ; and myself. Not long after, the mess was to be enriched by the addition of Captain Hardress Lloyd, of the 4th Dragoon Guards, as aide-de-camp to de Lisle.

My first job on Wednesday, the 14th, was to take the other Divisional motor-cars in tow and go by road to St. Jan Cappel, towards which the General and his staff rode across sodden fields. My road lay over the Mont des Cats and past the forbidding monastery at its top. I arrived in St. Jan Cappel ahead of the main body of our advance troops. The villagers gave the cars an enthusiastic reception. The German troops, after five days' occupation, had been driven out an hour before by the Queen's Bays. A dead German horse in the main street was the only sign of the fray.

The advance squadrons kept the enemy on the move, headquarters following close behind, and by afternoon we had crossed into Belgium and occupied Dranoutre, out of which the 5th Dragoon Guards chased the Germans at midday. As we neared the town a trooper unearthed a handsome Bavarian boy, whose horse having been shot and his knee hurt in falling, had hidden in the cellar of a house near by. He blushed like a girl as he was hauled forth, devoured with disappointment and chagrin at such an unheroic end to his campaigning.

MONS TO YPRES.

Headquarters were in a nunnery at Dranoutre, a dis-
spiriting habitation, rendered no more cheerful by the
cold, sullen rain.

News of Rawlinson's 4th Corps coming south-west
and not far distant led to an evening journey. De Lisle,
with " Mouse" Tompkinson, took a run towards Ypres.
Past Locre a patrol, aware that he was the " furthest
north " of his own command, impressed us that we were
on a road " where no English had gone." La Clytte was
mysteriously darkened, the inhabitants scurrying off at
the slightest sound. Dickebusch was little better.
Germans had been about all day, said one habitant.
Had he seen any English troops ? Not he. In Voormezeele we found the first gleam of intelligible information, and I began to be reassured that the 4th Corps was
not, after all, a phantom army. Deciding to draw Kemmel next, we ran as far as Groote Vierstraat, and at last
heard British voices in the dark. Prince Alexander of
Teck was the first officer we met, and he gave us warm
welcome. We found General Rawlinson at Wytschaete.

I chatted with many old acquaintances who had been
" chased around the biggest part of Belgium," as one
of them put it, with the 7th Division. Evidently they
could qualify in the severest of tests of pedestrianism.
Vague news of heavy German forces heading west was
rife. The German army that had faced Antwerp was on
the move, and other German troops as well, it was said.
The Belgians were badly smashed, as an army, was the
general verdict. Thirty to forty thousand of them were
between Ypres and the sea, stiffened by some French
Territorials. Time, the best judges averred, must be
given the Belgians before their recovery could be
expected.

" Big German forces coming west," was the recurrent
topic. Strange how Dame Rumour and Madame Coincidence take tea together at times. Von Beseler with
two or three Corps from Antwerp was, we found
later, marching on Ostend, and that very day passed

WITH FRENCH.

Bruges. That day or the next four new Corps had left Brussels for Courtrai, and were soon to be distributed on a front from Tourcoing through Menin to Roulers. Looking back, I can remember rumours afoot that night in Wytschaete which forecasted that movement with uncanny accuracy. But G.H.Q. had no information in corroboration of those tales, as was witnessed by Rawlinson's orders four days later to take Menin with his 4th Corps, unsupported. No support was available, for Allenby, Pulteney, and Smith-Dorrien had their hands full, and Haig with his 1st Corps did not disentrain at St. Omer until October 19th.

We returned at a late hour to Dranoutre, where I learned that the 18th Hussars were in Neuve Eglise, Captain Thackwell with C Squadron of that regiment having pushed on to Ploegsteert. The next morning I took de Lisle to Neuve Eglise, where the headquarters of the 18th and the 11th Hussars were located.

No word had come from Thackwell. Lieutenant Gore Langton, of the 18th Hussars, at the head of a patrol, passed Nieppe, on the main Bailleul-Armentières road, and reached Pont de Nieppe, a mile from Armentières, in the middle of the night. A small road came into the main highway from the north. Along it troops were marching, lighted here and there by flares. A barrier extended half-way across the street. The patrol halted beside it. A trooper dismounted and walked towards the files of soldiers tramping past. " Are you infantry ? " he asked of a dark form standing by the barricade. Peering towards him in the drizzle the man he had addressed took a step forward and suddenly ejaculated, " *Mein Gott, Englischer !* "

It was a German officer ! The passing troops were files of German soldiers bound for Armentières.

The trooper threw his rifle forward until the muzzle almost touched the German's body, and pulled the trigger. An uproar followed. Leaping into the saddle, the trooper and his fellows put spurs in deep and tore back along the roadway for dear life. Ping ! went a bullet beside them. Ping, ping, ping, came others, closer still. One found its mark, and a riderless horse sped on with the patrol. The scattering shots merged into a fusilade, but the troopers were well away, and not another man received a scratch. The flashes of the rifles behind died down. Sparks along the *pavé* told of pursuit. On sped the little band, German cavalry hard on their trail. Through Nieppe they dashed at full speed, then settled down to a steady gallop for Neuve Eglise, where they arrived safely. The Germans kept on until a few miles from the town, at daybreak returning whence they had come. A villager told us that he saw eight hundred of them passing, which gave us the opinion that their numbers may have been at least one hundred, if not two.

Crowther, a 2nd Brigade motor-cyclist, was dispatched towards Ploegsteert to find news of Thackwell's squadron. Crowther was a doctor about forty years old, who had been in charge of an asylum in Surrey before the war. A brave chap, very useful as a motor-cyclist dispatch rider. He was instantly killed by a shell a few days later while carrying a message along a road in front of the Ploegsteert Wood. In his quest for Thackwell that morning he rode to the village of Romarin, on the way to Nieppe. As he could see no one of whom to ask a question, he headed his motor-bicycle towards " home," placing it just behind a street barricade, and left its engine running while he started to pull down the barrier. He had worked at the pile of stone and earth but a short time when he descried a trio of German troopers ahead. They had not caught sight of Crowther. One hundred yards away they dismounted, and cautiously crept forward along the walls of the houses, apparently trying to locate the sound of the motor. Crowther jumped on the machine and made off.

When he returned without news of C Squadron of the 18th, some anxiety was felt for Thackwell, but later in

the day news came that he and his squadron were safe.
He had sent three messages to headquarters, each carried
by a bicycle orderly. The next day we found all three
dead along the road. Germans in ambush had shot each
one through the head at close range as he passed, and
piled man and wheel in the ditch by the roadside.

Care to stop when challenged by our own sentries at
night was impressed upon us by news of a French interpreter attached to one of our Brigades and his chauffeur,
who had rushed a sentry and been fired upon the night
before. Both Frenchmen were shot through each leg.

On Friday, the 16th, we ran to Ploegsteert, Messines,
and Wytschaete, little dreaming that in scarcely more
than a fortnight thousands of men were to be killed or
wounded in the defence of the three towns, two of which
were to be taken from us by the enemy. The morning
was foggy, preventing military operations of much consequence, but in spite of the weather Pulteney's 3rd Corps
occupied Armentières, meeting no serious resistance.

A Belgian said eight Germans had come to his house
at dawn and changed their uniforms for peasant garb.
Everyone was on the watch for the spies, as the eight
uniforms had been discovered and the Belgian's tale
corroborated. Howard had news of one of the Germans,
tracked him from village to village, and finally caught
him. After pretending for some time to be drunk, the
spy admitted he was a German soldier, and ended his
career against a wall.

A Belgian farmer came to an officer of the 4th Dragoon
Guards and reported that a German soldier was hiding
in his cottage. Surrounding the house, the officer and
four of his men entered it. A thorough search was made,
but no German was found. As they were about to leave,
a trooper looked up the chimney of the kitchen fireplace
and saw a heavy boot. Strong hands pulled until the
boot came down and left a stockinged foot dangling
above. Increased efforts were at last crowned with
success, and crash came the hidden fugitive into the

ashes. After a struggle on the floor, during which each member of the party received his mark of the prowess of the soot-covered captive, superior numbers triumphed. For a moment he lay with eyes closed, breathless, pinned hand and foot.

" Let old Jack Johnson up," said a trooper as he nursed a bruised eye, " and I'll hit him a crack with the butt if he tries any more of it."

At the words the prostrate man's eyes opened. He gave a start and yelled, " You bloomin' rotters, I thought you were dirty Deutschers ! Why don't you sing out who you are before you pull a feller's leg off ? " Then, catching sight of the officer, " Pawdon, sir, I come in here 'cause I saw some 'Uns comin' up the road. I was out alone and didn't 'ave no rifle, so I 'ooked it and 'id away. 'Ow was I to know, sir, that it wasn't 'Uns as got me ? "

The officer sat down and laughed heartily, while his squad took stock of sundry bruises and a tear here and there in tunic or breeches. " It would have served you right, young feller," growled an old non-com., " if we'd a-knocked in your foolish nut for you, but you *did* fight like hell."

From Saturday, October 17th, until the following Wednesday we were hard at work in front of the Ploegsteert Wood, facing the German position on the Lys. The cavalry fought dismounted, and were not to see warfare of other sort for many and many a long month. First we attempted to force a crossing of the river. Unable to do that, we held the enemy's attention on the Lys front while the infantry pressed north from Armentières on the further bank. Houplines fell to the 3rd Corps, but Frelinghien, the next point to be taken, remained in German hands, in spite of repeated attacks. Once or twice our infantry penetrated the town, but were always compelled to retire to a position in front of it.

Our cavalry attacks on Saturday and Sunday and

the attacks of our infantry on Sunday and Monday were productive of only partial results. Tuesday saw the inception of a German attack on our front, which had been stiffened by the 12th Infantry Brigade. Wednesday found the infantry east of the Lys still hammering in vain at Frelinghien, and the German attacks on the Ploegsteert line west of the Lys increasing in violence. On Wednesday morning the enemy had a decided success at Le Gheer, but the 12th Brigade snatched the fruits of victory from them before the day was over.

Running with the General and Colonel Home early on the morning of the 17th from Ploegsteert to Messines, de Lisle impressed it upon me that he was in a hurry. A sentry not far beyond the Ploegsteert château tried to stop us, and was waved aside. He persisted, standing in the centre of the road until the car was almost upon him. At Home's suggestion, the General told me to back to the insistent Tommy, and see if he had any particular reason for his action. When we reached him he said, " Sorry, sir, but I just saw a party of German cavalry in that village down there," pointing to St. Ives, a few hundreds yards distant. " Some of them rode out that way, the way you were goin'. I thought you ought to know, sir." How I did bless the lad and his pertinacious common sense.

We backed the car around in the lee of a wayside inn, ran to the château, and reported the proximity of the enemy patrol to the Colonel of the Essex Regiment, whose men were hard at work digging trenches.

Our Divisional headquarters moved to Ploegsteert to watch the forcing of the Lys. Briggs's 1st Cavalry Brigade were to cross at Pont Rouge, by Deulemont and Mullens, who had succeeded de Lisle in the command of the 2nd Cavalry Brigade, had orders to take the bridge at Frelinghien. A patrol of 9th Lancers had visited the Frelinghien bridge the night before. I talked with one of their number, who said they had discovered

the enemy well entrenched to the east of the Lys.
" Those bridge-heads will want some taking," said he.
A sound prophet.

On our left Gough was to capture Warneton and win
across the river at the eastern edge of the town.

The panorama of the battle lay before us from the
tall tower of the Ploegsteert château, high on its hill
above the wood. Our field-guns and the few sixty-
pounders at our disposal started the ball. Watching
their white shell-clouds made me long for a couple of
batteries of good big howitzers with plenty of nice fat
high-explosive shells. That was the proper medicine
for Huns entrenched and Huns behind the houses. Care
had to be taken with the shrapnel. An unlimited
supply was not at the disposal of the gunners. Allen,
responsible for the transportation of the ammunition,
spent his life in being cursed for the shortage, and
cursing in turn his inability to get what he wanted at
the base. He wore a haunted look and mumbled
things in passing. Was it imagination, or did I hear
him mutter, " God knows I don't *eat* the damn stuff.
I give the ungrateful devils all I can get of it."

The sky was leaden, though the daily drizzle had
ceased. The roads were awful. How motor-cyclists
stayed on them no one knew. Often enough they
failed to do so, but the cheerful dispatch-riders always
" showed up smiling " sooner or later, save now and
again when one of them " ran into " a shell. Heroic
work, that dispatch carrying over roads that never
knew complete freedom from shell fire.

Four German prisoners marched past. An R.A.M.C.
man and a bombardier, both unarmed, in some occult
manner took the four Bavarians, though each bore a
rifle. The two British soldiers came upon the Germans
unawares. Beckoning madly as for assistance to
imaginary companions behind them, they ran straight
toward the badly-rattled quartette, who put hands in air
with a will when they saw they had been discovered.

WITH FRENCH.

Odd little episodes, those " all-over-in-a-second " experiences. A quick brain and plenty of nerve worked wonders. Sometimes. The majority of us, however, would generally have " done it infinitely better " if we " had had a bit more time to think." Which, of course, accounted for the success of the flash-in-the-pan minority. Two unarmed men capturing four that were armed was by no means an unparalleled incident.

The village idiot busied our spy department for an hour or so. His antics were so identically those of the average Hun spy when fate placed him in British hands that the real was definitely established as counterfeit. The Ploegsteert padre rescued the unfortunate man from our " Sherlock Holmes contingent."

The net result of the day's fighting was that the Germans were pushed back to the railway that ran alongside the Lys on our side of it. We did not take the bridges. General de Lisle ran in the car to General Briggs' headquarters between Le Gheer and Pont Rouge. An hour before, the enemy had been there, and were but five hundred yards in front when we called. Rifle fire was constant. I was unaware of the proximity of the enemy until a horse beside me was struck in the shoulder by a bullet, when I at once assumed a humble attitude in a ditch until the General's departure. At Mullens's headquarters at Le Bizet we were treated to a shelling, so the day was quite sufficiently exciting to suit the most bored of onlookers.

Towards evening the 12th Infantry Brigade came up from the right and took over part of the line.

Sunday morning the weather took a slight turn for the better. From our headquarters in the Ploegsteert château we ran to Messines and called on General Gough. His troops had gained a foothold in Warneton. Operation orders directed Gough to watch the point of the advancing German column coming south-east from the Roulers-Courtrai region and give it a check. This advance was reported to have reached America, a

206

village six or seven miles from Messines. Gough was also to operate against the Lys front.

Sydney Green, of the R.A.C. twenty-five, by that time depleted to half that number by sundry resignations, was attached to General Gough's staff. He told me of a visit on the 17th to the east of Ypres. Rawlinson's 4th Corps was in force on the Ypres-Roulers and Ypres-Menin roads, and two Divisions of French Territorials, the 87th and 89th, were between Rawlinson's force and the Belgians on the north.

While we were discussing the situation in Messines, General d'Urbal's 8th French Army was that day forming on the British left in front of Ypres, to take the responsibility of holding the line from Ypres to Nieuport and the sea. This was to prove no mean task before the German onslaughts on the northern road to Calais were to wear themselves out against the stubborn resistance of the Allied armies.

The 18th of October was the date for Rawlinson to commence his futile movement against Menin, on the second day of which his advance had to be transformed into a hurried retirement in front of the onward surge of the German flood that Haig was soon to check so gallantly and with such narrow margin of success in the bloody first battle of Ypres. G.H.Q. was still unaware of the fresh German movement west from Brussels, or Rawlinson's attempt on Menin would never have been ordered.

Back in Ploegsteert château we had sufficient work to keep our minds off operations further eastward. About one o'clock the enemy sent half a dozen shells at the château tower. Those who were about the grounds had one or two close calls, though the only damage done, save to the turf, was the killing of one of Hardress Lloyd's chargers.

During the morning the 9th Lancers had attacked in front of Ploegsteert Wood, with the Inniskillings on their right. A Battalion or so of Germans behind the railway

embankment waited patiently until the 9th line had
come within 400 yards, then poured a deadly machine-
gun fire into the advancing troopers. Francis Grenfell's
squadron was in closest proximity to the withering
fusilade. He kept his men down, returning the enemy's
fire until they ran out of ammunition, and then lying
under cover of the rifles of the Inniskillings until our
gunfire made retirement possible. Of Grenfell's
squadron six were killed and ten wounded. Our total
casualties only reached the modest figure of thirty-two,
a wonderfully small number under the circumstances.

My work for the afternoon included bobbing back
and forth from the château to 2nd Brigade headquarters in front of St. Ives, carrying artillery officers up
to see the enemy positions and cavalry officers back to
the château tower to show the gunners where to drop
their shells. Enemy shrapnel splintered the roadway
thirty to forty yards from us once, but we came through
sound enough. When our observation officers spotted
the exact location of the Germans our shells soon found
them. The gunwork was exceptionally fine. From the
tower I counted shrapnel after shrapnel that burst over
the precise spot upon which the guns had been told to
direct their fire.

At daybreak on Monday the guns commenced where
they had left off at dusk the night before. German
" coal-boxes " were thump-thumping in Le Touquet, a
village to the west of the Lys, across from Frelinghien.
Le Touquet had been taken by our infantry after a
sharp fight on Sunday afternoon.

The din of the early morning battle came clearly over
the low river-bed as the pressure of our 3rd Corps on
Frelinghien increased. No effort was to be spared to
take the town.

Rumours reached us of Rawlinson, fighting hard away
to the east. The 2nd Life Guards had been badly
knocked about, said someone.

Our line was never really quiet. Machine-guns

General de Lisle's Headquarters after being hit by a "Jack Johnson"

Mr. Coleman's car hit by a shell outside Messines

rattled away frequently. The noise at Frelinghien overshadowed other operations near at hand, but as the afternoon wore away it died down and left a season of comparative quiet. At twilight Le Touquet was ablaze. The fire lit up the night for miles around.

Morning brought further entertainment from the gunners. Major Hutchinson, Brigade Major of the 1st Cavalry Brigade, called at the château at eight o'clock and pointed out three targets from the tower. A Belgian had told of a farm on our side of the Lys where an enemy howitzer was placed behind a stout stone wall. The exact location of the German trenches along the road from Deulemont to Frelinghien had been learned from another Belgian. An outpost had discovered that two enemy machine-guns were " dug in " in a clump of bushes at the corner of a burned factory on the edge of Le Touquet. All three points were plainly visible from the tower, and soon the fun began.

A dozen rounds went hurtling towards that part of the sky where once the sun was wont to rise. Wrapped in the contemplation of our own efforts, we forgot for the moment the enemy gunners. At least, two of our officers acted as though they had forgotten. Not content with the view afforded from the lower tower, where watchers were screened from sight, the two climbed higher. On the small landing at the tower's top they stood, eagerly marking the splendid accuracy of our shells, and incidentally exciting the Bavarian gunners to try their skill at so unusually fine a target.

Crash ! A hole in the lawn by the château. Bang ! An officer's horse hit in the drive. Crash ! A stifling black cloud drifted in the window. A man was brought round the corner of the building with a hole in his back. The headquarters horses scattered this way and that, one on three legs as a red stream poured from his fourth, badly torn by a piece of shell. Bang ! Bang ! Shrapnel. Then two more. Soon they were coming fast. Crash ! Another high explosive that jarred the whole hillside.

WITH FRENCH.

Hurried preparations were made for the shifting of headquarters. A quartermaster's clerk jostled the mess waiters, who bumped into the hospital orderly in turn.

I sped down the path to the lodge gates where a woman had essayed that morning to laundry my linen. Our six Divisional motor drivers were bunched by their cars. " What orders ? " I queried. " We are told to take the cars out at once," was the reply. " Force the lower gate and go out that way," I advised, and walked towards it with one of the drivers to see if the gate could be opened. We had not taken thirty steps when a smash behind us threw us forwards. A shell had lit by the group we had left, killing three of the drivers and rendering one unconscious from the shock of the concussion.

As I gathered my damp clothing together and climbed the path to the château, a horse near by, hit by a shrapnel bursting overhead, screamed with pain. Five or six other chargers lay here and there on the turf. Stretcher parties hurriedly gathered the wounded and bore them swiftly down the hill.

At last the place was cleared of men, horses, and cars. Two of the latter were well marked. A jagged sliver shattered a head-light on my car, and splinters marked one or two of the panels.

General de Lisle was the last to leave. While waiting for him, Colonel Ludlow, the Divisional A.A.Q.M.G., told me of a visit to the kitchen when the first shell fell. Our mess boasted a chef, a French soldier, among whose experiences was a trip round the world with Madame Melba. The first few shells had come and preparations for departure were proceeding apace. The chef's assistant, Hawes, was hurrying matters, or, at least, advising haste.

The chef was seated on a chair, his head bent low in earnest preoccupation as he wrestled with a refractory puttee, always somewhat of a trial to his unfamiliar hands. From his lips came calm advice to the impatient Hawes. " *Reste tranquil, mon ami,*" breathed the chef heavily as he began the maddening task for the third time. " *Reste tranquil.*" As he spoke the last word a big Black Maria went off just outside the kitchen window at his back.

With one dive he cleared the chair and landed on hands and knees under the kitchen table, ejaculating as he gathered himself together, half-dazed, " *Reste tranquil—reste tranquil !* " A combined examination by everyone in the vicinity was necessary before the chef could be convinced he was not a dead man, or, at least, well on the way towards becoming one. Fortunately for the mess, he had fully recovered by dinner-time, but to arouse his ire for days to come, the servants averred, it was only necessary to murmur, " *Reste tranquil—reste tranquil.*"

An old château further from the line and less exposed to the eye of the enemy became our headquarters. Beside it was a battery of sixty-pounders, the 31st Horse Battery of the Royal Garrison Artillery, which rattled the windows with loud volleys, deafening at such close quarters. A cheery grate fire was welcome, as the damp, lowering day grew quite cold.

At about three o'clock a heavy German attack developed all along the line. The air became charged with the continual crash of a modern battle. Enemy shells, our own guns, rapid-firers and rifles all merged into one *mêlée* of sound, utterly beyond the comprehension of one who has never heard it. The Colonel in command of the 12th Brigade sent a message asking for support in front of Ploegsteert, and the 11th Hussars were sent to his aid. Ambulances streamed back. In one of them I saw Captain Thackwell and Lieutenant Holdsworth, of the 18th Hussars. The 18th had suffered heavily from a fierce onslaught on their left.

Travelling on the by-roads, deep with mud and as slippery as they could well be, was slow work. On one trip back to headquarters the Queen's Bays passed me at a trot, to dismount not far beyond and go into the line in support of the 2nd Cavalry Brigade, which was in front of St. Ives.

Grenfell galloped up to where I was stationed and shouted, " Do you know, President, who is on our left ? "

" Tins," I answered, " or at least some of Goughie's lot." The Tins, as the Life Guards are called, was a composite regiment made up from the 1st and 2nd Life Guards.

Turning, Grenfell said, " Right! I thought so ! " Then, anxiously, " You are sure, are you ? "

" Not I. Don't take my word for it. I heard someone say they were there, but it may be wrong. Ask de Lisle. He is along the road a bit."

Grenfell started towards the General, but a trooper, riding hard, stopped him. With an exclamation the Captain tore off at a gallop.

A moment later I was despatched with a message to the château. As I arrived three horsemen pulled up at the door. One of them, a wounded officer, could not dismount without assistance. After he had been taken inside and turned over to the doctor, I said to the sergeant, " Who was that ? His face was a strange one to me."

" Mr. Wallace, of the 2nd Life Guards," was the reply.

" Where is your regiment ? " I asked.

" We were just over there a bit," he answered, " but we were driven out. The lot of us were in a proper death-trap."

When I again reached the General I learned that Grenfell and Colonel Campbell of the 9th had luckily got wind of the retirement of the left of the line in the very nick of time. Throwing a squadron across our left flank and bringing up another in support, they held off the enemy, who were coming straight for a battery under Major Wilfred Jelf, whose left had been completely exposed.

For an hour or so the fighting raged madly in that sector, but dark came on with the line very little changed. Our troops had fallen back from the more exposed low-lying ground to positions prepared for just such an attack.

At dark I took Generals de Lisle and Mullens and Colonel Home to the Ploegsteert château, out of which we had been shelled that morning. Its devastation, soon to be completed, was well begun. By candle-light the damaged walls took odd shapes, and shadows distorted twisted ironwork and ragged shell-holes grotesquely. General Mullens and his staff used the château as headquarters that night, but were shelled out of it at daybreak.

On the way home de Lisle stopped alongside McCarthy's batteries and told the tall Colonel-gunner his guns had enabled us to hold our line, which without them we would have lost. Once before, to my knowledge, McCarthy had been given a like message at the close of a hard day's work—at Tour de Paissy, on the Aisne.

At early light on Wednesday we were off to Messines to see Briggs, then back to Ploegsteert Wood to Mullens. A cold wet night had been followed by a strong attack at dawn on the Ploegsteert position. The Germans succeeded in thrusting a wedge in our front that gave them Le Gheer and a corner of the Ploegsteert Wood, but before the middle of the forenoon the Inniskilling Tommies, supported by the 2nd Cavalry Brigade troopers, had driven them back, and, in official parlance, had " straightened the line."

The sixty-pounders seemed to make more noise as days passed. The headquarters château rocked with the din. A great flash, a thin, sickly, brownish-yellow cloud that hung in the damp atmosphere, and a rever-berating crash ; then as the sound echoed, leaving ringing ears, the whistle of the big projectile, in pulsating waves, died in the distance as the shell seemed to limp along through the air.

Before noon word came that the Germans had moved four batteries across the Lys near Warneton and concentrated a large force in front of that town for an attack on Messines. Briggs, with his 1st Brigade, was ready. Mullens and his 2nd Brigade was to be relieved at once and hurried towards Messines as support. At once the guns were turned on the German attacking force and began hammering away with increased vim. It became apparent as the day wore on that they had arrested the threatened advance.

Fifty-five German prisoners, taken by the Inniskillings at Le Gheer, were marched to our château. With them a dozen of our own men were retaken, having been captured when the enemy took Le Gheer at daybreak. The Hun prisoners were Landwehr for the most part, and all Saxons. A few first-line men were among them. They were of all ages, and many wore glasses. A sober, serious group, drawn from a very good class of citizen. One told me in French he had been enlisted eleven weeks, and during the previous seventeen days had marched 250 kilometres. Their uniforms were faded and worn. A man of forty, a pair of huge spectacles over sad, patient eyes, seemed so miserable I tried to cheer him with some fatuous remark to the effect that he was safer far in an English prison-camp than in the firing-line. Earnestly he shook his head. " No," he said with unmistakable pain in his voice, " war is hard. I enlisted to fight for the Fatherland, not to be taken by the enemy. Better I had been killed, if need be." His face was a picture of real suffering. He believed his cause was just.

1st Cavalry Division Headquarters slept that night in Neuve Eglise. We said good-bye to Ploegsteert, save for itinerant calls, and set our faces towards Messines, where grim days awaited us. Before I went early to bed, de Lisle said to me, " Some of the troops that came with the Indian contingent are to join us to-morrow, President. I will load the car with a few of the new officers and take them round where the Black Marias are bursting, to acclimatise them." Whereupon I retired to dream of a weird run on some strange planet that seemed one mass of seething flame and smoke.

WITH FRENCH.

CHAPTER XII.

WHILE the fighting at Ploegsteert was growing daily fiercer, the Germans were pressing hard on our lines a few miles away at Messines.

On Thursday, October 22nd, the whole of the 1st Cavalry Division left Ploegsteert to the defence of Wilson's 4th Division. The Cavalry, with the Ferozepore Brigade of the Lahore Division of the Indian Corps in support, was assigned the task of holding the corner of the line that swung round Messines, where every day for a week and a half was sanguinary battle, culminating in the capture by the enemy of the Messines-Wytschaete ridge, and the consequent evacuation of Messines on November 1st.

In ten days of continual fighting against great odds in men and guns, one third of the 1st Cavalry Division was to fall, and the magnificent qualities of the British Cavalry were to be tried to the utmost. Tried in the fire they were with a vengeance, and never for a moment found wanting.

The closing days of October were well-nigh the bloodiest the world has ever seen. On the far right of Messines for six days Maud'huy at Arras held off an attack by Von Buelow in the hardest battle fought since the beginning of the war. Smith-Dorrien's 2nd Corps, facing La Bassée, was hurled back by the Bavarians in ten days of awful fighting, but held its new line in the face of hammering of a sort of which veterans of Mons and the Aisne had never dreamed. In front of Armentières and Ploegsteert the Germans threw battalion after battalion in overwhelming numbers against our line. To the left of the Messines position Von Beseler and his Antwerp Army, on the coast, all but crumpled up the poor remnants of the

MONS TO YPRES.

Belgians, saved from utter destruction by the guns of British men-of-war, d'Urbal's 8th French Army, and by the flooding of the canalised Yser. To the south of the Belgians at Dixmude, Admiral Ronarc'h and his 8,000 French marines saw fighting that was almost superhuman in its intensity and persistence. The Ypres salient at its northern re-entrant was held by part of Dubois' 9th French Corps, the tale of whose casualties in the combat for Bixschoote ran high. But Ypres, in front and on its right to where de Lisle held Messines, was to see the greatest conflict of all. Haig's 1st Corps, the 7th Division, and the 3rd Cavalry Division were to suffer casualties unheard of in the history of wars.

Thus the battle of those last October days, over one hundred miles of front, raged with unparalleled violence. One million German troops, well towards half of them of the first line, strove to break the thin ribbon of less than a fifth of their number of the soldiers of France, England, and Belgium co-operating as if units of one army.

There was heavy fighting all along the line on the 22nd. Early that morning Briggs, in Messines, told us of an attack at dawn, vigorously pressed and beaten off with equal vigour. Our line ran well in front of Messines, and the 2nd Cavalry Divison took it on north in front of Oosttaverne, past Hollebeke to Klein Zillebeke. News was brought from Armentières of an unsuccessful enemy assault on that front, beginning at eleven o'clock the night before, continuing for a couple of hours, to be renewed at dawn. Before night 1000 dead and wounded Germans lay in front of our line between Le Touquet and St. Ives.

An *estaminet* on the road from Wulverghem to Messines, about a mile from the latter town, was chosen as Divisional headquarters. The 1st Connaught Rangers, part of Egerton's Ferozepore Brigade, were set digging reserve trenches not far from the inn.

WITH FRENCH.

One of their officers ran to Messines to see the shell-fire, which was fairly hot that morning in the ill-fated town. He saw it. While he was in the square a shell lit on one side of it, killing four troopers of the 1st Cavalry Brigade. I stayed under the lee of a house wall near the square while he explored the town. I had no curiosity.

Coming from Wytschaete I met the first Indian troops I had seen in France. They were Wild's Rifles, North-West Frontier men, fine-looking soldiers. Their arrival on our front added to a motor driver's trials.

In Messines in the afternoon shells burst all about. A man who stood boldly in the streets, when cover was conveniently available, was foolish. He was likely to find a shell splinter mixed up with some part of his anatomy as a reminder of the proximity of German howitzers in considerable numbers. Spies were in the town. General Briggs was shelled from three houses in succession, finally repairing to a cellar to obtain peace and quiet. The manner in which the German gunners followed Brigade headquarters from one place to another could not have been due to coincidence.

Towards dusk I had another wait in Messines. I found the few troopers who were not in the trenches in front, or in reserve behind, were lying very close. A loose bull and an escaped canary were attracting marked attention. The bull was foraging and the canary apparently trying to find its home, perhaps also in search of food. M. Taurus was obviously ill-tempered, and was given a wide berth.

The General chose a spot at a corner near a barricade not far from the square, which we concurred was as good as any other in which to leave the car. Its good fortune during those days in Messines never wavered. Another headquarters car went by, its occupants continuing to the square, where two minutes later it was put *hors de combat* by a big shell. The passengers and driver had stepped from it and into safety but a moment before.

Machine-guns blazed away in front of Messines all the evening. As dark closed in the howitzers scattered huge "coal-boxes" all along the trench front, our guns flashing fitfully in reply. The 2nd Brigade relieved the 1st that night. At Gough's headquarters on our way to Neuve Eglise and a night's rest, I heard that during the day the enemy had launched strenuous attacks on FitzClarence's 1st Brigade at the extreme left of the British line near Bixschoote, on the 2nd Cavalry Division at Hollebeke and on the 3rd Corps front at Frelinghien. Smith-Dorrien had been fighting hard further south. The German struggle for a road to Calais had begun in earnest.

The interesting situation in front of Ypres so overshadowed all else that I was glad to spend Friday, the 23rd, in touring the line. I ran to Ypres by way of Wytschaete and Voormezeele. The roads for the first part of the way were crowded with tall Indians, each group surrounded by its quota of admiring Belgians.

General Haig's and General Rawlinson's headquarters were in Ypres, and the square by the great Cloth Hall was full of the flotsam and jetsam of armies. The town presented a busy scene. Bulfin was attacking towards Pilkem with considerable success. Near Langemarck the 1st Division was repelling a furious push forward by the enemy, and the 7th Division, by that time beginning to feel the strain of continued fighting and heavy casualties, faced a strong assault near Becelaere. Proceeding past Klein Zillebeke to General Makin's 6th Cavalry Brigade headquarters and to General Byng's headquarters not far beyond, I found the German pressure on the Hollebeke front, which Byng's 3rd Cavalry Division had taken over from Gough, had been so staunchly met the day before that nothing had been heard of it since.

As I passed Ypres, long lines of French infantry

were marching through the streets of the town to the eastward. Splendid troops, the 17th and 18th Divisions of the famous French 9th Corps, they ambled on leisurely to relieve the 2nd Division, so that the hard-pressed 7th Division could in turn be given aid and its front shortened.

Reports of the operations were so confused and varied that I obtained permission to return to Ypres on Saturday, the 24th. Passing Messines, Mullens said his brigade had repulsed two attempts by the enemy to break through to the town, one at seven the night before, and the other at two in the morning. At Haig's headquarters Bulfin's 2nd Brigade success of the day previous was declared to have been splendid. Six hundred German prisoners, a field strewn with 1,500 German dead, and the relief of the Cameronians from an isolated position were among the fruits of his victory. Little runs to points of vantage disclosed that the new French troops were advancing on the Roulers road and the 7th Division being pushed back, with severe losses, to the west of Becelaere and past the soon-to-be-famous Polygon Wood. Wounded poured along the salient roads in streams.

Ypres had not echoed to the crash of its first shell. The townsfolk were busy supplying the needs of their martial visitors, little dreaming of the devastation that was soon to visit every home.

Hardress Lloyd was beside me on our return homeward as we crept through Wytschaete, winding round chaotic Indian transport, then dashed on at a good pace towards Messines. Halfway, I heard a pop! behind. "Puncture," said Hardress. Pop! The second sound caused dismay. "Great Scott, another tyre," I groaned, as I released the clutch and applied the brake. Pop-ping-g-g. Pop-ping-g-g. Punctures. indeed! Punctures of a sinister sort. Someone was plugging away at us at close range. The last two bullets came alarmingly near. Pop-ping-g-g! One went between our heads, close enough to make us feel the swish of it in passing.

Ducking low we sped on. A dozen more bullets came over us, but in a few seconds we were out of range unharmed. Still speeding, we discussed the situation, which had its alarming features. The shots had undeniably come from our right. The Germans were on our left and a line of our trenches in between. Could the enemy have won the trenches and got over the road? If so, we were properly " done."

"Are you sure you are heading for Messines?" asked Lloyd. "You don't suppose you are on the Warneton road by mistake?"

"Road is right," I answered. "For that matter there is the Messines church tower ahead. Maybe the Huns have taken Messines."

"If so, we will know it soon enough," and Hardress grinned.

We were certain Messines could not have fallen and we not heard of it, but there was the disquieting fact that rifle-fire had come from the west of the road. Consequently, it was with some relief that we drew near the barricade in the edge of the town and saw a khaki-clad figure beside it.

"Fresh Indian patrol, probably," laughed an officer from whom we invited a solution of the puzzle. "Took Hardress for a German, perhaps, from the red band on his cap. Seems their markmanship has gone off, though, since I knew the Punjabis. I don't quite see why they didn't get one of you."

We left this comforting person to his regrets at the deterioration of the Indian markmanship, thankful to be whole of skin.

By Sunday, the 25th, Briggs was again in Messines and Mullens in support. Sullen days had been succeeded by a morning of bright sunshine. A pleasant breeze drove white clouds across a sky of pale turquoise. Before night the clerk of the weather had regretted this lapse. Rain was descending in torrents, promising an unpleasant night in the trenches, particularly for the Indians, who felt the chill damp of Flanders keenly. Casual fighting was the order of the day, no great change taking place for better or for worse.

On Monday Wytschaete was given its baptism of German shell-fire. We passed through not many minutes after. The roads near at hand were lined with fleeing inhabitants. Four or five shells had come into the town, killing a four-year old child and wounding Colonel Grey of the 57th Wild's Rifles.

I saw Captain Sadleir-Jackson of the 9th Lancers, signals officer of the Cavalry Corps, in Messines. He had endeavoured to utilise a quantity of fine German field telegraph wire. His men had run it through the square at Messines. Four times that morning zealous individuals had cut it, thinking it an enemy line. He had it put up for a last time, but had no better luck. In an hour a passing trooper had severed it at some point, and Jackson gave it up as a bad job.

That afternoon at three o'clock a big forward movement along the whole line was ordered. We were the pivot at Messines, and were to hold the trenches with Briggs' Brigade and the Inniskillings. Gough's 2nd Cavalry Division with the 129th Beloochis at his disposal, and the 57th Wild's Rifles and Connaught Rangers in support, were on our left. Houthem, two miles and a-half east of Oosttaverne, was Gough's first objective. Byng's 3rd Cavalry was to push south-east from Hollebeke and reach Kortewilde, just north of Houthem. The orders of the 7th Division, next to the left, directed their advance to the tenth kilometre stone on the Ypres-Menin road. Kruiseik, well in front of Gheluvelt, was the village they were asked to reach. Still further left, Haig's 1st Corps were to win Becelaere, after dislodging the enemy from the edge of the Polygon Wood.

MONS TO YPRES.

Had that advance succeeded as planned, a great change would have been made in the line.

The atmosphere was charged with tense anxiety. Eagerly we awaited news of the progress of the work as the afternoon wore away. From the failure of the line to advance on our immediate left, we knew something had gone awry ; but not until the following day did we learn that from daybreak until noon the enemy had struck blow on blow at the 7th Division front near Kruiseik. All that saved Zandvoorde and a bad hole in the line was a brilliant counter-attack by the 7th Cavalry Brigade.

Advance against such overwhelming odds was futile. The Hun was hammering for a pathway to the Channel forts, and for the next three days we had no thought, on our front, save that of holding the line against his threatened onslaughts. No day was free from fighting on some sector of the front, but not until the 29th did the full fury of the storm break on the Ypres salient.

On the 30th it was to spread to Messines. For seventy-two hours from the bursting of that tempest of mad fury, we lost all thought of operations on other battlefields. Each hour brought carnage and death ; each minute was pregnant with action. All that could be done was hold the line intact, and that at times seemed well-nigh impossible, but never hopeless.

So the intervening days, viewed in the fierce light of that after-period of gigantic conflict, seemed tame indeed. Yet each bore its story.

Messines was becoming a death-trap. Shells had fallen in every quarter of the town, which had been cleared of inhabitants. One resident told me the village had surfeit of wars in bygone days, and was razed to the ground once in the eleventh century and again in the seventeenth. Its demolition in the twentieth bid fair to eclipse its former woes.

While waiting in Messines for de Lisle, who visited the town many times each day, I became quite

223

accustomed to hot pieces of projectile falling within reach, and black, pungent shell-clouds drifting over and around me from the near-by explosion of a Black Maria. Experiences one afterwards deems narrow escapes are ludicrously plentiful in a town continually under bombardment. I have ducked nimbly round a corner to a doorway grown familiar as a shelter, and left intact but half-an-hour before, to find it choked with *débris* from the chaotic mass of wood and plaster to which a howitzer shell had reduced the interior of the dwelling. A walk across the square was never a leisurely procedure after I had seen a couple of shells light in it. But in reality no surer road to fatalism exists than work in such surroundings. The futility of haste or loitering is demonstrated a hundred times each day. A power far more potent than mere human gunners and the engines of their ingenuity guides shells. 'Tis just as well to leave it to Him.

A deep approach trench in front of Messines enabled the change of troops in the front line to be effected with but very few casualties. The garret of a house at the outer edge of the town, close to the end of the approach trench, was used as an observation station for our gunners. I spent some time there, standing well back from the little gable window to escape the watchful eyes of the enemy. From the window I could see our own trenches, and the German ones not far beyond. Shells often came near, once setting the next house alight. One evening General Briggs was in the garret when a shrapnel came through it, passing both walls and entering the adjacent house before it exploded. He left the building, which was hit by eight shells in that many minutes, the first one coming as he walked out of the door.

On Monday afternoon German shells, which for days had battered the great square tower of Messines' eleventh-century church, fired the ancient pile. The eastern sky grew ominously black. The red flames

The ruins of the eleventh century church in Messines

The fire-spared crucifix in the burned church at Messines

licking at the roof were pictured fantastically against the sombre background. White smoke poured upward as the conflagration grew, a study for an artist.

In the trenches in front of Wytschaete that night, a farm on fire near by, the great Messines church blazing hard in the darkness, bursting German howitzer shells lighting up the line, and the sudden flash of our batteries behind us made a pyrotechnic display of unequalled magnificence

A couple of days later I accompanied Generals de Lisle and Briggs to the ruins of the church and the adjoining convent.

Inside the doorway the bare, unroofed walls rose to a grey sky. The masonry and stone of the sturdy tower had withstood the storm of shell and the fiery ordeal it brought. At the far end, under the noble blackened arch, a heap of *débris* marked where the altar had been. The devastating conflagration had devoured all save the walls of stone, except one figure which the fingers of the fire had left strangely untouched.

On the facia of a column under the tower hung a life-size Christ on the Cross. But for a small hole in the side, made by a falling bit of masonry, it remained intact, unharmed. No single object in the ruins existed in its normal form save that figure.

A few townsfolk, allowed an hour in the town to collect belongings, stopped in the doorway. Their curious eyes were caught and held in awed homage. One group of garrulous women, chattering like magpies, stopped transfixed, on reaching the door, their voices hushed. Crossing themselves, they drew away whispering.

Major Hutchinson told us he stood as near the doorway as possible on the night of the fire. The interior was a seething mass. Shading his eyes with a bit of tin, he could see the figure of some saint of the church on the opposite facia, wrapped in smoke and flame, already almost indistinguishable. Across the floor, isolated on the bleak wall, the Christ on the Cross stood out in the clear light of the blazing fixtures that surrounded it, as if set aside by some hand that guided the tongues of flame away from it.

" Weird," the Major characterised it.

As I was standing in the doorway, knots of troopers, having heard the story, gathered to the ruins of the ancient church.

Pausing on the threshold, peering under the high, blackened stone arch above, each eye was raised to that commanding figure.

For a brief moment in the midst of turmoil, death and battle, many a mind was focussed, all-devout, on one great thought.

I saw more than one soldier, his head bared in respectful silence before that fire-spared crucifix, who plainly felt the Mighty Presence of the King of Hosts and Lord of Battles, whose cause, the triumph of the Right, was that for which he fought.

A major of Connaught Rangers reported after his initial experience in the front line the night before that his men had taken three lines of German trenches. His report attracted immediate attention. Questioned, he said: "The enemy had gone back before we arrived. The first line we got to was only waist deep. The second we fairly walked into. I noticed a funny thing about that line. The beggars had dug the trench just in *front* of a barbed wire fence. We had to cut through it. Devil of a job, too. The next line we had a bother with. Lot of sniping, though they got out of it as we came in. I didn't hold on to it ; but went back into the second line, as it was a better position."

I listened attentively, wondering. Walking into abandoned German trenches sounded too good to be true. De Lisle said little, but grunted once or twice. Later developments led me to characterise the sound as a snort. Days later, I heard the correct version of the incident. The Connaught Rangers, in "taking over" had found three trenches not long vacated by the Tins. In his occupation of them the inexperienced major had cut up a most carefully arranged reserve wire entanglement. Just sufficient sniping had come his way to make him think the enemy were in the fore trench—a not unnatural error in the dark. The yarn went the rounds, gathering detail, until it assumed unique proportions, but it served to raise many a laugh where there was little enough over which to make merry.

A major of the Queen's Bays, in the trenches before daylight one morning, heard a party of Germans approaching. " Come here ! " called out a voice from in front. " Come over here ! "

" Hands up," responded a trooper, though little could be seen in the darkness.

" Send on one man," was the shouted suggestion of another Dragoon Guardsman.

Unintelligible words were mumbled in reply. Curious, the major raised his head and looked over the trench parapet. A volley at close range missed him, and our men pumped bullets into the adventurous Huns in quick time. When day broke half a dozen Germans lay dead a few yards in front in witness to the accuracy of our fire.

The 2nd Cavalry Brigade was sent south to Smith-Dorrien on the 26th. The next day I ran de Lisle to Smith-Dorrien's headquarters at Hinges, behind the La Bassée line. On the 28th the newly-arrived Indian contingent attempted the capture of Neuve Chapelle, which had been taken by the enemy the day before. The Indians faced German shells for the first time. The 2nd Cavalry Brigade was in support. The 47th Sikhs bore the brunt of the work. The 9th Bhopal Infantry was in the fight, and two companies of the Indian sappers and miners.

The Sikhs charged magnificently. They got into the town, and the houses were the scenes of many a hand-to-hand fight. One big Sikh brought back three prisoners. He had cornered eight Germans in a room, he said, and went for them with the cold steel. Five of the enemy he killed outright. Asked why he stopped, he naively explained that his arm had tired, so he spared the remaining three and brought them back as evidence of his prowess.

Close-quarter fighting and individual conflicts in the buildings of the town scattered the Sikhs. Soon the Germans brought a couple of machine-guns into play at the end of a street, mowing down the big black fellows in squads as they came within range. Their officers were down, save one or two. No cohesive body could be formed to take the quick-firers, so back the Sikhs came, straggling and demoralised, the effect of their splendid charge largely nullified by their inexperience of this kind of warfare. Howitzer shells fell by the hundred. The 2nd Cavalry Brigade were sent into the scrimmage and fought hard till nightfall. They were relieved at daybreak next morning. Neuve Chapelle had been taken, lost, retaken and lost again. When night closed in the Germans were in possession of the greater part of the town. The cavalry suffered seventy casualties, a light list for that part of the world in those days.

Many of the 2nd Corps regiments on that front had lost all but a couple of hundred out of a full thousand. Men of that command had been fourteen days and fourteen nights in the trenches without respite, but the line had held, and the arrival of the Indians had greatly relieved the situation.

The enemy's plan of attack on the long front from Arras to the sea never varied. His guns shelled hard, preparing the way for his infantry, massed, often deeply, on a narrow front. Battalion came behind battalion, regiment behind regiment. The foremost body repulsed, the reserve stepped into the breach and continued the attack. Should the first onslaught prove successful, and a foothold be gained, reserves were brought up without delay to hold, and, if possible, widen the breach in the line.

Hurling back the initial attack and pounding to atoms each front line that pressed on was of vital importance in those tense days. Every foothold had to be torn loose, no matter what the bloody cost. Easier far to expend at first that strength which lay beyond what man had learned to term the limit of human endurance. No limit bounded the endurance and effect of the British soldier save death itself. The impossible was achieved so often in front of Ypres that its performance ceased to cause wonder, and hardly attracted attention.

Fighting became mechanical. Men lost their identity as men. Rank assumed less importance. Each atom fought, and fought, and fought, until to fight became as natural to the savaged Tommy as breathing. No explanation will ever be forthcoming as to why the Germans did not win through to Ypres. Time after time they won a hole in the line, blocked by no reserves, because there were none. Companies faced Brigades of the advancing enemy, and somehow held them off. Never had so much killing been done. The dead seemed to outnumber the living at times. Yet the line held, in some way. It was beyond comprehension.

The Menin road and Gheluvelt, on the 29th, was the scene of an all-day battle, to be renewed at daybreak on the 30th. The storm centre drifted our way. Gough was driven out of Hollebeke. De Lisle sent the 4th Dragoon Guards and 18th Hussars to Wytschaete to aid Gough, if he found help necessary to hold the new position in front of St. Eloi, to which he had fallen back. The day was big with action all along the line. Reports came of stubborn resistance by the 7th Division at Gheluvelt, costly to us and trebly so to the enemy. New German units had been brought up, and the Kaiser was with them, we heard.

I noted a score of wounded Wild's Rifles, almost to a man shot in the left hand or arm. One of their officers told me this was due to the peculiar way the Indians shield their head with the left arm when firing. The Beloochis got home with the bayonet one morning, inflicting frightful execution and repelling a determined attack.

A message came from the 11th Brigade at St. Ives that the enemy was advancing in great numbers. The 11th line was broken that day, to be made good by the Somersets. With Gough on our left in need of reinforcements and Wilson's 4th Division on our right barely able to hold its own, the 1st Cavalry Division was faced with a grave situation at Messines, where showers of howitzer shells were followed by massed attacks hourly increasing in intensity.

Saturday, October 31st, was not two hours old when the German bugles were heard in a dozen places in front of the Messines line. Lanterns could be seen darting back and forth like glow-worms in the black night. Shouted orders were borne on the wind to the British trenches. The rhythmical cadence of German soldiers' voices in loud marching chorus told of singing columns moving forward to the attack.

The 9th Lancers were in the front trench. On their left were two short trenches facing the left front and left flank, occupied by the 5th Dragoon Guards. On the right of the 9th the trench line continued in a gradual curve to the southward, the 57th Wild's Rifles holding that section of the line.

The enemy reached the Indians before daybreak, pouring over their front like a flood, and driving the 57th back into the town in some confusion. Messines had been shelled all night long. Driven from their position by overwhelming hordes of singing Huns, whose ranks, mowed down, filled up with numberless others from the blackness beyond, the poor Indians found the path of their retirement led straight into an inferno of scattering earthquakes that spread death over the whole district like a mantle. The blinding flash and nerve-shattering roar of the big howitzer shells, ever punctuated by the dozens of wicked, whirring shapnel that searched every quarter of the town, might well have demoralised troops of much more experience of the new gun-cult of modern warfare.

In support of that part of the line was a reserve company of the 57th and a squadron of the 5th Dragoon Guards. These two contingents went into the Germans with the bayonet most gallantly, but were hurled back by overpowering numbers.

Every European officer of the Wild's Rifles was killed, making a rally of that regiment impossible.

Also before dawn a column overran the 5th Dragoon Guards' position on the left. There pile on pile of German dead blocked the way of those who followed after, never wavering until the trenches were won and the gallant regiment forced back inch by inch, dealing death at every step.

The 9th Lancers beat off the first attack on its front. As the night began to pale the German bugles were sounding and their lanterns flashing behind the 9th and towards the town on both right and left. With the first streaks of dull light began a fight on three sides of a square that was to cost the Germans dear. On came the enemy, steady as if on parade, a maxim at each end of the advancing grey line belching forth a stream of fire at every few yards. Every man in the 9th—cool as a cucumber and full of that glorious pride of regiment that makes the super-soldier—fired shot after shot into the oncoming mass, every bullet bringing down its mark. Once the pressure on a flank uncovered the end of the trench, but the enemy's brief advantage was won back by a hand-to-hand struggle.

Then the shells came. The air was one mass of rending flashes. Shock succeeded shock, and deadly missiles fell like hail—so fast and thick no living thing could remain long untouched beneath the torrent of metal that sprayed over the trenches.

Back came the 9th, firing as they retreated. Shrapnel followed them every inch of the way. The enemy's gunners never showed better markmanship. At the edge of Messines, Francis Grenfell turned, and with some of his squadron started back down the approach trench. One trooper who went with him said to me an hour later, "I didn't know where the Captain was going, but he said, 'Come on.' It looked to me as if he was starting off to take the bally trenches back with a bloomin' pistol." Grenfell had noticed the enemy were not advancing, and had heard a storm of fire from the trench ahead. He knew someone had been left behind and was still fighting hard, so back he went to get into the fight.

He found the lost trench momentarily re-won. A corporal in charge of one of the 9th machine-guns had placed a low bush above it to hide its position. When the regiment was ordered to retire by Colonel Campbell, the corporal had stayed in the trench by his gun. Waiting until the Germans were almost upon him— until some, indeed, were climbing the parapet not far on his left and piling into the trench—he loosed off his deadly quick-firer. He poured a thousand rounds into the enemy at such close range the execution was beyond realisation. Men were mowed down like grass. The surprise of the manœuvre added to its effectiveness. Leaping back out of the death trap the Germans rushed rearward in a close crowd for cover, the machine-gun in the corporal's deft hands playing on them as they ran.

By the time Grenfell reached the trench the

MONS TO YPRES.

Germans had peppered the corporal and his bit of ordnance until the gun was pierced with a dozen Mauser bullets, six or eight of which had punctured its water jacket and rendered it useless. Not long afterwards the corporal passed me outside Messines. He was carrying the tripod of his abandoned gun and almost wept as he spoke of having to leave it, useless, behind him and in the hands of the adjectived Germans, who had again come on in force to the trench, not to be denied by the few of the 9th who were left to face them. The corporal was subsequently awarded a well-deserved V.C.

De Lisle was worried. He left headquarters for Messines that morning at an early hour. On the way he called on General Hunter Weston, of the 11th Brigade, at Ploegsteert. Weston ordered two companies of Inniskilling Fusiliers to be so placed at once that his line would extend its left to near Messines. This gave de Lisle his own Division and four Battalions of 2nd Corps troops that arrived in Neuve Eglise during the night for the defence of the town and that part of the Messines-Wytschaete ridge which our line covered.

Reinforcements, without which the line could not be held much longer, were coming. Second Corps troops from the south and the French 16th Corps from the north, with Conneau's French cavalry as well, were on the way. The need was sore, and their prompt arrival a matter of more than life or death.

As we sped on from Ploegsteert, we tarried a moment by McCarthy and his guns. He nodded his grizzled head when asked to help. McCarthys were rare in any army. Oh for a dozen of him in that war of guns!

As we came in sight of Messines, smoke-clouds rose from every quarter of the town. A dozen houses were ablaze, the flames leaping high in the light breeze.

Swinging up to our reserve trenches, narrow, deep,

233

and so placed as to be well concealed, turbanned heads peeped above the level of the unharvested beet-field, for all the world like khaki cabbages in a row.

Straggling Indians were all along the road, many of them wounded. At one point a procession of the poor fellows were rapidly filling a convoy of horse ambulances gathered at the roadside. A big Punjabi, covered in blood, came up, pale and tottering, supported by a comrade. Most of the wounds were in head or arm, allowing the men to navigate rearwards under their own power. One passed, insensible, borne on a door by four of his fellows. The next was in a motor-car, half lying on the front seat, huddled with pain, a blanket between his set teeth : a brave chap, horribly wounded, but holding on with sublime courage and never a groan to tell of his awful agony. Many a hero tramped by among those black soldiers of the King so far from their own land. Their stretcher-bearers, with their incessant gabble, gabble, gabble, sounding like a flock of excited turkeys, did yeoman work in their own Oriental way.

As we entered the town, a German war balloon loomed high in the near distance, a line of gaily coloured flag-signals suspended from it.

The black cross showed clear from the under wing of a German aeroplane droning above.

I saw Basil Blackwood, attached to the 9th Lancers, taken past, shot through the shoulder. Francis Grenfell, an ugly bullet-hole in his thigh, was also sent back. The 9th had suffered heavily. Seventy-five per cent. of their officers and a third of their men had been hit that morning.

A moment in the edge of Messines, where the fighting had reached the barricades at the eastern edge of the town, and we were speeding back to our own headquarters inn a mile behind.

A squadron of the Oxfordshire Yeomanry arrived that morning, and went up towards the front, a splendid looking lot. They were to take their places in action with the finest cavalry in the world, and to make a record of which the oldest veterans would be proud.

Coal-boxes began to search the country round more persistently. A dozen dropped on a ridge not far on the right of our *estaminet*. They were feeling for McCarthy's guns, and coming close to him at times. As I was watching the ridge I saw a wagon, loaded full of men, women, and children, leave a spacious farm and start for the rear. A sharp flash, a great black column rising, rising, and the double rumph-rumph of the howitzer shell, told of a hit in the road in front of the fleeing farm folk. Two seconds later another flash, again the mounting, twisting column of black, right over the wagon. Out from the shell-cloud galloped a horse. One or two scurrying forms dashed from the lane, and scattered like frightened rabbits over the fields. I turned from the sight with a shudder.

Clatter, clatter over the cobbles, the remainder of the Oxfordshire Hussars went up at a trot.

A dirty, cheery, devil-may-care motor cyclist pulled up with a message from Briggs' headquarters in the burning town.

" How is it up there ? "

" Absolutely bloody."

But the Germans had not won the town. They were in an edge of it, but there they stuck, every sally thrown back at heavy cost. Every minute the firing grew heavier. More shells rained on the blazing buildings. The rattle of small arms rose to a high continuous note and hung, piercing the booming din of the howitzers and the racking fury of their bursting shells. At times the "coal-boxes" burst so fast, it seemed a fierce thunder-clap had spread itself over minutes which imagination lengthened into miniature ages of nerve-tension.

" Looks up there as though most everyone is hit

or scratched," said the cyclist as he started back. "Absolutely bloody, that damned Messines So long!" A grin, a nod, and off he dashed, straight into the thick of it.

Ambulances full of wounded wheeled slowly back to Wulverghem, dumped their shattered freight at the dressing-station, and returned at a trot into the zone of shell-fire.

A couple of wounded troopers bumped and jolted about on a bundle of straw in the narrow box of an empty limber that rattled rearwards for a fresh supply of ammunition. An officer came slowly down the road, supported by his subaltern. He was shot through the shoulder. "Only a scratch," he said, with an attempt at a smile as he staggered on.

News reached us from Weston's headquarters of Germans massing in front of Frelinghien and Le Touquet for an attack in force. Too much was going on in Messines to allow even a passing thought of what might transpire elsewhere.

Two armoured cars, attached to the Oxfordshires, moved up, to retire discreetly shortly afterwards. Messines was no place for an armoured car. A healthy, full-grown Black Maria would scatter one to the four winds.

By ten o'clock the six-inch howitzers went slowly back, their attendant transport wagons following soberly. A couple of days before those howitzers had come up fresh from the base, the gunners eager to "get into it." The change in their position to the region of the Kemmel road meant that the enemy had come too close for the sixes to be used effectively.

The 9th Lancers filled the trenches of the reserve line not many yards in front of headquarters. If we fell back from Messines those trenches would mark the new line.

A hurried dash to Messines and back in the car was found to be unwise, and a stop was ordered at the bottom of the hill leading into the town. Bullets were singing overhead. The struggle for each street was a battle in itself.

Colonel Ludlow drove up. Two battalions of Worcesters were in Neuve Eglise, he said, and the Scots Fusiliers, Northumberland Fusiliers and Lincolns had pushed on half an hour before for Kemmel. Good news that. Seventh Brigade and 9th Brigade troops of the well-tried 3rd Division. Reinforcements from Smith-Dorrien's hardened lot, well worth having, every man of them.

I chatted with Colonel Campbell and Major Beale-Browne of the 9th for a few minutes, then strolled back towards the headquarters *estaminet*. By dint of great persuasion we had induced the proprietress to send away her four-year old daughter in charge of an elder sister that morning. The woman herself, her husband, and a girl of sixteen remained, though repeatedly advised to take up safer quarters.

I passed Pat Armstrong in the road. "Where away?" he queried. "Only to the car to sit and scribble," I replied.

The car stood by the inn.

"Bang!" went a Black Maria sixty yards from us. General de Lisle was in the roadway. "How far from us was that one?" he asked. Pat and I turned to him to reply, both laughing as each paused, waiting to criticise the other's estimate.

Before the answer, a crash that beggars description came without warning, sudden as a thunderbolt. A howitzer shell had struck the house fifteen to eighteen feet from where we were standing.

I distinctly felt the shock of the concussion. Others by me did so and others, even closer, said they felt no shock.

My head was driven violently downwards.

I jumped the roadside ditch as I recovered my balance and ran for the shelter of a haystack a few yards away. I think my idea was to avoid a possible second shell. I hardly knew what had happened. My chin was bleeding, grazed by some flying bit. The air was choked with dust and *débris*. A black, stinking pall hung over the *estaminet*, a farm across the road, and all between.

Women's screams came shrill and high from the thick bank of smoke. I could not, at first, see the outline of the inn or what, if anything, remained of it. No voices could be heard for a second or two, save the heartbreaking shrieks from the women.

Leaping back to the road I saw the General standing on the bank. As I joined him the smoke drifted. The house showed dim, then clearer. Its eastern end was torn away. A skeleton-like frame of rafters remained where the roof had been. The interior was a confused heap of *débris*.

Major Davidson, of the R.A.M.C., who stood in the road a few yards beyond the inn, said it opened up like a stage house blown asunder by an explosion in melodrama, tumbling inwards and collapsing as a house of cards falls.

The screaming women were extricated. Though badly hurt they could both walk and were led off toward the dressing station. The aged owner of the *estaminet* was severely wounded.

Corporal Smallman, one of the 2nd Cavalry Brigade motor-cyclists, was in the kitchen. Both his legs were blown away, and he died in terrible pain on the way to the field hospital. His grim pluck never failed, though when he knew that both limbs were gone and no chance of life remained, he asked through set teeth for a release from the warping, frantic agony in the shape of a kind bullet to hasten the inevitable end.

Smallman was one of the very best of our motor-cyclists. No finer epitaph could be given him.

We lost another motor-cyclist by that shell, killed in the road close to where I was standing.

MONS TO YPRES.

When the shell came the largest of the two rooms
in the front of the house was empty, for the first time
any member of the staff could recollect. An occupant
of that room would have met instant death. Colonel
Home and Percy Hambro were in the smaller, further
room. Both were buried in the falling *débris*, but
clambered from the window unhurt after digging themselves from under a pile of bricks and mortar.

A chair Hambro had adopted as his own stood in
the larger room. The explosion hurled it high in the
air. Alighting on the ruined roof it hung there on a
splintered rafter, mute evidence of the fate that would
have met one who had been its occupant a few minutes
before.

Captain MacFarlane, of the Queen's Bays, was the
Divisional signals officer. As the black cloud over the
scene lifted, MacFarlane came from the farm gates,
black from head to foot. I thought some new form of
Hun explosive had dyed him. "What's happened to
you?" I asked in amaze. "I jumped out of the signals
office in the barn to see what was up," said Mac. "I
couldn't see a foot ahead of me in the muck, and
stepped plump into the centre of that stinking stagnant
pond in the farmyard. However, I'm none the worse,
bar looks."

I turned to my car. The raised hood was smashed
under a load of brick and splintered beams, about
which were wound a woman's bodice and odd bits of
feminine headgear. Jagged holes in the panels showed
where pieces of shell had torn their way through the
sides. Pulling my muffler and Burberry from under
débris that covered the front seat, I found each had
been pierced in more than one place by shell-splinters.

The car was equipped with a self-starter, a mysterious
device that sometimes started, sometimes not. Eager
to get away, still fearful of another shell, a movement
of the starting lever proved that it was to be a case of
sometimes not. I went to the starting handle and

gave it a swing. As I did so I heard a shout of warning, and involuntarily ducked my head. Close under the mud-guard I crouched. Swish, swish, swish came the shell. I strained forward, bracing myself for the crash. But swish, swish, swish was all that came. In a twinkling I realised that the half-hearted efforts of the self-starter were turning the engine slowly and jerkily. No shell was near. Guiltily I peeped under an arm and saw Ludlow, across the road, bent double in laughter. "That look of anticipation on your face, President," said he, "was certainly the real thing."

I moved my load of brick to Wulverghem, where I took stock of damage and cleaned the car. I scrapped the broken hood, but otherwise the car's usefulness was unimpaired. A mud-guard was splintered and its general appearance marred, but it would run.

From Wulverghem I could hear the incessant din of the never-flagging battle.

A couple of German prisoners were brought back. Their uniforms were dirty and faded, but the men looked sound and fit. One captive said he had had no food for three days, but his appearance went ill with the story. Another German taken during the day told of orders received direct from the Kaiser that Ypres must be taken by Sunday, November 1st. A prisoner stated that his contingent had come from Verdun, *via* Lille. He told of eighteen German howitzers that he had seen in front of Messines operating in lots of three.

What a difference eighteen howitzers at our disposal would have made!

By early afternoon Briggs reported the Germans holding the eastern part of Messines, while he held the west side with his 1st Cavalry Brigade. The Inniskillings had regained their trenches on the right, and were within half a mile of Messines, firm as a rock. On the left, toward Wytschaete, the 4th Dragoon Guards and the King's Own Yorkshire Light Infantry

In the front trenches facing Wytschaete

French 16th Dragoons in the trenches at Lindenhoek

1st Corps (Haig's); Men coming out of Ypres trenches during the
first great battle of Ypres in October

A hidden British Howitzer

MONS TO YPRES.

held the southern part of the ridge, with the London Scottish, lately arrived, in the fields behind in reserve.

The heaviest of the street fighting fell to the lot of the Queen's Bays and 11th Hussars.

The wounded poured through Wulverghem in a never-ending stream. One complete convoy of ambulances was filled with troopers of the Bays and a couple of their officers.

I asked one of them if he had seen any Germans.

" Loads of 'em," was the reply. " Brave beggars, that lot. Three of us were in a house facing the square. Close behind us, a few yards down the street, was our barricade. We saw the Germans start another charge from clear across the open. We pumped a few rounds into 'em, and as they came on we hooked it for the barricade. When those chaps came round the corner where we could get a pot at 'em, how many do you think they was ? Just eight! It seemed a pity to kill the plucky mugs. Eight of 'em ! Just think of it ! Charging like as if they was a whole damn army. I wouldn't minded takin' 'em, but we couldn't. It wouldn't 'a done. Besides, maybe *they* wouldn't. So we wiped 'em off."

" But "—he shook his head sagely as he climbed aboard the ambulance—" they was plucky beggars, if they *was* Germans. *I* don't want to see no pluckier. They've been killed off like pigs up there, in that town, and they keep on comin'. They fight stiff, that lot—they fight damn stiff ! "

Weeks afterwards I read a letter, written by a German officer to a friend in Zurich, which paid a counter-tribute to that trooper and his comrades.

It read as follows :—

On November 1st, Messines was stormed by our troops, with great losses on our side, for the English had erected wonderful barricades, which defied all attempts to break down. As we went to the attack we were told to spare the village as much as possible, but this order proved easier to give than to

241   R

obey, for the English had so ingeniously hidden themselves on all flanks that they were able to shoot down our men as they approached without our being able to locate their whereabouts. On finding that it was impossible to oust the enemy in this manner, we brought our heavy artillery to bear on the village, thus clearing the path somewhat and enabling us to move forward with less molestation from the enemy's deadly snipers. Still, even after two hours' bombardment, every house had to be stormed singly, and it was well into the evening before the place could be deemed anything like safe.

If we Germans were given to understand formerly that the English soldiers were not to be feared, then that idea may now be banished from our minds, for the general opinion of those who have fought against them in these districts is that one Englishman is more dangerous than any two of the Allies.

After a luncheon of bread and black coffee, the best fare procurable in the Wulverghem inn to which head-quarters had been shifted, de Lisle took the car to General Briggs's headquarters in the hollow behind Messines. As we reached the cover of the little valley a company of the King's Own Scottish Borderers trudged past and started up the hill toward the inferno above. The short distance to the scene of the conflict was emphasised by the frequent "Sing-g-g" of a Mauser bullet.

At dusk de Lisle had a talk with Mullens, whose 2nd Brigade was to relieve Briggs' 1st Brigade at dark. With the depleted 9th Lancers, 18th Hussars, and 4th Dragoon Guards, Mullens was to have the King's Own Scottish Borderers and the King's Own Yorkshire Light Infantry. General Allenby wanted the position held at all costs, even if it became necessary to give up the town. "De Lisle could evacuate Messines, for that matter," said Allenby, "if he held the ridge from Messines north to Wytschaete." But to lose Messines, said de Lisle, would be to lose the ridge with it, so the town must needs be held.

The situation was bad. The Germans had a strong position on the eastern side of the town. A night attack was planned, the King's Own Yorkshire Light

MONS TO YPRES.

Infantry on the right, the Cavalry in the centre and the King's Own Scottish Borderers on the left. Pulling up a field-gun to within a few yards range of a German barricade was discussed, and the idea abandoned. Curiously enough the Germans adopted that very procedure during the night, blowing away an old barricade behind which, luckily, only a couple of men were posted. Neither of them was hurt.

To the north of Messines the London Scottish carried the line along the ridge from the left of the 4th Dragoon Guards to the right of the 4th Cavalry Brigade, a part of Gough's 2nd Cavalry Division. The 4th Brigade consisted of the 3rd Dragoon Guards, the "Tins" (Composite Regiment of Household Cavalry) and the 6th Dragoon Guards (the Carabineers). The last-named regiment was on the extreme right, next to the London Scottish. The keeping of the centre of the precious ridge was chiefly in the hands of these two regiments.

On our return to Wulverghem we heard that the 1st and 2nd Division headquarters had been shelled near Hooge that day, Generals Lomax and Monro being wounded, and half a dozen Staff officers killed. Three Divisional headquarters struck by enemy shells in one day was certainly a record. During the morning I had overheard a Staff officer joking about Staff school teaching, that Divisional headquarters should be well out of range of interruption and distraction of thoughts from the work in hand. A grim joke in the light of the day's events.

The line in front of Gheluvelt had been lost by the 1st Division, and regained by the 2nd, said the news from the Ypres salient. The 7th Division was holding on by the skin of its teeth. The French in front of Zillebeke were in like case.

Twice that night I ran to General Allenby's headquarters at Groote Vierstraat, and was greatly cheered by the sight of long lines of Conneau's Cavalry on the

243

road. Reinforcements were close at hand. A French officer of cuirassiers told me of thirteen Battalions of the 16th French Corps well on the way to join hands with us on the morrow. Nevertheless, I went to sleep on a bundle of straw in a house in Dranoutre that night with anything but a light heart.

Could we hold the line?

What price could Germany pay to break it?

I was not the only one to ponder those questions that night in Flanders.

We rose at daybreak on Sunday, November 1st.

General de Lisle was at breakfast when General Allenby and Colonel Barrow came in.

"I hear things are much the same in Messines this morning as they were last night," said the Corps Commander.

"The night attack was only partially successful," de Lisle admitted. "We gained part of the convent, but could make no headway on the left. We have bettered our position in the town, though we were unable to drive the enemy from it."

"Well," I said to myself, "things might be worse."

The French were attacking in two places that morning between St. Eloi and Wytschaete to relieve the pressure. The 32nd Division of the 16th Corps, containing some of the finest soldiers of France, were pressing forward to the attack. The sacrifice of the past days had not been in vain. The line had held, and help was in sight—at least, so it seemed.

By six o'clock I had started for Wulverghem, de Lisle alongside and Colonel Home in the tonneau.

As we pulled into the town a grey-haired colonel, without a cap, ran into the road ahead.

"Is this General de Lisle?" he asked.   To whom do I report? I am Colonel Malcolm, of the London Scottish.   The Germans are through," he went on, speaking with some excitement.   "They are through the 4th Brigade.   They came across the Messines-

Wytschaete road, and broke through. My lot out there have stood an awful shelling—Black Marias, shrapnel, every kind and sort of shell we had—all outside any trenches, for we had no trenches to get into. We drove them back twice, and got into them with the bayonet ; but they came on the third time in such numbers we could not stop them again. I lost my two majors and I don't know how many of my poor men."

" Where have the Germans got to ? " de Lisle broke in.

" They are right out there a little way," said Malcolm, pointing beyond the church to the north-east.

From the din of small-arm fire I thought he was right, and that they were " out there," but a *very* little way.

The General ordered me to push on sharply. He chose a lane by the church too narrow to allow the passage of the car. Leaping to the ground he seized a near-by horse and galloped across the field, sending Colonel Home post-haste to Neuve Eglise to bring up the good old reliable 1st Cavalry Brigade. No matter how battered Briggs' lot might be, it was a host in itself. In a short time we had finished that job, and had come back hot-foot to Wulverghem.

De Lisle returned. He had found a fair-sized contingent of the London Scottish, who had been driven well back by the heavy shell-fire, but were eager to take a further hand in the fray. They had seen severe fighting. While they inflicted heavy losses on the Germans at close quarters, accounting for many of the enemy when they " got in " with the bayonet, the rush of overwhelming numbers, their unfamiliarity with the position, the darkness and the awful storm of shell to which they were subjected at dawn, had pressed them back some distance from the line.

They rallied like veterans when de Lisle called on

them. One of their number told me afterwards a wave of quiet laughter went over those of his comrades who heard their Major say: "The men have had no breakfast, sir." De Lisle replied: "They will find plenty of breakfast over that ridge in front. They look the sort that would thrive on that kind of food."

As they started off with two squadrons of the Oxfordshire Yeomanry, dismounted, to give the enemy a further taste of their mettle, the Major said to de Lisle, "The Colonel and the other Major are dead, sir, I'm afraid."

"No, no," answered the General; "they will show up all right."

"But," insisted the Major, "the Colonel is gone. I have *reported* him dead."

"Now, Major," laughed de Lisle, "you will find it will take a lot more than that to kill him. I have just left him in Wulverghem, sound as a drum."

The London Scottish and the Oxfordshires were in support of the Lincolns and Northumberland Fusiliers for most of the day, and both acquitted themselves nobly.

At 7.30 the General decided to go towards Messines and find General Mullens. We lost no time on the journey. I bumped at good speed past the ruined inn that had been our headquarters. Just beyond we flashed past the 9th Lancers, grim and determined, in the reserve trench which was soon to be the front of the battle line.

When we reached the brow of the hill which stood across the dip in the ground on the western edge of Messines, the road was so swept by bullets that de Lisle ordered me to back quickly behind a heavily foliaged tree. Dismounting, he walked down the slope to Mullens' headquarters, where we had visited Briggs the day before.

That was a warm corner. Turning the car in the narrow road, with bullets singing over me in dozens, was a nervous business. I could see the Germans coming over the ridge not far away on the left. The enemy held the north part of the town. Having broken our line on the ridge further to the north, they were starting to come westward past Messines, while our troops were still fighting hard in the south-west corner of the town.

The Mauser bullets came so fast and furious, it was not difficult for me to imagine I was the target, though more than likely I was merely sitting in the line of fire, unnoticed by an enemy busy with far more important game.

The whizzing pellets came lower. I took to the ditch, and from it watched couples and trios of wounded and stragglers trickling rearward along the ditch across the road from me. Sing-g-g! sing-g-g! went the little devils. Zip-p-p—zipp! as one cut its way through the leaves. Pawk! One hit the tree trunk. A sharp slap from across the road and a quick " Hi!" from a passing Tommy told of a bullet that had found a billet. The boy who was hit was helping a wounded comrade. He fell when hit, but rose and hurried on. He would not stop and let me bind his wound.

Still lower the fire came. One or two hit the cobbled road-bed. I lay on my back in the damp ditch. Twigs and leaves cut off above me floated down lazily. Of all that stream of fire only two bullets hit the car.

It was only 7.35 when the General walked up the hill to the car. It seemed as if he had been gone three times as long. I jumped into the seat in a hurry.

"No rush," said de Lisle. "Wait for the Colonel." A tall figure in khaki was coming easily up the rise, unaware of our delay on his account. I longed to shout an invitation to him to quicken his pace.

At last we were off, and soon back safely in

Wulverghem. Divisional **headquarters** was moved at eight o'clock to the Station Inn, on the Kemmel-Neuve Eglise road, beside which, in a field, a battery of 6-in. howitzers was making a deafening row.

I stayed in Wulverghem with Colonel Home until nearly nine o'clock. The wounded poured through the village. Many fine London Scottish lads were among them. An 18th Hussar officer went by, his jaw tied with a reddening bandage. He made as if to speak, spat out a mouthful of blood, then shook his head and waved his hand as he rode on. Two old Belgians made useful trips to the edge of the town, to return supporting tottering soldiers to the ambulances.

Indians appeared in twos and threes at intervals. Unable to speak English the poor fellows knew not where to go. One lay dead on a bank outside the town, a worn-out comrade crouching huddled beside him.

Crean, V.C., the R.A.M.C. officer with the 1st Cavalry Brigade, one of the bravest men who ever won the cross, was doing the work of a dozen.

Thinking Wulverghem would soon become unhealthy he started moving the wounded from a temporary hospital in an *estaminet* which faced the end of Wulverghem's main street. Inspired by some intuition, he hurried the ambulances up and filled them in unusual haste. The last wounded man was out of the house and the last ambulance fifty yards down the road toward Neuve Eglise when crash came a howitzer shell, crushing the *estaminet* like an eggshell.

Major Wilfred Jelf, who had succeeded Colonel Drake as our Divisional C.R.A., did a good piece of work that morning stopping the fire of a battery of our guns that were hurling lyddite into a part of Messines occupied by the King's Own Scottish Borderers.

At 9.15 the General went up to the line again. McCarthy's batteries had been hard at it all the morning and the German gunners were searching madly for them. The enemy were within rifle-range of the left of our reserve line. Between the shells and the spent bullets no place held much security.

The ridge was gone. The enemy's success in breaking our line between the London Scottish and the 2nd Cavalry Division could not be gainsaid. Holding on to Messines meant a useless sacrifice of men's lives, for the town had been held only to make the ridge secure, so at 9.30 de Lisle ordered our troops back from the edge of the town.

We had to content ourselves thenceforth with holding our strong reserve line.

Wytschaete had been captured by the Germans when the ridge was taken. The Beloochis on the left suffered heavily and fought like demons. A barn along the line became a point of vantage. The enemy drove the Indians from it. They rallied, charged, and retook the building, killing or wounding every German in it.

The 3rd Cavalry Brigade relieved the 4th Brigade, in turn to be relieved by the French troops.

Wytschaete that day saw a charge of the 12th Lancers, supported by the 3rd Hussars, in which scores of Germans were put to the bayonet.

There, too, the Lincolns and Northumberlands were caught by a tornado of German shell, which cost them many casualties.

The French attack, after one abortive effort, won the town at midday, and cleared it of the enemy. The place was rendered untenable by howitzer fire, and once more it was evacuated and a line taken to the west of the town.

Our new line of defence, since the incessant bombardment of Messines, Wytschaete, and the ridge between had won the ground to the enemy, ran from the west of Wyschaete, past a hill known as Hill 75 (from its designation on our maps), to our carefully prepared position to the east of Wulverghem. From there it circled round St. Ives and the Ploegsteert Wood to Le Gheer, and thence beyond to the trenches in front of Frelinghien.

At eleven the General took another spin to the line. En route we met General Allenby's car, and behind it General Wilson of the 4th Division. The three commanders held a roadside conference. When we arrived at the ruined *estaminet*, the enemy's shrapnel was bursting in dozens over the 9th Lancers in the trench line.

Germans could be seen digging in the open near a windmill on the Messines ridge. Major Hambro jumped into the car and told me to hurry him over to McCarthy, whose guns were provided a splendid target by the busily-entrenching enemy.

I dropped down the hill outside Wulverghem like a shot, and piled through the town at a rate of knots. I did not expect to meet another vehicle in Wulverghem, but as I swept toward the corner a big car came toward me at good speed.

I tried to swerve to the right, but the slippery cobbles threw me round. The space between the houses on the left and the approaching car seemed small indeed, but no alternative existed save a smash. I dived left and through, winning the passage by a hair's breadth. As I escaped I caught a horror-stricken look on the face of the driver of the other car, whom I recognised as Jimmy Rothschild, driving one of General Pulteney's staff.

At noon, returning to headquarters, we passed long lines of London's motor buses debouching infantry near Neuve Eglise. Reinforcements in plenty had arrived. Though they came too late to save Messines and Wytschaete, they were in time to nullify the German gain and hold the enemy to the ground so dearly won.

Early in the afternoon airmen reported the enemy

MONS TO YPRES.

forming for attack at Gapaard, a village east of Messines. French guns and English guns hammered at them for an hour or so, and the threatened attack fizzled out.

Visits to the ruined inn on the Wulverghem-Messines road became more and more exciting. Wulverghem was shelled at frequent intervals. Coal-boxes dropped everywhere. No field was free from a miniature cellar or two excavated by the howitzer shells.

"If they begin shelling you, move out," was de Lisle's usual caution. Move out, indeed! Little would be left to move if a Black Maria came too near. Fifty yards from where I stood two great black fellows ploughed the turf. Yet not a splinter came my way.

A run to La Clytte late in the day, to General Allenby's headquarters, took me past innumerable French foot soldiers. They bred confidence in their sturdy appearance, crowding along swiftly in undulating lines. They looked eminently business-like.

Passing through Kemmel at dusk de Lisle saw a detachment resting in the ditch at the side of the road. Pulling up, he said :

" What troops are these ? "

" London Scottish," came the answer.

" Is one of your officers with you ? "

" Yes, sir," and Colonel Malcolm rose and came to the side of the car.

" Ah, Colonel," said the General, " you are on the right road. La Clytte, where your regiment is to reform and get some rest, is only a couple of miles ahead."

" On again ? " said Malcolm. " My men have had no sleep for three nights, and we have had no rations to-day."

But before he had finished, word had passed from mouth to mouth along the line of sturdy youngsters that food, rest, and, best of all, the gathering of their

251

comrades scattered in the charge, were but two miles away. Cheerily prodding sleeping forms, stretching weary limbs, they jumped into the road and were off in a jiffy. Their temper, when so completely worn and tired, was good evidence of the fine stuff of which they were made.

One day they were to be brigaded with the 1st Division, Haig's lot of seasoned heroes. In that collection of regiments, whose fame was one with Britain's greatness, I was, months later, to hear a veteran officer of the line say with feeling, "No better Battalion of soldiers exists in the whole army than the London Scottish"—high praise indeed, and well earned before it was won.

So the battle of Messines ended. Our losses were great, and those of the enemy far greater. The 1st Cavalry Division had nearly forty per cent. of its numbers killed or wounded, and the Battalions brigaded with it suffered almost as heavily.

MONS TO YPRES.

CHAPTER XIII.

The Germans attacked the line of the Ploegsteert Wood and Le Gheer violently on the morning of Monday, November 2nd. The detonation of the heavy firing came dully through the rain to us. Early in the forenoon the noise of battle lessened, the rain ceased, and the sky brightened.

One who had been talking with Sir John French told of the conversation. " The war surely cannot last *much* longer," he reported the Field-Marshal to have said. " The butchery is too frightful. The losses in themselves will stop it sooner or later. The enemy cannot stand it long."

So it *must* have seemed to one who knew what price the enemy had paid to win the few miles of ground he had so far won on our front in Flanders.

The Germans were pressing hard on our line in front of Wulverghem to Hill 75, west of Wytschaete, and north to our positions before St. Eloi. The sound of the guns was incessant.

A cyclist from the 11th Hussars passed our headquarters on the Neuve Eglise-Kemmel road and told me of his regiment, which had been shelled out of its trenches. A First Brigade motor-cyclist supplemented this information. A gap between our strong line of trenches in front of Wulverghem and Hill 75 led across soft ground that presented great difficulties. To prepare it for defence in the sodden state of the low levels was well-nigh impossible. The 11th had been told to hold that part of the line, and had dug themselves in as best they could during the night. The German howitzers had torn the soft fields to bits in the morning, utterly destroying the trenches. Half of the 11th were hit or buried, and the remainder of the regiment was withdrawn to save it from total annihilation.

The enemy tried to follow up the advantage thus gained, and grey lines could be seen pushing west from Wytschaete. The French seventy-fives were in action, however, and our own guns were reinforced by batteries from the 2nd Corps. Shells rained on the front towards which the German attack was directed, and it soon fizzled out in front of the wall of fire and smoke that barred the way.

A Belgian staff officer drove past, pausing to tell us of the flooded Yser. From the sea southwards almost to Dixmude, he said, the land was inundated. Germans were drowned in hundreds, their guns were sinking in the all-enveloping mud, and the coast route to Calais was closed to the Huns.

A run to General Conneau's headquarters near Kemmel showed that the road would not long be passable for cars. Great cellars in the *pavé* road had been dug by the Black Marias, which were falling at frequent intervals all about the district.

The Kaiser had been in Hollebeke the day before, we were told. Incidentally came the news that our airmen had dropped one hundred and ten bombs on that village during the day in honour of His Imperial Majesty's presence. Who could hear such rumours without hope that one of the aerial missiles had found its mark and ended the mad career of the man responsible for the carnage he had come to engineer?

Tuesday morning I spent behind the ruined wall of the *estaminet* that had been our headquarters on the Wulverghem-Messines road. A house on the eastern edge of Neuve Eglise had been dynamited out of existence to clear the line of fire for one of our batteries thereabouts. As we passed the pile of *débris* that marked where it had stood an officer was trying to get a snapshot in the dull light. Later I saw the result of his efforts in the form of a picture in a London paper. Under it was

the inscription, " The work of a German shell." A
large amount was advertised to have been paid for the
photograph.

Shells came so close to the ruined inn during my
sojourn behind it that I took to the ditch, snuggling
down behind the dead body of a red cow that had
been thrown from the field to the ditch the evening
before.

The 1st Cavalry Division held the Wulverghem line,
the 3rd Corps on the right and Conneau's Cavalry on the
left. Sir John French had sent a commendatory dispatch
to de Lisle's Command, asking us to " hold on." It
might be a matter of days or only hours before support
came ; we were to keep the position at all costs until
its arrival. The 2nd Cavalry Division was in billets, to
be called upon by the 1st Division if its assistance
became necessary.

While the day was young the enemy forced back the
French line on our left. De Lisle ran to the headquarters of a French general, whose troops were bearing
the brunt of the attack, and sent the 1st Cavalry Brigade
up on his flank. French wounded littered the highway.
The seventy-fives were firing with wonderful rapidity
from a dozen positions near by. Kemmel came in for a
rain of howitzer shells that made the vicinity a most
unhealthy spot.

Foch attacked on Conneau's left, hoping to drive the
enemy from Wytschaete, and then press on to retake
Messines. Excitement reigned. A wave of optimism
engulfed everyone. Our 2nd Cavalry Brigade could see
the French attack from their trenches. De Lisle moved
up to the ill-fated *estaminet*. All eyes were on the
French. When they could be seen approaching Messines
de Lisle was to let the 2nd Brigade loose. The 1st Cavalry
Brigade would also attack Messines from the south-west
and the 3rd Army troops close in from the west.

The ceaseless roar of guns intensified in fury. Stray
shells began dropping in threes and fours close to our

headquarters. Pieces from one of them spattered the walls and rattled on the tiles of the roof.

At General Mullens's headquarters back of Wulverghem shells were falling in even closer proximity. One splinter came through a window of the cottage occupied by Mullens and his staff and found the slim form of Jeff Hornby, but fortunately damaged him so slightly as to wound his feelings more than his attenuated anatomy. The irrepressible spirits of the 2nd Brigade staff bubbled forth in unquenchable hilarity at this incident, and messages of mock condolence were showered on Hornby, as though the very war itself were one huge joke.

In the midst of the fun the laughter subsided abruptly on the arrival of Lieutenant Chance of the 4th Dragoon Guards. The boy was covered from head to foot with dirt, as though he had rolled in a mud bath. His hand had been painfully smashed by a shrapnel bullet. He came in to report that he had been compelled to pull his squadron back from the line to a position not far behind it.

Chance was one of the many junior officers who were in senior positions in those days of heavy casualties. His squadron had been on the right of our line, adjoining Conneau's Frenchmen on his left. His task was the holding of the soft sandy ground that had been so shell-swept the day before. Digging a deep trench line, his lot " sat tight " under a bombardment that had been terrific. A senior officer on the left of that position told me later in the day that for thirty-five minutes the bursting shells over Chance's squadron formed a curtain of fire that hid from sight the windmill just beyond.

Eight, sixteen, twenty-four, and then again eight, sixteen, twenty-four came the Black Marias in line. The ground in front of the trench was thrown up as by a series of mines. Then close behind the trench line, eight, sixteen, twenty-four, until the soft ground caved

At the corner of the Cloth Hall, Ypres, in November, 1914

A shell hole in front of the Cathedral in Ypres

The Cloth Hall and St. Martin's Cathedral, Ypres, November, 1914.

in in all directions and no trenches were left. Men were buried alive in squads.

Digging out those who had not been buried so deeply as to be hopelessly immured, Chance led his men back, through a hell of shrapnel fire, to the protection of a road-bank a little to the rear. Not a rifle was unchoked, and some time had to be spent in cleaning them. Wiping the sand and dirt from their mouths and eyes, they cheerfully followed the young officer up to the ruins of their trenches and began digging themselves in again.

Once more the German howitzers were turned on them, and once more they were buried in their obliterated trenches. Again Chance took the remnants of his squadron back to the road-bank. Realising the futility of further effort to hold the line where the trenches had been, he adopted the new position and improved it as best he could for defence. The wound in his hand, received during the early part of the morning, became so painful he came back to get it dressed, but before seeking the doctor he called on Mullens to acquaint the General of what had taken place, and to apologise for having to give up the part of the line that had been assigned to him.

Chance was only one of many youngsters who showed such mettle. Truly an army containing a multitude of youths of that mould may be well termed invincible. The lads among the officers were given full opportunity in the Messines fighting to show their worth. The few days on that front cost the 1st Cavalry Division seventeen officers killed and sixty wounded. The total Divisional casualties were not far from seven hundred.

It was evening before we gave up all hope of the success of the French " push," but it could not get on. Guns, guns, guns, all day. Aeroplanes sailed over friends and foes. The latter dropped streamers in the sunshine, and at dusk fire-balls, over us. Shells, shells,

shells, till one wondered if the supply was inexhaustible. One of our airmen reported that our guns hit a German battery twice *sure*, and possibly three times. Our gunners said the Huns did our batteries no harm, in spite of the incessant shelling.

A G.H.Q. summary recorded that " the absence of men in the active list from amongst the prisoners captured during the last month is remarkable, and seems to point to the exhaustion of that class. Between the 14th and 20th of October 7,683 German prisoners have been interned in France, excluding wounded. News from Russia continues to be good."

That was the news from the outside world to us. Our news in return was no more or less than that we had " held on," and darkness had come on another day of continual struggle.

In the night the dismounted French cavalry filed past us in two long lines. On one side of the lane little fellows trotted along in red trousers, light blue tunics, and high-peaked blue caps to match, armed with short carbines and big sabres strapped to their backs, with a great blanket roll atop. On the other side marched the orthodox cuirassiers, tall forms in dark blue coats and capes, their helmets cased in cloth covers.

With every hour the enemy was to find our thin line growing stronger and his last chance of breaking through on that front fading away. The day cost the 4th Dragoon Guards two officers killed and two wounded and over thirty casualties among the men. Only seven officers in the 4th Dragoon Guards were left. The 9th Lancers, too, lost a couple of officers and several men from the everlasting shell-fire.

Conneau's attack brought his line 500 yards nearer the enemy.

Late at night the 2nd Cavalry Division took over our trenches, and we stood in support of them, the men gaining a momentary respite from five days of incessant battle, during which hardly a man, from general officers to troopers, had his boots off.

A sad incident marked the next day. Lieutenant George Marshall, of the 11th Hussars, an aide on General Allenby's staff, and a universal favourite, went to Ypres with a fellow staff officer, as Cavalry Corps headquarters was resting. General Haig's headquarters were in a hotel in the square at Ypres. A big shell lit just outside, killing Colonel Marker of Haig's staff, and also instantly killing Marshall.

Our headquarters had been moved to a comfortable château—just in time, it proved. During the morning the Germans shelled Neuve Eglise, our former home, killing seven and wounding more, immediately in front of the house which had been our domicile for some nights past.

After a second day in support, our troopers again took over the trenches, which meant a night of hard work in the rain and mud. A night attack on the French position on Hill 75 had resulted in some success to the enemy, which made the connecting of our left with the French right a troublous matter in the wet darkness.

The morning of Friday, the 6th, was quiet ; at least, judged by the standard of its predecessors. British optimism was at once forthcoming, as always, when given a ghost of a chance. A glimpse of the sun made all forget the mud underfoot. A G.H.Q. officer was authority for the rumour that the Germans were evidently preparing to " get out," and moving their howitzers back with that idea in view. All were willing to accept any cheerful interpretation that might be offered.

At noon the French gallantly attacked Hill 75 and won it nobly. With a trio of staff officers I tailed along across the fields ankle-deep in mud, watching the advance of the lines in blue. We could see little enough, but quick rushes up slopes not far ahead were now and then visible, and the rattle and roll of small-arm fire so close in front was inspiring. French troops charge over almost impassable ground with unbelievable rapidity.

Our first big 9.2 guns arrived, whereat there was unlimited rejoicing. For days after the arrival of the first one or two to be apportioned to our part of the front, marvellous tales of direct hits far inside the German lines were current.

Visits to the trenches near our old headquarters inn in front of Wulverghem were daily increasing in interest, as that locality was never free from danger. A dozen howitzer shells fell round the ruined *estaminet* that day as we approached it, but luckily no more followed. The road beside the dead red cow, that I had adopted as shelter in the ditch, was torn by a great shell hole, and paving blocks had been scattered broadcast. Rifle-fire became an added distraction while I was waiting on the hillside, stray bullets cutting leaves from the tall poplars that lined the roadway.

Heavy firing away to the north told of battle towards Ypres. We ran to General Allenby's headquarters on Mont Noir that evening and heard of fierce fighting in front of Klein Zillebeke. The French infantry had been violently attacked and driven out. The 7th Cavalry Brigade had been sent in to make good the line, as the retirement of the French uncovered the right of Lord Cavan's famous Guards Brigade. The 1st and 2nd Life Guards and the Blues had won back the lost ground, but it had cost them dear. Colonel Wilson, of the Blues, and Hugh Dawnay, who had left French's staff to command the 2nd Life Guards, had been killed. Seventeen of the officers of the two regiments had been killed or wounded, and many of their men. To Lawford's 22nd Brigade also was due a good share of the glory of snatching victory from defeat.

Thus swung the tide of battle. One day, in one part of the line, it seemed the rush of onslaught had been stemmed, only to break forth with increased fury in another sector.

What would be the end ?

We crawled home to our château through a heavy fog. The mud, the deep ruts in the broken *pavé*, the great shell holes in the road, French troops and English along the way, horse and motor transport, an odd battery or two of guns changing position under cover of the night, motor-cars and motor-cycles, all without lights, made such a run a trial of temper and of skill.

Colonel Seely called and provided some amusement to offset the strain.

Saturday, the 7th, came, wrapped in cold fog. All night the rifles had spat into the darkness, each side firing at the flashes when they showed dim through the mist.

Once more we poked our way to the ruined *estaminet* that was our daily port of call. Just before nine o'clock Hardress Lloyd came back from the trenches, where he had gone with de Lisle. He said the General had walked down the line, and we were to make a detour through Wulverghem and meet him on the road to Wytschaete.

In the outer edge of Wulverghem we found a barricade across the street, which had been so solidly constructed that there was no question of pulling it down and getting the car through. Consequently Lloyd suggested that I should put the car under such shelter as I could find, while he walked down the road and explained to the General why we did not come further. I left the car in the lee of a wall while I went on a tour of inspection. I found no one in the village ; at least, no one alive. There were four dead soldiers in the tartan of a Scottish contingent down one street, and three dead soldiers who had been laid out, with a sheet put over them. I discovered I was the only live person in the town, which was by no means consoling. A sharp burst of rifle fire started not far on the left, and I returned to the car. Our field-guns had been hard at it since daybreak, and so had those of the enemy, and the small-arm fire had also been heavy at intervals. The French were attacking, and the heavy high explosive German shells were going off with their double rrrumph-r-r-rumph not far away.

I sat on the step of the car, took out my note-book, and scribbled. My notes recorded the events of the next few minutes in detail that tells of effort to forget my nervousness.

"9 a.m.—Across the road from me is the convent building which was used as General Allenby's headquarters for some days recently. It is a sight. Every pane of glass in the first story windows is shattered, and many of those in the windows of the ground floor. A great gaping hole in the roof is surrounded by scores of smaller holes in the tiles. The roof as a roof is not of much further use.

"Bang! A shell has fallen in the town. Whizz! Bang! Another one just over me. To go on with my description of General Allenby's house (Bang! another), a big hole has been torn in the wall of the upper story (Bang! one has fallen closer still), and a sister to it appears in the side of the lower story.

"The four shells that last came this way appear to be shrapnel. The French guns are replying, and so are ours. Whizz! There went one that did not burst. Now for the other three to make up the quartette, as the German batteries are apparently firing in fours.

"9.5 a.m. Bang! That is number two. Close and just on my left. It exploded. Quite a shower of bits of *débris* and pieces of shell fell over me. Nasty sound. Bang! Number three. That was a good shell as well, also a bit to the left of me and a little further beyond. A couple of bullets from that one hit the convent. Whizz! and a crash just at my side. That was No. 4. Well over and in a fine position. Fortunate that it did not explode, as it could not have been more than eight or ten feet from where I sit, and just across the thin

MONS TO YPRES.

wall which is the best protection that I can find at this point. If it hadn't been a 'dud' they would have more than likely had to cart me out of this rotten town.

" 9.8 a.m. Sometimes the German gunners stop after firing a series of eight, and sometimes after a series of twelve. Rarely with this itinerant shelling do they send more than two lots of four, or at the outside three lots of four. There are occasions when they keep it up for a long time. I wonder what will be their policy this morning as regards Wulverghem ? One more right where the last one lit would do the business so far as I am concerned.

" 9.11 a.m. Beginning to feel better, for it looks as though the eight finished the salvo.

" 9.13 a.m. The German shells are searching the vicinity of the town on both sides and in the front and all behind it, but the eight did finish that lot. What luck ! They are looking for the French batteries which are firing steadily from quite a number of positions hereabouts. A French artillery officer has come up the road and greeted me with great cordiality. He asked me if I had seen another French officer in the uniform of his battery hereabouts. I have not, and told him so. We passed a joke about the fact. Wulverghem is a nice healthy spot at the moment, and I told him I thought the shell-fire had for the moment ceased. I was constrained to knock on a piece of wood beside me as I made the remark, which brought a curious glance from the Frenchman. Superstition apparently has no nationality.

" 9.15 a.m. I dislike being the only occupant of a town that is being shelled. If I could have held the French officer for company I should have done so, but he has returned to his battery, after wishing me good luck.

" 9.17 a.m. Here, at last, is the General, and I can get out of this place, and back to our headquarters, which I shall not be loath to do."

WITH FRENCH.

The General told me, as we returned, that he had been interested in watching the shelling. He too had been wondering whether the Germans had commenced a consistent bombardment of the town which would last for some time, or whether they were only dropping a couple of rounds of shrapnel thereabouts. He said, " When I saw they were shelling the town I knew that you would be having an engrossing few minutes, so I remained in the trenches a little while. It was quite as interesting to watch the shelling from that position as it would have been to observe it from Wulverghem, and I did not want to steal any of the enjoyment from you."

The K.O.S.B. and K.O.Y.L.I. went past us during the forenoon on their way to the line. The former regiment suffered heavily during the last hours of the fighting in Messines. A captain told me all but two of his fellow officers were hit and the strength of the Battalion reduced by nearly 150 men.

French infantry moved to the right of our Wulverghem front and planned an attack on Messines for the afternoon. General de Lisle rode up to watch the progress of the French, and said I could come as far as our familiar ruined inn, see what I could, and bring him home when the show was over. At the French General's headquarters I learned that the attack on the slopes of Hill 75, where the line was swaying back and forth each day, was successful. A good length of trench was taken the Germans leaving scores of their dead in it.

At the smashed *estaminet* howitzer shells were falling in sufficient numbers to dispel any illusions as to the withdrawal of the enemy's big guns from the Messines area. Odd rifle bullets hit a tree or a broken wall with a nasty smack, and the wicked zipp-zipp of the little fellows came every few seconds. Once a German machine-gun spattered that part of the hill, but the damaged house wall was good cover from any such missiles. The sound of Black Marias shrieking not far above and crashing into the pasture beyond was disconcerting, but they were doing no real damage.

By chance I discovered that a deep trench had been dug in the lee of a haystack that stood at the corner of the ruins of the farm across the road from the inn. There was safety. The field about the stack was littered with dead cows, and monster shell holes were thickly spattered in front of it.

I could see the French and German lines on the sides of Hill 75, not far across a ravine at the foot of the steep slope surmounted by my haystack.

The noise of the bursting German shells and the sharp barking of a number of batteries of seventy-fives behind me was painful. Black Marias fell near in search of the French guns. The noise really hurt me.

When under shell-fire, I have more than once tried to sense the pain of the constant banging as one might define physical suffering. My brain was sometimes numbed, sometimes made acutely sensitive to it. When the howitzer shells came in dozens and scores the sound waves have caused me positive agony of a mental sort. The sensation was indescribable. A tearing at my nerve-centres seemed like to wrench apart some imaginary fabric of feeling and sensibility. It grew unbearable, but generally subsided with a lull in the shelling, leaving me tired, as if having suffered physical pain.

The Oxfordshire Yeomanry were in our front trenches not far away, and one of their officers was on observation duty behind the stack. He saw a company of Germans file down a cross trench a couple of hundred yards in front of the French line on Hill 75, and at once told the French gunner who was observing in the trenches. Back ran the Frenchman to his battery, to point out the exact spot. In a moment the seventy-fives were sweeping the ridge in front of the French trenches. Back and forth and back again went the devastating shower of shrapnel. " Some observation," remarked the Yeomanry officer with a grin.

As de Lisle had suggested my going into the trenches and " talking to the boys " if I became lonesome, I crept along the roadside ditch that served as an approach trench. " Keep down," came the sharp order as I drew near. I stooped lower. In a tiny dug-out I chatted with a couple of Oxfordshire officers.

One of them, Lieutenant Gill, I had heard mentioned as having handled his men with great coolness on the morning we lost Messines, the first day the Oxfordshires were under fire. Shelled while lying in a beet-field, Gill had quietly moved his men a hundred yards from the path of the howitzer shells, which followed him to his newly-chosen position. Thereupon he as quietly moved the men back whence they had come, losing but few of them. Repeating this manœuvre at intervals saved his squadron heavy casualties, and taught them that disregard of Black Marias on soft ground which is so hard to learn, but so comforting when once one has thoroughly absorbed the idea.

The French attack on Messines " made some progress," but was stopped a long way from its objective.

News came at breakfast on Sunday the 8th of the heavy Ypres fighting of the day before. Byng's 3rd Cavalry Division and Lawford's 22nd Brigade were specially commended. Owing to them we regained practically all our lost line at Klein Zillebeke. The French on Haig's right had a terrific struggle and gained a mile.

On our immediate left Conneau reported that the enemy had evacuated some of the Wytschaete trenches, leaving their dead in considerable numbers. The attack on Messines was again to be pressed.

Taking advantage of the cool bright day, General de Lisle ran to the headquarters of the Indian Corps at Hinges. Twenty-three thousand of Willcocks' men were in the line, I was told. General gossip told of

MONS TO YPRES.

Seaforths whose trenches had been invaded by Germans, only to be bayoneted to a man, and of Ghurkas who hated shell fire, and could not understand why they should sit still under it without retaliation of a personal sort.

The Germans pushed our 3rd Army troops back to the edge of the Ploegsteert Wood during the morning.

The French were confident night would find them in Messines, but were doomed to disappointment.

Waiting outside General Allenby's headquarters at Westoutre the next morning, a 3rd Cavalry Division officer told of a captain in his regiment, killed in front of Ypres, whose body had been found next day robbed of coat, cap, and boots. A listener retailed a story of a visit paid to a French battery by an officer in an English staff uniform. He spoke good French, and showed no less intelligence than interest in the position and the battery's work. Two other British officers came past. Noting the khaki, they called out a query as to the route to a near-by town, and were answered in French. Neither of them had any proficiency in the Latin tongue, and said so feelingly.

" What swank ! " said one to the other ; " the beggar must want to show off in front of the French chaps."

" Please direct us in English," he concluded to the staff officer. " Sorry to have bothered you."

But not a word of English could they obtain in reply. About to depart in mystification and somewhat ruffled in temper, one became suspicious.

A moment sufficed to prove the pseudo staff officer a sham. He was no other than a German spy in British uniform.

A subaltern of the Warwickshires rode up asking the way to Bailleul. The 2nd Royal Warwicks, the 2nd Queen's (West Surreys), the 1st Royal Welsh Fusiliers, and the 1st South Staffords composed Lawford's 22nd Brigade, which had loomed large in despatches. We piled question on question. The Brigade was retiring from the line for rest, said the Warwick lad. Of its original 124 officers only fourteen were left, and its men were reduced to less than half the strength in which they had left England. When the enemy broke through between Cavan and the French the 22nd Brigade and the 3rd Cavalry Division were hurled into the breach. Out of the fourteen officers left in the 22nd eleven were killed or wounded, leaving only three, including Lawford himself, who led one bayonet charge in person. "The general," said the young officer, "plugged on ahead of all of us, waving a big white stick over his head and shouting like a banshee. There was no stopping him. He fairly walked into the Germans, and we after him on the run. We took the German trench in front of us and held it, but they mowed us down getting up there. How Lawford escaped being hit is more than anyone can tell. I can see him now, his big stick waving in the air, and he shouting and yelling away like mad, though you couldn't hear a word of what he said above the sinful noise. My Sam, he did yell at us ! Wonder what he said ? "

The boy rode off down the road in a brown study. It had just struck him he hadn't heard a word his chief had been shouting. He had come through that awful charge alive—one of few to do so. Yet he forgot all that. His own part in the fight never entered his head. " Wonder what he said ? " And he rode away thinking.

Oh, such men ! Could the whole world beat them ?

That afternoon I met General Lawford himself in Bailleul, looking fit as a fiddle. After great efforts I persuaded him to dine with us that night at our château, on condition that I should convey him there and back, and " not keep him more than an hour," as he was busy.

Someone from St. Omer told me the " Terriers " were coming out in increasing numbers. The 10th Liverpool, 5th Black Watch, and Leicestershire Yeomanry were across the Channel, soon to be followed by other Territorial Battalions.

General de Lisle had watched with increasing interest the splendid observation of the French gunners and the terrible execution of their seventy-fives. Taking Major Wilfred Jelf, our Divisional gunner, he ran to the ruined *estaminet* in front of Wulverghem to spend an hour or so watching French gun practice.

As I pulled up at the familiar spot I saw ample evidence that the Germans had been paying marked attention to our former headquarters since my last visit. Six or eight new and good-sized shell holes showed black in the soft earth of a nearby field.

The rickety old chair I had rescued from the *débris* a few days before and placed in the lee of the wall was smashed and tossed aside. A stretcher which had stood against the wall for some days was broken in pieces. The *pavé* road was badly battered, the grey stones of the surface being spattered with holes of varying sizes and ground to white powder. Odd-looking little holes those, and sinister in appearance, telling of flying splinters of stone, not less deadly than pieces of shell.

As we crossed the road and entered what had once been the gateway of a farm, one of the buildings, a mass of ruins well burned out, was blazing fitfully.

Two partially burned rifles were mute evidence that some soldiers had been about when the building had been struck.

Of the two buildings that still bore some semblance of their original form, one had been as completely demolished by high explosive shell as had its fellow consumed by the flames. It had not caught fire, but shell after shell had passed through it till the mere skeleton of a building was left.

A signal corps man in a trench behind a haystack at the corner of the farm reported that his wire had been cut half a dozen times by shells that afternoon. While cut off from all possibility of communicating with his fellows, he busied himself by counting the German shells. During the first thirty minutes he had counted fifty that had fallen within a short radius.

The German gunners were evidently of the opinion that the French batteries were closer to the *estaminet.*

In order to reach the French observation officer we walked down the road in the direction of the front trench. The enemy trenches at this point were about four hundred yards from our line. It was growing dusk. We covered a quarter of the distance, when a shrapnel, followed closely by three more, burst almost over our heads. Had we been in the field on the other side of the hedge beside which we were walking we should have been in the direct path of the shrapnel bullets. All three of us stepped down into the ditch that ran by the roadway. I ducked as low as possible as we quickened our pace to the trench in front of us. Four more shells, closer it seemed than the first four, burst over us just as we reached the shelter of the trenches. The General and Jelf went into a tiny dug-out with two officers of the 2nd Life Guards, and I crawled on my hands and knees into the mouth of the main trench. This trench was fairly deep, and at the bottom the men had hollowed out a snug shelter underneath the front wall. The men, lying head to feet at the bottom of the trench, well under the cave roof, were quite secure.

The French batteries behind us began a fast and furious reply. The enemy's fire quickened in turn until shells were bursting with nerve-racking regularity over the roadway immediately behind us.

I could find no room in the bottom, so lay in the approach part of the trench. How I did wish for a foot or two more depth to the end of the trench that was left to me!

The French batteries continued to fire steadily. They were shelling a farm in the near distance in which the enemy had placed a group of machine guns. As dusk approached apace, the Germans were afforded an increasingly better target by the flash of the seventy-fives close behind us. After fifteen or twenty minutes of nerve exercise the General decided that he must return to the car. So many successive quantities of shrapnel were bursting over the road that to return by the way we had come seemed suicidal. The Germans now and again turned their guns on to the ruined inn and the farm. I told Jelf I was sure they knew we had to go back there for the car. But jokes fell a bit flat in that atmosphere.

Finally the General tried a detour. Walking down the road a few yards, we turned across it, when we reached our trench line on the further side. I glanced down in the trenches as we went behind them. The men were lying tight and close at the bottom. A French observer who was in the hedge by our side warned us to keep low on account of the French shells that were screaming over our heads.

As we turned back towards the car the French guns seemed to throw more vigour into their firing. The swift rush of the shells and the sharp bark from the muzzles of the seventy-fives so little distant made one think uncomfortably of prematures. Once in a while shells will burst before their time and scatter from the very mouth of the field-piece death and disaster to him who chances to be in the near foreground.

A bough from a low tree under which I was standing was cut by one of the French shells. I ducked and involuntarily jumped for a near-by trench. I was at once called back by the General, who was off across the open space before I could catch up. As I stepped through the hedge a rain of German shrapnel, from twelve to sixteen coming at once, burst over the part of the field just ahead of de Lisle.

We could not veer further towards the French bat-teries, as to cross their line of fire at any closer proximity would have been madness. It was equally unwise to stay where we were. To return to the trench which we had been occupying might very well have landed us in difficulties, and, at all events, would find us no nearer our objective—the car and " home."

The General walked steadily across the field, unmindful of the shrapnel. I was never more sure of being hit. I hardly know whether I was paying more attention to the French guns roaring away and their shells whizzing over our heads or to the enemy's shrapnel bursting in front of us, on our right, over us, seemingly everywhere about us. I kept my eyes strained in the dusk for shell holes which were deep enough to offer some shelter. Had I been alone I would have run, I think, rabbit-wise from burrow to burrow rather than walk so steadily and with such maddening slowness across that awful beet-field.

In the centre of the field we suddenly stumbled across an empty trench. Much to my delight the General suggested that we should retire into it for a moment. As I lay prone in the bottom of it the shells continued to come over, bursting not far above. We were quite secure unless a shell actually came into the trench and burst, in which circumstance we would have been, as Jelf said, " finished up properly and consequently beyond all worry." Turning their attention from the field for a moment, the Germans began to burst shrapnel over the ruined *estaminet*. Time and again the Major, after a particularly violent burst of shell, remarked, " That lot finished the car thoroughly, I think." De Lisle was of like opinion. I said that I hoped that the Germans would keep on firing at the car. It was much better than to burst big and little ones all around *us*. " But," said the General, " I certainly don't want to walk home." " I do," said I. " I would be quite willing to walk home and walk back again to get out of this."

Once or twice we started to leave the trench, but each time the French batteries seemed to quicken their fire and the enemy shelled back violently in return. When it was almost dark we cut across to a line of trees, then up towards the road, leaving the tree line for the temporary shelter of a low haystack in an open field not far from the motor. I sallied forth to the car, losing no time. I started the engine, jumped quickly into the seat, and dashed away from the *estaminet.* Pausing a moment to pick up the General and Jelf by the haystack, I sped down the hill towards safety.

Inspection of the car on the following morning showed a couple of jagged holes in the sides of the body. A large piece of shell had gone through an empty petrol tin, and ruined a rug in the tonneau. So but little damage was done after all, save to my nerves.

We were gaining the belief that German high-explosive shrapnel defeated its own object. The propulsive power necessary to scatter the bullets was often counteracted by too powerful a bursting charge.

Lawford dined with us as promised, and told us something of the hard times that had fallen to the lot of the 7th Division, which had but forty-four of its officers left and only 2,336 of its 12,000 men.

The 1st Cavalry Division was once more in the trenches on the morning of Tuesday the 10th. General de Lisle started early for the front. We passed Neuve Eglise, running to the Brewery Inn on the Kemmel road. Marks of shell-fire showed this spot an enemy target, so it was voted unhealthy for headquarters. A point near Wulverghem was reconnoitred, but dead horses were near-by in such numbers and state that we returned to Neuve Eglise and settled in our old home. German shells came daily to Neuve Eglise, a fact that caused some thought to more than one member of the staff.

The location of headquarters for the day having been settled, we visited General Briggs on the Kemmel road, then ran to Wulverghem.

De Lisle rode in front, beside me. Hardress Lloyd was in the tonneau.

At the entrance of the town I glanced at the General

questioningly. " Surely," I thought, " he is not going
up to that unmentionable ruined inn again. The place
is a death-trap."

" Straight on," said de Lisle. Yes, he was going to
the *estaminet* after all.

I set my teeth and " let the car out."

Three seconds later, " Crash!" a shell exploded in
our faces. The sound of splintered glass and of the
shell striking the car mingled with the deafening blast
of the explosion. Bullets whizzed past, striking on all
sides. A French soldier close to whom we were passing
dropped with a groan.

I felt a sharp blow in the chest and a twinge of pain
as I caught my breath.

I reached for the brake. " The General," I thought,
" *must* be hit. Lucky *I* appear to be all right. Now to
back round and clear out before number two shell comes."

" Back out of it," came from de Lisle, with sufficient
emphasis to show *he* was alive, right enough.

I tried to put in the reverse, a maddening process on
my car at the best of times. Force! Force! the gear
would *not* go in. Any moment number two and
numbers three and four, for that matter, might arrive.
At last the reverse grated home and I started back.

Turning, I saw de Lisle was sound and unhurt. But
Hardress! His face was in his hands, his head bent.
Hit! And in the head! I was sure of it. But no, a
moment later he assured us he was all right bar bits of
glass from the splintered screen that had got into his
eyes.

Backing as fast as I could, I narrowly missed a French
soldier who had fallen behind us, sorely wounded.
Swinging the car round, I headed for Neuve Eglise.
No need to stop for the French boy, whose comrades
were close at hand. Away we dashed. " Crash!" came
another shell as we tore out of the town. I never
learned where it struck; all I know was that we were
clear of it.

MONS TO YPRES.

A good-sized piece of shell had hit the heavy plate-glass screen, shattered it to bits, and luckily glanced past the General and struck me in the chest. Had I known of its coming the night before I could hardly have been better prepared. Feeling the cold weather intensely, I had worn an unusual amount of clothing.

A heavy flannel vest, a thick winter khaki shirt, a weird sweater, double-breasted, annexed in Rheims, and my tunic were covered by a double-breasted Irish freize coat. This last had been sent out to me by mistake, as it was dark grey in colour. So unorthodox a garment could not be worn along the lines without a plentiful display of khaki. Consequently I had wrapped round my neck a huge khaki muffler of thickly-knitted wool, tying its ample folds at the chin, and letting its double ends provide me with a wide front of the prevailing shade.

The piece of shell tore its way through the double folds of muffler and played havoc with the great coat. None of the remainder of my voluminous wardrobe suffered, but my breast-bone felt the shock. It was some time before I could believe that it or various ribs attached to it had not been broken. Time proved that a bad bone bruise was the extent of my injuries after all. As the General hadn't a scratch and Lloyd's eyes were none the worse, all ended merrily, save for the car.

A halt at a French headquarters along the road showed that a shrapnel bullet had penetrated the radiator, passing through it, and leaving a clean hole, from which the water was spouting.

" No water of any sort at this farm," said a French staff officer. I hurried on to Neuve Eglise, and from there took the damaged vehicle back to the base for repair.

A halting, limping run found me in St. Omer by afternoon, *hors de combat*, but hoping soon to be ready to return to duty.

CHAPTER XIV.

WEDNESDAY, November 11th, marked the onset of the great attack on Ypres by the Prussian Guard.

The Kaiser had spurred his Bavarians, Landwehr and Landsturm to superhuman efforts. No troops could have fought with greater bravery, but they fought in vain. Their failure to hammer a hole in the thin British line left William the War Lord but one arrow in his quiver—the Guard.

The onslaught of Germany's most seasoned veterans was in keeping with their proud name.

The enemy hurled itself simultaneously against the line held by Haig's depleted 1st Corps, the 32nd and 9th French Corps on his left and the 16th French Corps on his right. Heroic charges were repulsed with enormous loss to the oncoming Battalions, which dashed themselves in solid masses against men to whom fighting had become as natural as drawing breath.

Haig's troops met the brunt of the fight along the Menin road, in the vicinity of Gheluvelt. One Division of the German Guard Corps, a portion of the 15th German Corps and a portion of the 27th Reserve Corps surged forward indomitably, and drove our 1st Division from its first line of trenches, only to have the most of the ground gained torn from them by such counter-attacks as warfare had never seen before.

The story was told simply and effectively by Haig's general order of the 12th. This read as follows:

"The Commander-in-Chief has asked me to convey to the troops under my command his congratulations and thanks for their splendid resistance to the German attack yesterday. This attack was delivered by some fifteen fresh Battalions of the German Guard Corps, which had been specially brought up to carry out the task in which so many other Corps had failed, viz: to crush the British and force a way through to Ypres.

"Since their arrival in this neighbourhood the 1st Corps, assisted by the 3rd Cavalry Division, 7th Division, and troops from the 2nd Corps, have met and defeated the 23rd, 26th and 27th German Reserve Corps, the 15th Active Corps, and finally a strong force from the Guards Corps. It is doubtful whether the annals of the British Army contain any finer record than this."

De Lisle's 1st Cavalry Division came out of the line in front of Messines on the evening of the 11th for a well-earned seventy-two hours' rest. For ten days little or no opportunity had been given to take stock of heavy casualties and refit.

The men left the trenches on Wednesday afternoon, and at dinner on Wednesday night orders came to Headquarters that the Division must move to Ypres at once in support of Haig's men, to whom, after three weeks of constant battle, had fallen the task of repulsing the fiercest attack of the whole war.

The 1st Cavalry Brigade was on the road to the north by 11 p.m and the 2nd Cavalry Brigade an hour later, all thought of the seventy-two hours' rest forgotten, eager to press on to the succour of their gallant comrades, with such strength as in them lay. That strength was not to be gauged by their attenuated numbers, for the troopers, who had held on to Messines till the ridge was lost and their withdrawal ordered in consequence, were equal to a force of the enemy outnumbering them by six to one.

The 12th they spent in the salient in reserve, and on the 13th, Friday, they took their places in the line and showed their temper to the Prussian guardsmen.

My shell-smashed radiator temporarily repaired, and my chest better for a few days' doctoring, I rejoined the Division on Friday evening, as it was going into action.

The days required for the repair I had spent in St. Omer, at G.H.Q. Rain fell unceasingly. The work on the car was carried on in the open, regardless of the storm, the mechanics standing ankle deep in a quagmire of ooze and mud. Efficient repair seemed well-nigh impossible under such circumstances, though the men worked like Trojans. Oftentimes they toiled far into the night, for no matter how diligently they strove, broken down cars surrounded them in droves, their impatient drivers clamouring ceaselessly. Poor Scott, the A.S.C. Captain in charge of the repair park, was vainly trying to do the work of ten men.

Hieing to the cosy Café Vincent I delivered myself to the tender ministrations of a pretty auburn-haired waitress, who had become the pet of junior officers at General Headquarters. The soup was excellent, and then came sardines. Heavens, was I never to escape them ! Sardines, alternated with their more lowly blood-brethren *maquereaux*, had dogged our footsteps for months. Even in the most opulent hostelry in St. Omer they followed me relentlessly.

After a careful search of the town I found a yard stick marked with inches, the property of a local draper. From it I made a tape measure. With a friend's assistance careful figures were compiled and despatched to my London tailor. A winter uniform was a necessity. Aghast at such a falling off in my ample proportions, the man of scissors and thread in London town obeyed my behests. A month later the new clothes arrived. To my horror they were so small I could not get into them. Research showed the St. Omer yardstick to have been a delusion and a snare. Its inches were marked for profit, not for accuracy.

An evening in the Hotel du Commerce at St. Omer was great fun. Harry Dalmeny, Shea, Baker-

MONS TO YPRES.

Carr, Hindlip, and kindred spirits gathered at dinner.
Marlborough was sometimes present. Jack Seely
discoursed at length on subjects concerning all and
sundry, Dalmeny ever joking him unmercifully. A
stranger whose ears caught the conversation would
have been shocked to hear Seely told that all ills of
the Army were due to rottenness of the administra-
tion of his office on the part of that Minister for War
who held the portfolio the year preceding the outbreak
of hostilities. But Seely was imperturbable. Nothing
ruffled him. Not even Dalmeny's oft-told tale of
Seely—" I am Colonel Seely. I have been directed
by the Commander-in-Chief to receive and impart
information." This, according to Dalmeny, was the
invariable formula hurled at staff officers dashing past
in the heat of battle or in the stress of frantic hurry at
some critical moment of the retreat. It was all good
fun. Every man present knew Seely as a very gallant
officer. F. E. Smith's languid sarcasm glanced off the
hardened front of this gay gathering like feathered
shafts from a coat of mail. Freddie Guest and Guy
Brooke were neither of them strangers to the party.

An unusually severe downpour made my departure
from St. Omer for Ypres a wet business on Friday, the
13th. I missed the comfort of a hood. A new hood
for my car had been ordered from England, but was
to lie, mislaid, at Woolwich Arsenal for many a long
week.

Past Cassel on its hill-top, the road lined with
camions awaiting French reinforcements, soon to
disentrain from the south, I sped to Steenvoorde and
Poperinghe. A veritable nightmare, that run. Of all
the maddening road obstructions the Algerian horse
and cart column easily took first prize.

At Poperinghe application to Headquarters of
Echelon B of Haig's Corps produced the information
that the 1st Cavalry Division was " somewhere on the
Menin road, east of Ypres." I was recommended to

"proceed through Ypres and push on east a few miles, then enquire again." Cheerful!

A newly-fledged fleet of Red Cross ambulances worked its way autocratically on toward my goal, and I fell into its perturbed wake. At last, a block—impassable. West of Ypres, at the railway-crossing, traffic was banked up like a log-jam. French horse-transport, side by side with ubiquitous British lorry drivers in considerable force, tried to forge eastward over, around, or between a column of French cavalry and a Brigade of British field-guns, which were persistently disputing the right of way to the west. French officers shouted orders to English gunners, who swore softly, while a British officer ploughed through the sticky mud and drenching rain, urging reason on French cuirassiers, who politely wondered what in the world he wanted. A tired jehu behind the wheel of a lorry laughed loudly as a flare showed a mud-plastered sergeant who had lost the road, his footing, and his temper. At the roar of merriment his woe-begone appearance produced, he let loose a searing blast of reproof that was in itself a liberal education in expletive. The driver's laugh subsided to a chuckle, then died in wonder at the storm it had unwittingly raised.

Entranced, I watched the scene till I caught sight of Major Macalpine-Leny, of the 1st Cavalry Division Staff. Hailing him, I learned de Lisle's whereabouts, and pushed on, when the block cleared, to Divisional Headquarters on the outskirts of Ypres.

From Ypres the flash of guns showed through the pitch dark of the rainy night in front, to left and to right. German shells were falling in most unexpected quarters. No rule or reason seemed connected with their arrival, save to make night hideous with their din and chance a hit at bodies of troops or transport moving in the night.

Howitzer shells exploding near at hand, momentarily

Cleaning a machine-gun in the Ypres front
line trenches

Using a periscope at 45 yards from the German
trenches at Ypres

One of the trenches in front of Zillebeke

The Battle of Ypres ended in a blizzard; cold weather in
the trench line

flashing from the blackness ahead, produce a picturesque effect for all their terrifying detonations.

The 1st Corps units our Division relieved were sadly cut to bits. One Battalion consisted of but two officers and sixty men. Another had only one officer left, and numbered less than two score all told. We found a Brigade headquarters with a major in command, whose brigade-major was a subaltern.

On all sides stories could be heard of terrible slaughter inflicted on the enemy. The Guard had come as if on parade, men said. Whole regiments had withered away under a stream of fire, and others relentlessly advanced over their dead bodies as if unmindful of their own certain fate. A gunner told me one Battalion of the Prussians had broken through our line and marched straight towards our guns. Coming within one hundred yards of his battery, they had literally been blown back from the very cannon's mouth, leaving 500 of their dead in ghastly heaps to mark the limit of their bold advance.

I saw half a hundred prisoners, huddled in the rain, examined by lantern-light. Fine, big men, broad-shouldered and tall. They looked defiance on their captors, as if to remind the hated English they were German Guardsmen still, though their teeth were drawn and their comrades littered the slopes they had thought to win.

Haig's heroes were generous in their tales of German bravery. Death held no terrors for the Guard, they said. I was often reminded of this as the days wore on. The German line would surge up to our trenches, only to be swept away, the remnants staggering back from the withering fire. Recovering from the shock of the recoil, small detachments, twos and threes, dozens, or perhaps a score, would come trudging back where death was being dealt out with lavish hand. Some marched boldly, more came doggedly. Many were seen advancing with an arm across their eyes. These futile manœuvres, always ending in the total annihilation of such a group, were inexplicable until a captured German officer gave the key. Men of some Battalions, he said, ever remembered that their regiments had never known and never could know retreat. Death, yes, but not retirement. There was no place at the rear for them, so they went on to join their fellow comrades in a glorious death.

It was better so, from our standpoint. Every dead German meant one less with whom to deal. It may have been magnificent, though none but Prussians would have called it war.

Haig's troops held men who never thought they would have an active *rôle* in the Ypres fighting. Cooks, orderlies, officers' servants, and transport men were called into the line to reinforce the thin Battalions.

I saw soldiers who had spent eighteen continuous days and nights in the actual firing line without respite or reprieve. No billets for them, save the water and mud in the bottom of the trenches, to which they were hanging by tooth and nail. Bearded, unwashed, sometimes plagued with vermin, the few who remained in that front line were a terrible crew.

One of their officers, unshaven, unkempt and unbelievably dirty, told me the remnants of his command might be divided into three classes. One or two had succumbed to the frightful physical strain and were broken past all probable recovery. The rest were sullen or fierce, according to temperament, equally to be dreaded as fighting units. Whether they killed with a lustful joy, half-wildly, or with the deadly matter-of-fact calm of desperate determination, killing had become the one paramount business of the hour, and never ceased for long.

Such was the handful of bull-dog breed against which five to one and even heavier odds of the flower of the greatest Army in the world's history threw itself in vain.

No more glorious achievement rests to the credit of the British Army than that of Haig's sorely tried 1st Corps in the first battle of Ypres.

The fight was by no means over by the 13th. For four days more the struggle was waged with unvarying effort, on the part of the Germans, to break through.

The early morning of Saturday, the 14th, gave me my first sight of the destruction wrought in the ancient Flemish city. Great cavities in the streets and piles of *débris*, ever increasing in number, made Ypres barely passable for motor traffic. The Menin road was under constant shell fire, which made me thankful that our Headquarters were on the Zonnebeke road, between Potijze and Verlorenhoek. A room in a modest dwelling served as headquarters. A stream of wounded soldiers, French and British, rolled back towards Ypres. Ambulances passed and repassed, crowded with shattered forms. They had little room for a wounded man able to walk back to a dressing station.

The British line crossed the Menin road about a mile west of Gheluvelt. The irregular front followed the eastern edge of the woods on both sides of the road. The position was well "dug in," and tunnels and underground rooms were scattered here and there.

South of the highway, the opposing lines, a few yards apart, ran through the grounds of the Herenthage Château. The château was held by the enemy. Our troops were in possession of the barn. By a fierce attack during the morning the Germans captured this barn, and we heard of the organization of a night attack to regain it.

The salient was alive with French and English batteries. The noise of their firing was ever with us, augmented by a continual shower of enemy shells.

WITH FRENCH.

Sharp intermittent bursts of rain hourly spread a thicker covering of slimy mud over the road surfaces. The temperature fell rapidly, and night closed in cold and dreary.

The Northumberland Fusiliers made the attack on the Herenthage Barn. It failed, and the officer who led the assault was killed. A gunner officer volunteered to wheel a field piece to within a couple of hundred yards of the barn and smash it at close range. Five shrapnel were hurled into the stronghold, and a sergeant led the Northumberlands a second time to the attack. This time the charge was successful, and the position was won. The shattered building was a shambles. In addition to its defenders, it had contained a number of wounded when the five shells came crashing through it. Not a soul within its walls was left alive.

An effort to reach Ypres after dusk landed us in a hopeless tangle on the Zonnebeke road. A column of Yeomanry transport, badly handled and very badly driven, was the initial cause of the trouble. The mud in the roadway was ankle to knee deep, and the ditch alongside full of black slime. An R.E. lot from one direction and a long column of French cavalry from the other added to the confusion. One cuirassier became mired—his horse fell, and he disappeared beneath the mud in the ditch. The driver of a mess cart, who constantly reiterated that he was of the " 'Erts," tipped his vehicle over in the midst of the *mêlée*. Hours passed before the tangled skein was unwound. A dozen shells had fallen along that road a few hours before. A dozen more would have caused trouble awful to contemplate had the German gunners known of the jam.

We dined to the accompaniment of bursting Black Marias, though none fell nearer than a couple of hundred yards from us.

Sunday brought a driving sleet. A run down the

MONS TO YPRES.

Menin road and back found it so torn and smashed as to be practically impassable for a car. All day shells traced its length from the trenches back to Ypres. No man who traversed it in those days finished his journey without wondering he had not been hit. Hourly I "strafed" the respective shells that had smashed my hood and screen. The sleet made the work of driving bitterly cold.

Still the troops held back the German attacks, and piled up their dead in front of our trench line.

Our own part of the line saw less fighting than other sections that day. An attack by a party of sixty or seventy of the enemy was pushed on as if forced from the rear. One of our staff officers suggested that the German commanders might find it necessary to promulgate some sort of an attack each day, no matter how small its area or how remote its chances of success, "to provide the daily notes for their official diaries."

Numbers of German dead lay close to our trenches. An officer of the 4th D.G.'s was asked why he didn't clear away one corpse that could be reached by a bayonet from the trench. " Oh, sir," the officer replied naively, " he is quite inoffensive."

Lord Cavan was almost a demi-god in the eyes of his devoted men, whose position adjoined ours. What was left of the West Kents, Munsters, Grenadiers, Coldstreams, Irish Guards and London Scottish were in Cavan's force. His personality had figured largely in the stubborn defence of the line. No words could paint his services in too glowing colours.

The German snipers merited and soon gained our full respect. From thirty to one hundred yards from our line in their own trenches, or concealed individually in the wood, woe to the man who unduly exposed himself in front of them. Some of them had notorious records. One at a point in front of Cavan's force had hit nine West Kents, two Grenadiers and a Munster. None of our men could locate him.

WITH FRENCH.

Sniping at the Germans was most diverting work. An officer of the 9th Lancers took out a trio of sharp-shooters, and in an hour was offered a target at one hundred yards, which enabled his men to "get" four of the enemy.

Monday one of our Brigades was in reserve. The men busied themselves in more or less futile efforts to dry out. The rain never ceased for long.

French troops arrived hourly, and the ferocity of the German attacks seemed to wane somewhat. That night the 1st Cavalry Brigade was relieved, and sent back to billets in the Flemish farms north of Caestre and Flêtre. The next night, Wednesday the 18th, the 2nd Brigade followed to billets in the Mont des Cats-Berthen area.

The ground was white with snow. Incessant rains had turned to freezing blizzards. The Prussian Guard had failed, and the line had held. The first battle of Ypres was finished.

The French troops took over the whole of the Ypres salient. To the British Expeditionary Force was assigned twenty miles of front, to be held by four Infantry Corps. The 1st Cavalry Division was promised four days' rest before a few days in the trenches in front of Kemmel.

MONS TO YPRES.

CHAPTER XV.

A SIMPLE, impressive ceremony took place at the Mairie in St. Omer on November 16th. Lord Roberts's death touched a very tender chord in all hearts in France and Flanders. French and British, Englishmen and men of India did heartfelt homage that cold, dull, dispiriting day when, the short service over, the veteran General's body started on its last journey homeward.

The sun burst through the lowering clouds as the cortège was starting, and a brilliantly-hued rainbow appeared for a few moments, its bright arch standing forth in sharp contrast against the black sky.

Its sudden coming and its almost as sudden disappearance, as the funeral party filed out of the bleak square, seemed timed supernaturally for the occasion.

As the 1st Cavalry Division was in billets, I had come down to G.H.Q. for a new radiator, brought out from England by Oscar Morrison, of the R.A.C. Corps. I was glad to get it, for the repair of the shell-smashed one had been a sad business.

Heavy snow set in. Sir John French was ill in bed with a cold, unofficially. On the 20th I paid a visit to Hazebrouck to see the splendid Du Cros ambulance convoy sent out by Arthur du Cros, M.P., and officered by two of his brothers.

The small light vehicles with canvas tops were just what we required at the front. My call was made interesting by the enemy airmen, who dropped eight bombs on the town. Their total bag was one poor civilian, an old man whose legs were blown off. The following day I rejoined General de Lisle at a château near St. Jan Cappel.

A crash when passing the hospital in Bailleul caused

a halt. Entering, I found an aeroplane bomb had been dropped right in the hospital. A hall built against the side of a church wall was filled with thirty odd wounded, at eleven o'clock. A fleet of ambulances came for them, and before 11.30 all had been removed but two. Then the bomb came. The room was frightfully smashed. Each of the two wounded men was badly hurt, one being hit by eight shrapnel bullets. Two hospital orderlies were in the room, and though both were hit by splinters neither was seriously injured. The airman who dropped the bomb was pursued and captured by one of our flyers. When told that one of his bombs had smashed into a hospital ward he expressed great regret, declaring he was aiming at the railway station.

On the night of Sunday, the 22nd, the troopers of the 1st Cavalry Division went into the trenches in front of Kemmel for a couple of days, after which they were promised a long rest. General de Lisle, with four of his staff, took temporary headquarters in a little dwelling in La Clytte, where he could be close to the Division.

We were fortunate in being allotted a part of the line where the Germans were using a very poor lot of shells. At certain points not one shell in ten was really effective. Quite fifty per cent. of them failed to explode.

The weather was bitterly cold, with hard frost each night. Our headquarters house showed a deep religious fervour on the part of its owner. A crucifix stood over the mantel of the main room, religious images of some size flanked it, and cheap coloured prints of sacred subjects adorned the walls.

The 2nd Cavalry Brigade, numbering 600 rifles, went into the trenches at dark, joining the 1st Cavalry Brigade and relieving the 6th Cavalry Brigade. Approaching Kemmel by the light of the thin crescent moon, the snow-covered fields showed black patches on either side where rows of horses waited for their riders to come from the trenches. I bumped into a huge shell hole in the darkness. By great good fortune I had fallen into its edge and not its deep centre. Gun flashes from all sides, and in front a blazing farm, gave a touch of colour to the picture. In the distance the sky was alight where the old Cloth Hall in Ypres was burning.

For a couple of hours the " taking over " proceeded steadily and without the least excitement. Some few wounded, hit by itinerant snipers, were helped back, but for the most part the change was made with clock-work regularity and in a deep silence born of long experience.

As the 3rd Hussars, coming out, passed the 9th Lancers, going up, low-voiced greetings were exchanged.

" Nothing much going on up front," said a big trooper, " bar snipers."

" How's Nobby ? " queried an acquaintance.

" Nobby ? " came the low reply. " Oh, Nobby. 'E stopped one. But not proper—only with his 'and." And he trudged on into the snow-rimmed blackness.

Everybody was cheery.

Cold, dark, but dry, the night wore on.

" It's warmer in the trenches," said the departing ones. " Plenty hay ; not half bad."

Food went up and ammunition. All as orderly as such events can be when every man knows his job and sets about it silently and seriously.

The General strolled up, walking first here, then there, seeing that the detail of the work was being carried out efficiently.

All the while the sniping went on merrily. The bark of the rifles near by was given an added sharpness by the cold, tingling atmosphere. Our field guns not far away fired at regular intervals.

At last we were " in " and our predecessors " out."

I slept in La Clytte. I chose a very soiled mattress

close to the diminutive but energetic stove. Cecil Howard was condemned to a bed much too short for him, to which he attributed a powerful and persistent nightmare. The quarters were far from luxurious, but we soon dropped to sleep to the sound of the ever-lasting sniping, which kept up all the night through.

The world was hidden in a mantle of hoar frost in the morning. A bottle of Vichy in a suit-case in the tonneau of my car was frozen solid.

We ran to Kemmel, and walked from there towards the trench line. General Briggs was indignantly bemoaning the stupidity of his chauffeur, who had covered the engine of his car with straw and in some way set it afire when starting in the morning. Result, car burned! Most drivers kept their cars in going order by a liberal mixture of methylated spirit with the water in the radiator—an excellent wheeze.

Tramping the white fields was inviting trouble with snipers. I returned to Brigade Headquarters, and gossiped about the new rifle grenades. Our hand grenades were very effective—much more so, we thought, than those of the enemy. The latest German device was a big valise-like thing, thrown by some means unknown, that came hurtling end over end and lay before exploding for two or three seconds after its arrival. The noise it made "beat a Black Maria hollow," a trooper said. The smoke from one of these projectiles lay and drifted low in great clouds. Its energy seemed wasted, however, for while it tore a great hole in the earth it apparently scattered no pieces of projectile about. At least that was the verdict of those who had close acquaintance of it.

A German prisoner had a rare fairy tale for us. He reported eight cases of self-mutilation in his company, the strength of which had been reduced to fifty-six. After hearing him talk one might imagine that all Germans would soon be on strike against further war-fare. His efforts to retail welcome information were unfortunately a bit overdone, particularly when one knew of a fierce German attack on Hollebeke the day before. But he meant well.

At mid-forenoon the quiet of La Clytte was shattered by eight German howitzer shells. One fell thirty yards short of our house, showering pieces of shell in the front yard. Another lit across the road. Not far from us a woman was beheaded and an old man killed.

A few minutes before the shelling, Major Steele, our Divisional R.A.M.C. officer, and Baron Le Jeune, our French liaison officer, had called. Le Jeune came to obtain the General's signature to a permit for a few days' leave. News spread that seventy-two hours in London was forthcoming for all of us in turn, whereat was great rejoicing. Le Jeune told me his little boy had been brought by his mother to Paris, where the Baron was to join them on the morrow. Everyone was happy in anticipation of soon seeing the loved ones at home. Gay quips and cheery laughter were on every lip.

Shortly after the brief shelling, Major Davidson, of the R.A.M.C., came in and told us that one of the shells had lit a few yards down the street, at the cross-roads, where General Short, of the Artillery, had his headquarters. One of his staff looked out of the door to see where the shell had struck. Lying in the road-way were the still bodies of Major Steele and Le Jeune, who had been passing at the moment the shell came. Poor Steele's left arm and shoulder were shattered, and he was badly wounded in the side and leg. Le Jeune was suffering horribly from a piece of shell that had torn its way through his body. Another bit of the shell had made a hole in his head. Both of them died—Steele on his way to the hospital, and Le Jeune soon after his arrival there.

Colonel Home, Hardress Lloyd and "Mouse" Tompkinson were starting for England, on leave, the day following. We had all been "bucking" about our "last day under shell-fire for a bit." Such hard luck for Steele, a greatly beloved and very gallant chap, and poor Le Jeune made everybody quiet.

More shells came in the afternoon. Towards evening we started for "home" at St. Jan Cappel. As we stepped into the car a shell screamed through the air and landed with a loud bang just in front of us. One last Black Maria had "come over" only a few yards above our heads, and sent up a high column of dirt and smoke from the corner of a field fifty yards distant. It was in perfect line.

The seconds dragged by with leaden feet until the General's order came to "let her go." Our way led down the street to the crossroads, where our two friends had been killed a few hours before, then left to Reninghelst. Number two was overdue, I thought, as I gathered speed. I took the corner on two wheels, and Home sung out from the back seat as we left La Clytte behind: "Those are my sentiments too, President."

That evening in Bailleul a Flying Corps officer told me a story of one of his airmen, named Blount. Blount was sent on a prosaic daily air reconnaissance. He duly returned, entered the office of his chief, and reported so many trains here, so many there, a column on this road, that road clear, and so on, as usual. Nothing seemed out of the ordinary in his story, or his manner of telling it.

As he turned to leave the room he said, " Coming back, I had a bit of a brush with a Bosche flyer."

"Hold on," called out the officer to whom he was reporting, "don't run off. What happened?"

"He was killed sir," was the laconic reply, and the airman opened the door.

"Wait," said the officer. Then, as he noticed blood dripping from one of Blount's hands, "What's the matter with your hand?"

MONS TO YPRES.

"Oh, nothing much," Blount answered modestly. "The German chap got me with one shot and took off the end of a finger." The two upper joints were gone. "I am going to have it wrapped up." And with that he departed, as if glad to escape from the necessity of giving further details.

The encounter had taken place over Bailleul, in good view of the aero sheds not far from the town. It caused immense excitement and enthusiasm, and the officer found no difficulty in gathering a much more complete story from Blount's fellows.

Blount discovered the enemy airman when returning from the reconnaissance, and at once gave him battle. A very pretty fight ensued. Gradually Blount mounted higher and higher, until he was above his antagonist. Then circling round and round the German, both firing all the time, Blount forced him lower and lower. At last, just before the German came to earth, one of Blount's bullets found its mark, and the enemy airman fell over and crashed to the ground with the ruins of his machine.

The coveted seventy-two hours' leave came at last. Three days at home at the end of November soon passed, and on our return we took up headquarters at a château between St. Omer and Cassel, some miles from the groups of farms and one or two villages in which the Division was billeted for the winter.

On December 3rd the Division was visited by His Majesty the King. The mounted troopers, swinging swords in high circles and cheering strenuously, made a fine sight as the King walked down the road between the lines of horsemen.

The next day I encountered a friend in sombre mood. "What's wrong with you?" I queried.

"I am just back from a jaunt with a batch of newly-arrived subalterns, who were turned over to me for map instruction," he said gloomily. "I daresay they are all right, but some of them are wonders. One of the cheerful idiots couldn't find a stream I pointed out to him, and after muddling along a bit, burbled out: 'Why, I thought all the rivers on a map ran north and south.'"

The days passed quickly. Shooting parties were formed and a steeplechase organised. Evenings found us frequently battling over chess or draughts.

The casualties for the Division to December 1st had been 1,544. The Queen's Bays, 5th Dragoon Guards, and 18th Hussars had lost over 200 each, the 11th Hussars nearly 250, the 9th Lancers 288, and the 4th Dragoon Guards 323. New drafts were daily arriving, and the regiments busying themselves getting the fresh men into shape. Continual exercise kept horses and men fit, everyone spending much time in the saddle—from the General himself to the troopers.

Every man in the trenches means three to five men behind the line. An army "resting" finds itself well occupied if the enemy still faces it. The actual "business" of an army teems with detail. A Divisional headquarters receives 700 letters and communications per day at times. Every other day de Lisle "did the rounds" of the Brigades. Many days I was left to my own devices. Permission to visit friends of other units was sometimes granted.

On a trip to Armentières, I heard the following story:—The town was lighted by electricity generated in Lille. For three weeks after the occupation of Armentières by our troops they found their use of the electric light uninterrupted. At last the Germans in Lille discovered that "their" town's supply plant was supplying the "juice" for lighting "our" town, and they forthwith put a stop to it. Some of our officers in Armentières, who chortled over the unique situation, suggested that a message should be sent to the Huns, asking for the bill for electric current.

Young Von Tirpitz, son of his notorious father, was taken prisoner, said a gossip in Armentières. The youthful Von T. tried to escape. Discovered and baulked, he found that his guard became increasingly attentive. Baffled and angry, minor restrictions goaded him to frenzy. Forgetting himself, he spat in the sentry's face.

The guard was a Jock of considerable proportions. He stared a moment, then quietly laid his rifle by his side, unbuckled and took off his accoutrements and gear, and spat on his hands. For a few minutes thereafter, the fur flew, or, at least, von Tirpitz's fur would have flown, if he had been a fur-bearing animal. The Jock was intent on giving the scion of the noble house of T. a severe lesson. Young Germany was inclined to show fight, but was promptly thrashed soundly, and finished off with a belting—his own belt being used for the purpose. As a fellow-Jock, a spectator, said, " Man, it was a noble beating."

Well castigated, but by no means injured, young Von Tirpitz was sufficiently an ass to report the occurrence and demand reprisals. The sentry was, of course, court-martialled. The full facts were laid bare. The sentence was given sonorously. " Twenty-four hours' imprisonment for laying aside your arms while on sentry-go," was the penalty.

Such yarns were typical, and, if not always true, were entertaining.

A jaunt in the Ploegsteert Wood was a muddy experience. I was told to leave my car behind a house in the village and walk to the point where the corduroy pathway led away through the trees. Winding in and out of the southern edge of the wood were the trenches. All about were broken and splintered branches and tree trunks—a weird place. Various paths were placarded with such names as Regent Street, Oxford Street, Piccadilly Circus, Hunter Lane, etc. The Tommies in the trench line were knee-deep in water. Men passed rearward plastered in mud. An officer told me a Tommy's overcoat, weighed in the village, had tipped the scale at forty-five pounds on his return to billets after forty-eight hours' trench duty! Withal, every man was cheerful. As an observing friend remarked to me, "You can't *beat* these soldiers. No amount of hammering, casualty, or hardship seems to affect their splendid spirit in the least."

I asked this friend what impressed him as of greatest interest in the trench-warfare. He replied, " The wonderful *assortment* of shells and projectiles one sees."

At tea-time one day I found the regimental censor hard at work over the letters of a yeomanry squadron.

" Hear this," he said. He read at length from an interesting letter written under shell fire, in the trenches. " Mother," it commenced, "you could not imagine the noise. Bang! There came one only a matter of feet from me. Shells are bursting every second, and pieces are flying all about." After a page or so of detailed excitement, the writer drew a line, then added an explanatory note to say that at the point indicated he had been bowled over by a huge Black Maria, but had miraculously escaped a wound.

" Very good," was my comment. " Writes jolly jolly well for a trooper, doesn't he ? "

" Yes," agreed the officer who was acting as censor. " but he's a farrier who hasn't been within three miles of the line. If he has heard a shell, it's been a long way off. He was mad all through because he couldn't go up with the regiment, which is in the trenches now. So he has taken it out in epistolary zeal. It's pure imagination. What am I to do with it ? "

" Pass it," cried the mess in chorus. " It will do no harm."

So pass it he did.

A couple of months later he showed me a soiled clipping from a Midland newspaper. A glance at the well-fingered excerpt showed it to be a verbatim reproduction of the farrier's letter. " The best joke is that he keeps the good work up," said the yeoman. " Not a week passes he doesn't curdle the blood of the old folks at home with some yarn. We quite look forward to 'em. The paper fairly eats 'em."

An epidemic of stories of distress in Germany ran through the army : English interned who scribbled : " Food scarce ; panic here," and hid the message with a postage stamp ; veiled hints of food shortage in letters from German residents ; tales from neutrals of hard conditions ; reports that placards were put up in the streets of Berlin at night bearing such legends as : "Stop the War," and so on *ad infinitum.*

Anything in the way of cheery news or a hopeful report spread like wild fire. A pessimist seldom got a hearing.

Water in the trenches and the cold spell made for bad feet. I saw whole detachments whose feet were so swollen after their turn in the front line that a couple of days without boots was an absolute necessity. The general health, bar feet, of the whole Army was exceptionally good, in spite of the conditions. This was due to the inoculation for enteric, wisely made compulsory. No sensible man who spent that winter in Flanders and who kept his eyes open would declaim against inoculation.

On December 14th the Division stood by in reserve while an infantry attack was launched on the German position in front of Wytschaete. The 8th Infantry Brigade and some French troops on its left made the sally. We paid about 500 casualties for an advance of about 500 yards in one little wood. The ground would not allow of a really successful offensive. After the men had gone a hundred yards across a field each foot was so caked with mud progress was impossible.

As December passed the "nibbling" continued. The Lahore Division at Givenchy, the Warwickshires at Bas Maisnil, the 11th Brigade at Ploegsteert, the French at Notre Dame de Lorette on the south, and

Pilkem on the north of us, all reported minor gains. The official summaries recounted slow progress, thick fog and hard frost from day to day.

Gun-fire was held down by limiting the rounds allowed each gun for each day, and units in the trenches made a report of the rounds of small arm ammunition used.

On December 19th the Indian corps at Givenchy had a nasty time. The Indian line from north to south was composed of the Garhwal Brigade, Dehradun Brigade, Sirhind Brigade and Ferozepore Brigade.

The trouble started on the morning of the 19th, when the Garhwal Brigade made an attack. It captured about 300 yards of the German first-line trenches, but was promptly bombed out and forced to evacuate what it had won. The Dehradun Brigade left its trenches, and, though the Sirhind and Ferozepore Brigades had advanced in the general forward movement, they were compelled almost at once to retire. A portion of the Dehradun front, the whole of the Sirhind front, and most of the Ferozepore front, together with the village of Givenchy, were soon in the hands of the enemy.

On the 20th heavy shell fire began at daybreak. The Sirhind Brigade fell back to Festubert, and it seemed that Givenchy was hopelessly lost. Finally Givenchy was recaptured by the Manchesters and the Suffolks. The remainder of the Corps reserve was moved up, and counter-attacks organised feverishly. In spite of all efforts the front of the Meerut Division was broken, and the Black Watch and the 58th Rifles were sent to its aid.

The next day the whole of the 1st Division was hard at it retaking Festubert and Givenchy, a task which they eventually accomplished.

So much for the bare outline of a story that was told in almost as many ways as there were men engaged in the fighting.

MONS TO YPRES.

I visited the Festubert area to gain some first hand knowledge of what had transpired. I learned that the Indians had fought much better than the bare accounts would indicate.

The trenches in that sector were full of mud and water. One officer I met had discovered in the thick of the fighting that of a hundred rifles in his trench but three were sufficiently free from mud to be usable.

Another officer told me his men had exhausted their ammunition. A box of ammunition arrived. The men carrying it were jarred by a howitzer shell that fell a few yards away just as they reached the trench. They dropped the heavy box into the trench with a splash and straightway it sunk many feet into the soft ooze and mud, all efforts at its recovery seemingly only serving to immerse it more deeply.

The awful conditions of the ground and of the trenches out of which the Indian troops were driven were largely responsible for their initial repulse. They counter-attacked well, and in most instances gained their objective. Unaccustomed to the all-important work of immediate consolidation of an enemy position, they were much harder to withstand when charging than to dislodge by bombing after the completion of the actual attack.

From close questioning in various quarters and quite a general survey of the locality, I became convinced that the Indians worked at great disadvantage when so scattered, and particularly when the Brigade Staffs were so far from the front line.

If one point could be selected for criticism it would, to my mind, be the faulty Staff work, owing in great measure to the much too great distance of the commands from the various Staff Headquarters.

The loss of their line was a sore disappointment to the poor Indians, who had been rendered unbelievably miserable previously by the awful weather and unusual climatic conditions. No criticism could

WITH FRENCH.

possibly be launched at their valour. That they required more and closer supervision in such a kind of warfare was as undeniable as it was to be expected in the first place.

Christmastide found the British Army becoming accustomed to the stagnation of a winter campaign in sodden Flanders.

On Christmas Eve, at midnight, the Germans in the trenches in front of the Ploegsteert Wood began to sing Christmas songs in chorus. The Somersets faced them. Some of the Somersets were old acquaintances of mine. Theirs was the first infantry command, with the Inniskillings and the Rifle Brigade, to arrive at the Ploegsteert Wood in the autumn, when the 1st Cavalry Division was fighting hard to hold the position.

A couple of Somerset bandsmen, who had left their instruments in England and were assigned to stretcher-bearing, told me a day or so after Christmas what occurred at Ploegsteert on Christmas Day.

The Saxon Christmas songs of the night before had odd results.

"The songs was fine," one of my informants declared. "They sang a lot. But the best was to come. A German bloke had a cornet, and he could play it grand. He just made it talk. The songs and the tunes the cornet feller played seemed more and more like ones we knew. Some of the songs I could have sung myself. At last out came that cornet with 'Home, Sweet Home,' and nobody could keep still. We all sang—Huns, English and all."

The night spent in song produced a general peacefulness of spirit all round. As day broke the Somersets saw the Saxons on top of their trenches. Soon they called out, "Come over and visit us, we are Saxons." No shots were fired.

"None of our chaps started for the German trenches," continued the bandsman. "We had heard all about

300

the white flags the Bosches had fired from under and all that. But our medical orfficer is a funny cove, and he got an idea in his head that started the whole thing. He said he saw a chance to give a burial to some of our dead that had been lyin' between trenches no end of a while.

" So he told me and my pal here to follow him, and afore we knew where he was goin', up he pops on the trench parapet. The Bosche trenches was only fifty to seventy yards in front, and up we had to get and over after that doctor. The Saxons was right there, in plain sight. I never sweat so, nor never did my pal here. We was sure there was a game on, and we would get it good as soon as we was well out of cover. Some of our dead had laid out there for eight or ten weeks, and was in a awful state. We picked up a Inniskillin orfficer, a captain, and got him on a stretcher —a big job—and got him back all right. No one fired a single shot.

" So out that doctor sends us again. We got over near the Bosche trench and up jumps a stocky little heavy-set German orfficer with a bushy black beard.

" He steps forward and says rough-like, with a scowl like he was goin' to eat us, ' Get back to your trenches, we have had quite enough of you. Get back there at once.'

" He spoke English all right, *he* did. We didn't need no interpreter for *him*. His looks went with what he said, too. We went all right. And I won't forget goin', not in this 'ere life, you can bet. That few yards seemed a sinful long way. Every step I thought ' Now I'll get it, right in the back,' but I didn't.

" We got into our trench right by our major in command, and told him what old whiskers had said and how he said it. All the major said was, ' I didn't think they would really let us get our dead. I'm not surprised.'

WITH FRENCH.

" But that little trip of the doctor's had fair started it. Half an hour later I could see some of our lads on our right going right over to the Bosches in the open. The major saw 'em too. When he got 'em in his eye he said, 'You can go on now, you men, and get some more of those dead in.'

" We went. We never saw the black-bearded chap any more, either. One of the Saxon fellers who spoke pretty good English sung out and said we could go right on with what we were doin'. He said all of us could bury dead till four o'clock, and they would, too. And sure enough they did get at it pretty soon afterward.

" Of course with us all kicking round each other out there in the open, lots of chaps got to talkin'. The Saxons was friendly enough.

" One chap said to me, 'You Anglo-Saxons, we Saxons. We not want to fight you.'

" I thought I'd land him one, so I said 'What about the Kayser, then, old lad ? What do you think of Mr. Kayser, eh ?'

" ' Bring him here, and we'll shoot him for you,' said the Saxon feller, and we all laughed.

" But I didn't take no stock of that. I knew he was only trying to be pleasant.

" Some of our chaps changed cigars and cigarettes with them Huns, and had talks about all sorts of things. At four o'clock we all took cover on both sides, but there was no firing on our front that night. The next morning we kept up the callin' business. We didn't stop it for a matter of eight days.

" Then the Saxons was relieved by the Bavarians. The Saxons warned us agin them Bavarians.

" One of the Saxon blokes said to one of our sergeants, ' Saxons do not like Bavarians. Shoot them like hell.'

" There was one Saxon chap, off a bit to our left, I heard one of our lot tell about that wouldn't have no truce. He was in front of the Rifle Brigade. He kept hammerin' away all through the piece, no matter what the Saxon chaps in front of us did "

An exchange of rations was a frequent occurrence during that remarkable period. Both sides agreed that tinned " bully " had no serious rival.

" Would the men who made friends with the Saxons fight them as hard afterwards ? " I asked.

" Sure," was the reply. " If our chaps got a chance to put the bayonet home in one of those fellers, there wouldn't be no difference in the way they would do the job. All the first moves come from them, not from us. They even said they would fire high if they got orders to fire on us. We didn't make no such foolish promise.

" Our lot wanted to see the German trenches bad. They wouldn't let us right in, but we saw a lot and learned a lot. We could get right up to their wire, which was no end better than ours. But it ain't now. Wait till they try goin' against our wire, and they will find we learned a thing or two." And the little group chuckled in anticipation.

The most amusing conclusion to this Christmas truce, in its various phases here and there along the facing lines of trenches, was the trio of severe orders promulgated from three high Headquarters.

Sir John French's order was short and sharp, but very much to the point. It expressed great displeasure at such carryings-on.

General Joffre issued an order not a whit less severe in condemnation of such tendencies.

But fiercest of all, and threatening direst penalties, was the order issued by the Kaiser.

That all three orders were necessary might give food for thought to psychologists.

That they were issued should, in kindness, have been told to Henry Ford.

WITH FRENCH.

APPENDIX.

Lieutenant A. Gallaher, of the 4th Dragoon Guards, affectionately dubbed Golliwog by his messmates, had a mad Irish experience at Audregnies.

More than once he told me details of it, the last time while he was convalescing from a second shell wound in the head received in front of Ypres long after the retreat.

" We were watering in Audregnies when the order came to mount and charge," said Gallaher. " I was at the head of the second squadron. It was quiet enough before that. We were dismounted in the village street, watering from buckets wherever we could find one. We jumped into our saddles and tore off down a narrow lane without in the least knowing where we were going or what was up. The dust was thick, so thick one could hardly see the man in front.

" We went off in a rush all right, and rode down that choking lane with no other thought than keeping going. We had no order to draw sabres, and just galloped in a bunch. Before we reached the end of the lane men began to fall. The bullets were coming from in front and seemingly from one flank as well. More men fell, but we couldn't do anything save gallop. At the end the lane curved round a cottage to the right. I remember seeing Colonel Mullens, and Major Solly Flood beside him, at the turn. Mullens cried, ' Not there—not there! ' but it conveyed no meaning to me. We dashed on after the leading squadron round the corner and into a very inferno of shell and small-arm fire. It *was* hot. No time to wonder what was doing. Shrapnel was bursting right in amongst us and men falling every inch

of the way, it seemed. Not far beyond the corner I
saw a flash which seemed right in front of my eyes, and
my horse went down.

" When I came round I was lying on my right side,
with one leg under my dead horse. My head was bad.
Alongside me was a French officer who had been attached
to us—a Count, someone said. He was dead. A
bullet had hit him right in the centre of the forehead.

" All was quiet for a moment. Dead and wounded
lay all around, and everything seemed strangely still.
Down the lane I saw Major Tom Bridges ride out into
view. He stopped, shaded his eyes with one hand, and
gazed about oddly. The Germans saw him and opened
fire on him, the bullets singing by him as he turned and
galloped away to safety. Months afterwards I learned
that he had been hit in the head during the charge,
stunned, and taken into a cottage. The Germans came
in the front door as he regained consciousness. They
were a bit too late, for he jumped out the window as
they came in the door of the room in which he had
been lying. He found a horse, mounted hastily, and
after finding which way the enemy bullets were coming,
made off in the opposite direction and escaped without
a further scratch.

" I struggled out from under my horse and tried to
run towards the point where Bridges had disappeared,
but my leg was so numbed and sore I fell. Another
attempt resulted in another fall, so I crawled on my
hands and knees to the nearest shelter, a cowshed by
the lane. Creeping inside, I found a wounded French
interpreter and two wounded troopers. The shell fire
began again and rifle bullets whizzed all about. One of
the cows in the shed was hit in the back by a bullet,
and with a startled effort broke the chain by which it
was tied and rushed out.

" A moment later a German officer and two German
soldiers with bayonets on rifles came through the doorway. In the officer's hand was a tiny popgun of a

pistol, which he kept pointed at each of the four of us as he went from one to the other. Reaching my corner, he stooped and relieved me of my revolver and my map case, the latter containing a notebook in which were an entry or two that I knew would hold his big round blue eyes. Running through my pockets, he came to a sovereign purse with seven sovereigns in it. This he tucked back in the pocket of my tunic, then stepped out the door to examine my notebook in the fading light. The moment his attention was well engaged, one of the German soldiers lost no time in extracting the sovereign-case and its contents from my pocket in a manner that left no suspicion in my mind that he intended replacing it.

" A squad of fifteen or sixteen wounded and prisoners —mostly cavalry troopers or Cheshire Tommies—were marched up from an adjacent house, hands in air. As they reached the door one man fell, a bullet through his raised arm—maybe a chance shot. I saw Sergeant Hynes of my regiment in this lot. He told me that in the house where he had been lying with a broken rib or two, injuries received when his horse fell sorely wounded in the lane, a Belgian woman had become so incurably hysterical that the wounded men had put a sack over her head to keep her quiet. They hoped against hope to escape discovery. The Germans found them in due course and liberated the frantic woman, who ran screaming down the lane, only to fall from a German bullet before she had gone far.

" A cook - wagon came up. After methodically milking the cow standing near, the Germans killed her, cut her up, and consigned her to the pot, foragers contributing turnips in profusion from the field hard by. Two great stacks of hay across the lane from us were lit at dark. The Germans threw British rifles and saddles on the blazing piles, with the result that a merry popping of small-arm ammunition commenced, bullets whizzing in all directions. At first our captors scattered, leaving us lying well in the line of fire, but soon they returned and shortly produced plentiful supplies of red and white wine. As the wine passed round they danced about the burning stacks to the music of a couple of accordions, a weird sight in the fitful light.

" On the arrival of an officer the hilarity subsided. The slightly injured British soldiers were marched off to collect the dead and wounded, friend and foe. The more serious cases were taken to the convent in the village. The sergeant and myself were the last two to be moved. I was carried on the shed door. Before I was taken away, the German officer, who spoke no English, came over to where I lay and gave me first a drink of water, then a drink of milk. Stiffly and awkwardly, he reached down and shook me by the hand as he departed. I never saw him again. Not a bad sort, I suppose. Meant well probably.

" Sergeant Hynes had fared worse. One of his arms was black and blue from the blow of a rifle-butt, delivered by a Hun for no better reason than that Hynes was the only one of a handful of wounded who had sufficient strength to sit up.

" Audregnies boasted two convents. To one some 190 British wounded were taken, while an almost equal number of wounded German soldiers were placed in the other. The Audregnies fight was on Monday. On Tuesday and Wednesday I lay in the convent hospital occupied by the Germans. There was no doctor for a day or so. The sisters worked like Trojans and the Catholic father was never idle. Both convents gave their morning toll to the cemetery.

" The priest exhumed the body of Lieutenant Garstin, of the 9th Lancers, and brought it for identification outside the window near which I lay. The villagers had given the poor chap a slight and hasty burial; the father transferred the body to the proper burying-ground, as well as those of two Cheshire officers. These, too, he brought to me for identification before interment. He carefully wrote down the names as I took them from the marks on the clothing, and the places of burial bear them, no doubt, to-day. A kindly soul, that priest. He would bring me an egg and a crust of bread at night under his robe. I was fortunate in having a request for transfer granted, and by Thursday was taken to the convent over the way which housed the British wounded. Two Belgian doctors came from Brussels. One was taken ill at once and incapacitated, but his fellow was a splendid chap and an indefatigable worker. He had hardly any bandages or anæsthetics. Four other officers, all of them Cheshires, were in the hospital, badly wounded.

"My damage was not serious. A shell had torn up my scalp a bit, but I felt sound enough, although my leg was very painful. I put it down to a sprained ankle, and bound it tightly with a couple of puttees. The doctor had too much work to do for me to bother him with it. Not for some days did I discover that one of the bones in the lower part of my leg was broken, though the pain at times brought me to the conclusion that a sprained ankle was a most unpleasant injury.

" Only a handful of German guards were about. The sisters tended us, and I suppose they had the feeding of us as well. By the end of the week I had planned to escape, and to take Sergeant Hynes with me. Monday, a week after the day of the fight, was chosen for the attempt. The four Cheshire officers were our only confidants. They suggested saving their food on the final day, so that we might take some provender with us.

" During the morning a convoy of ambulances, due on Tuesday, pulled up. That they had come a couple of days before we had been told they would arrive seemed likely to upset my plans. All was bustle. Those best able to be moved were placed in the ambulances at once. My heart sank. The doctor came to me, and as he examined me I felt sure he would send me away then and there. By luck, my eyes were terribly bloodshot from the explosion of the shell that hit me, making me look much worse than I really felt. After a moment's consideration the doctor passed me over, saying I was to go with the second convoy, which would come at daybreak the next morning.

" Sure enough it came. As a forlorn hope, I asked if I could hobble down to an orchard not far away and pick some apples before leaving. Permission granted, I limped through the trees, Hynes close behind. Under the fruit-laden branches we passed, with no eyes for the red cheeks of the fine apples within reach. Step by step we drew near to the hedge at the far side. No one was in sight. A last glance behind, a final effort to pull ourselves together, and we ducked through the leafy barrier, wriggled over a low wall, and rolled into a deep ditch beside it. Crawling as fast as we could, we followed this ditch for some hundreds of yards, lying flat and worming along wherever the varying depth made us nervous of possible discovery. We were convinced we would be shot if found by the Germans. The few guards at the hospital, the many dead each morning, and the confusion of evacuating the wounded might, we hoped, result in our escape passing unnoticed.

" All day long we lay in the moist, muddy ditch-bottom. I had begged a map from a Sister on the plea of locating some guns within earshot. She had torn a map of sorts out of the back of a railway guide, and it proved of inestimable value to us. We planned to strike north, cross the Mons-Condé Canal, and then make for some of the large Belgian towns to the north-west.

" It was stiff, tiresome work lying quiet in the ditch that day, but with brambles pulled together over us we were in comparatively little danger of discovery. At dusk we crawled painfully out of our hiding-place and slowly headed northward. Every sound meant

Germans to us, and our first mile was a succession of limping and halting sallies forward, interspersed with sudden dives underneath the hedge by the roadside. At last we approached the point where our road crossed the main highway from Mons to Valenciennes. The moon was shining. From our hedge shelter we could see long lines of dusty shapes moving slowly towards Mons. Clank of harness and the gear of guns and wagons sounded regularly along the way. Now and then a rough guttural voice rasped out an order or an oath. We waited for hours before a gap in the long, ghostly line gave us courage to cross. We passed safely enough after all, and skirting a couple of villages, reached a haystack near the Mons-Condé Canal before daybreak. We were not far west of the town of St. Ghislain. Before us lay the broad canal, spanned a few hundred yards distant by a ruined railway bridge, and a little further on by another bridge, over which we could see Germans passing in the growing light. At our backs was the home of the owner of the stack. He made his appearance at an early hour, and we hailed him. First he bolted back into his house. After a bit he gingerly approached the stack, and finally we induced him to mount the slight ladder against it.

" A little man he was, with a thin black beard, great rings in his ears, and piercing shifty eyes. Only a few moments passed before we found our host was like to cause us trouble. He was all for giving us up to the Germans, and said so frankly. To be discovered harbouring us meant his house burned and death for himself, he said. For a time no argument could shake him. I told him the British were advancing behind us and would soon be in Mons again. If he gave us up, or allowed harm to come our way, woe to him when our troops arrived. It was a silly argument, but it won. He agreed reluctantly to let us stay unmolested until night, when I promised we would swim the canal and make our way northward. We lay close together as he piled bundle after bundle upon us, until the sergeant felt certain the little Belgian was trying to ensure our being smothered.

" That was a tiring day, a hungry, thirsty day, but we lay as still as mice. From out the straw we could see German transports on the road, and what appeared to be guards on the bridges, which hourly reminded us of the necessity of keeping close cover.

" That night, about nine o'clock, we climbed down from our hiding-place, went to the edge of the canal, undressed, and waded out neck-deep. At the very moment I was about to start across Sergeant Hynes had to confess his injured side would not allow him to swim twenty feet. It was a bitter disappointment. To return to the stack held little hope. To try to go on might mean the death of one or both of us from drowning. Choosing the less sure road to disaster, we dressed and regained our nest at the top of the stack, where we lay all night cursing our bad luck and improvising futile plans of escape.

" On Wednesday morning the stack shook with the weight of someone ascending the ladder. ' Germans,' whispered Hynes. ' That light little Belgian never made such a commotion.' The perspiration broke out on my forehead. An age passed before the head of our visitor came into view. With inconceivable relief we saw the smiling face of a Belgian lady of most ample proportions. Blackbeard had told her of his unwelcome guests. The widow of a Belgian officer, she was as brave as an army. Rating the little man for his idea of surrendering us, and prevailing upon him to give up all thought of so doing, she had hastened to us with a bottle of red wine and a plate of beans. The Germans had taken everything eatable or drinkable from her house save these, she said. As to crossing the canal, she took on that contract with alacrity. Having a bit of money in her house, she told us she would arrange for a skiff to be ready for us at nine o'clock that night.

WITH FRENCH.

" The day seemed brighter after her visit, and we
rested much more easily. Nine o'clock came at last.
With it the ample form of Madame, who, alas! could
find no one who for any sum would venture to take us
across the canal. But her resources were by no means
exhausted. An urchin on a bicycle reconnoitred the
bridges, and brought back word that no guard could be
seen on the railway bridge. Though it had been blown
up and rendered useless for trains, it afforded means for a
crossing if we could climb over one or two obstructions
and escape being seen by the guard on the road bridge
beside it. We started without delay or demur, after I
had thanked our brave benefactress in my best and
most effusive French.

" We found the bridge sadly damaged. Twisted
metals were coiled over the way, and many of the
timbers were torn bodily from the trestle work. A
barricade presented difficulties which were soon over-
come, and within a few minutes our feet trod the north
bank of the canal. We had crossed safely and, apparently, undiscovered. Working northward, we struck
the road from Mons to Tournai. At midnight we
found we had made good time. Just how, I don't
know. We went round all the villages and learned to
anathematise all dogs in so doing. My leg was growing
more painful, but a great stick helped me to hobble
along at a fair pace. At first we were unduly nervous.
Faint moonlight played strange games with our fancies.
Once a tree trunk held us at bay for some minutes
before we discovered it was not a German with a rifle.
A restless cow, changing her pasturage, sent us flying to
cover. A startled rabbit dashed across the road, and I
found myself face down in a gully before I knew it.
The night made odd sounds, each one of sinister import
to us. The wind sprang up, and in the exercise of its
privileges caused our hearts to jump into our throats
half a dozen times.

" By midnight we had reached and circled round the

village of Basècles, half-way from Mons to Tournai. We
were sadly in need of food and drink. Approaching the
house on the far side of the little cluster of dark
dwellings, we lay by the door and under one of the
windows listening for the heavy breathing that might
betoken German occupants. All seemed quiet and pro-
pitious, so I gave a gentle knock and explained in a low
tone that we were English and wished to enter. Sounds
of commotion came from the cottage. A light flashed
from the windows, and a woman's shrill voice advertised
our presence. A moment later, as we still waited for
the door to open, a light appeared in the next house,
then the next. More feminine voices passed the words,
" Anglais ! Anglais ! " We had no desire for such a
reception, so hurried off towards Tournai as fast as our
disabilities would allow. Well it was we did so, for
no sooner had we reached a point some two to three
hundred yards up the road than several shots were
fired, and a few sinister bullets sang over our heads.
We strained every nerve to hurry. Fortunately there
was no pursuit. Nearly exhausted, and in rather bad
case, we slowed down after a time, only to become a
prey to all our former fears of night noises. A good-
sized bird flew close to my head and gave me a shock
that lasted many long minutes. Plodding along the
highway, the clatter of hoof-beats coming towards us
sent us to the roadside, where a ditch offered welcome
refuge.

" We jumped in, close together. At the bottom we
hit something soft, which turned beneath us and gave
a whistling grunt as our combined weight came down
upon it. We had jumped full on top of a man. Who
he was or what he was doing there were of no moment to
us. A sound from him might mean recapture. The
sergeant grappled him and crushed out what breath
remained in him. I lent a hand. As a troop of German
cavalry drew nearer we were well on the way to choking
our chance acquaintance. At that very moment the

Uhlans slowed from a trot to a walk. We held our breath. At least I held mine, while Hynes held his own and that of the third member of our party. Gradually the horsemen drew abreast, then past, then away. We waited until they were well in the distance, and then examined the man underneath. If we had been scared to have jumped on him, he was more than scared to have had us do so.

" The relief when we found him to be a Belgian farmer, frightened out of his few wits, was truly comic. The Germans had imposed severe penalties on inhabitants who moved about between 8 p.m. and 6 a.m., he said. His quest remained unexplained, except in so far as a sack of something we did not examine might explain it. We advised him to remain where he was until daybreak, and pressed on. Before dawn we took refuge in a shed behind a house not far from Tournai. The distance we had covered must have totalled from fifteen to eighteen miles, evidence of what strength fear and desperation lend to tired and broken feet. The owner of the premises which we had chosen as sanctuary was a fine man, courageous and full of resource. Learning who we were, he took us from the outbuilding to his garret, where he fed and tended us with a will.

" The Germans, he said, were not in force in Tournai, being chiefly interested in obtaining provisions therefrom. One train went each day to Bruges, leaving just before eight in the evening. Belgian guards were at the station, and the Germans were unlikely to trouble their heads about who left by the train during those days. Our host obtained a cart, in which he secreted us, driving to the station in such time that he arrived at the very moment of the train's departure. The engine whistled as we jumped through the station door and made for a carriage. But we were not to get away so easily after all. We were capless. Our clothing was torn to rags by thorns and brambles. Truly we presented a sorry sight. We careered into a couple of

MONS TO YPRES.

Belgian guards with fixed bayonets, who seemed thereupon about to use them. Up went our hands, and we panted incoherent protestations that we were English. A look of utter incredulity came over the faces of the stolid civic guards. Someone yelled out that the Germans had come. Pandemonium reigned. Two Irishmen jumped from the train and recognised that we were really what we said we were. They were getting through as refugees, but they managed to put us right with the two with the bayonets. The commotion that had been started, however, was not to be easily subdued. Passengers piled on to the platform in a hopeless panic crying aloud their fear of the Huns. The crowd made for the door of the station and there jammed. More cries came from the outside that the Germans were coming. It was most unpleasant. A resourceful chap dashed up to the engine-driver and explained who we were. We were hustled aboard the train, and without more ado it pulled out, leaving most of its intending passengers behind. We threw ourselves back on the soft cushions and heaved deep sighs of relief. We were safe. At least it looked so.

" A wire sent to Bruges brought the Mayor and two soldiers with the inevitable bayoneted rifles to the station to meet us. Only one train per day ran into Bruges from the edge of the war zone. Thousands of anxious Belgians awaited it in a great square, eager for news of relatives and friends.

" Our appearance in a carriage with the Mayor and what appeared to the assembled multitude to be two guards gave rise to the belief that we were German prisoners. Booing grew from a deep murmur to an angry roar. The crowd surged forward. Things looked bad. The Mayor leapt to his feet. The crowd stopped the carriage. Mounting a cushion the Mayor, by dint of great exertion, gained a moment of comparative quiet and told the people we were escaped and wounded English soldiers. All was changed in a twinkling. The crowd made its onward rush—but to embrace us, not to tear us asunder. Before we were through we became afraid there was little to choose between the two. Our troubles were over once we won through the square, however, and next day we were sent to Ostend and from there home, to good old London town."

MAP OF THE DISTRICT
DEALT WITH IN

"FROM MONS TO YPRES
WITH FRENCH"

By
FREDERIC COLEMAN.

INDEX.

INDEX.

INDEX.

INDEX.

INDEX.

INDEX.

INDEX.

INDEX.